CRITICAL AND CULTURAL THEORY

CRITICAL AND CULTURAL THEORY

THEMATIC VARIATIONS

DANI CAVALLARO

THE ATHLONE PRESS
London and New Brunswick, NJ

First published in 2001 by
THE ATHLONE PRESS
1 Park Drive, London NW11 7SG
and New Brunswick, New Jersey

© Dani Cavallaro 2001

Dani Cavallaro has asserted her right under the Copyright, Designs and
Patents Act, 1988, to be identified as the author of this work

British Library Cataloguing in Publication Data
A catalogue record for this book is available from the British Library

ISBN 0 485 00438 0   HB
0 485 00628 6   PB

Library of Congress Cataloging-in-Publication Data
A catalog record for this book is available from the Library of Congress

Distributed in The United States, Canada and South America by
Transaction Publishers
390 Campus Drive
Somerset, New Jersey 08873

Typeset by Acorn Bookwork, Salisbury, Wiltshire
Printed and bound in Great Britain by
MPG Books Ltd, Bodmin, Cornwall

This book is dedicated to
Barney, Paddy and Tristan
(in alphabetical order!)

CONTENTS

CONTENTS

GENERAL INTRODUCTION

THE TITLE

i. Critical and cultural theory

There are no universally accepted definitions of the phrases 'critical theory' and 'cultural theory'. This is because critical theory and cultural theory are not sciences governed by precise sets of rules and procedures. In fact, they are multi-layered discourses that integrate diverse themes and approaches. Moreover, the issues they tackle do not reflect the concerns of any one self-contained discipline, for those issues are actually central to a wide range of disciplines: Literary Studies, Cultural Studies, Linguistics, History, Art History, Politics, Sociology, Anthropology, Geography, Media Studies and Science Studies, for example. Thus, critical theory and cultural theory have redefined traditional disciplinary boundaries by drawing together disparate fields of study. In the process, they have created scope for creative exchanges amongst subject areas once considered separate. In fostering interdisciplinarity and intellectual cross-fertilization, they have also encouraged the emergence of new perspectives and facilitated the development of academic programmes based on such perspectives.

This book seeks to highlight the interdisciplinary character of critical theory and cultural theory, by showing that they have infiltrated a number of fields, that their principal themes have been the object of heterogeneous interpretations, and that their own meanings are open to redefinition over space and time. For example, the phrase 'critical theory' is often historically associated with the activities of the Frankfurt School. These were carried out between the early 1920s and the late 1950s with the aim of moving beyond purely functional and pragmatic readings of Marx's theories through a self-critical approach that would consistently examine the relationship between those theories and contemporary culture. Today, the phrase 'critical theory' is generally used in a far less specialized fashion. Indeed, employed in tandem with 'cultural theory', it describes a cluster of approaches which – especially since the 1970s – have prompted a radical reassessment of notions of meaning, history, identity, power, cultural production and cultural consumption. Several subject areas and doctrines have participated in this process: philosophy of language, semiotics, aesthetics, theories of representation, political theory, psychoanalysis, feminism, ethics, epistemology and science.

Changing understandings of phrases such as 'critical theory' and 'cultural theory' remind us that it is important to register the shifting connotations of scholarly labels. This can help us approach history as a dynamic process rather than as a static collection of *facts*. Much as a culture – any culture – is shaped by its past, it must nonetheless be willing to question and modify past meanings and interpretations. After all, the past tends to reach us through inconclusive narratives, and historiography itself does not function as an ultimate guarantee of truth. Moreover, it is by viewing the past as a dimension amenable to ongoing redefinition that we may also begin to entertain the possibility of an open-ended future.

ii. Thematic variations

The examination of theoretical perspectives and methodologies provided by this book is structured on the basis of themes drawn from the interrelated fields of critical and cultural theory. These themes are discussed both in terms of their relevance to contemporary thought and practice, and in terms of their place in ongoing speculations about language, society, identity and related systems of knowledge that span classical times to the present. Accordingly, each chapter included in the book addresses a concept as a theme, with reference to a variety of philosophical positions, their principal proponents, and their social, historical and ideological contexts. As a theme-based introduction, the book offers its readers an alternative point of entry into critical and cultural theory to the one supplied by several existing texts whose focus is on movements, schools, trends, prominent names, intellectual gurus and cultural icons. So much for the use of the word 'thematic'.

As for the use of 'variations', this is inspired by a desire to show how several of the discourses and techniques developed by critical and cultural theory can help us vary our take on objects and ideas which we may otherwise conceive of as fixed. Music and painting arc not the only arts that flourish by producing variations on a theme. The art of interpreting the world and its manifold systems of signs, and of figuring out our individual and collective roles therein, requires us to consider the multiple variations which any human being may be in a position to produce on a given theme. The themes addressed in this book could all be regarded as coordinates within which our grasp of reality takes shape, and within which disparate experiences come to form specific cultural paradigms.

A number of traditional scholars have found critical theory and cultural theory daunting due to these discourses' commitment to a radical questioning of conventional concepts of truth, value, unity and stability. Indeed, both critical theory and cultural theory, in various degrees, have challenged the notion that language conveys stable meanings and, relatedly, have argued that both personal and collective identities are impermanent. Moreover, both have emphasized the constructed status of anything we may call 'reality'. Neither literature nor art nor the human mind, for that matter, are seen to mirror reality in a transparent fashion; in fact, they represent reality on the basis of conscious, semi-conscious or even unconscious codes and conventions. However, these positions should not be regarded as a nihilistic denial of meaning. In fact, they intimate that our sense of reality may be enriched by an understanding of its inconclusiveness, its ambiguities and *gaps*.

READING *CRITICAL AND CULTURAL THEORY*

The book is constructed so as to make its chapters open to two kinds of reading. On the one hand, the eighteen essays can be read sequentially as parts of a whole. On the other, they can be read individually, and in any order, as discrete entities. The choice of one or the other type of reading will depend on the reader's own interests and research priorities.

i. Linear route

The structure of the language in which this book is written requires propositions to unfold in a linear fashion. Following this logic, the text can be seen to trace a sequential trajectory, and its three parts can be read accordingly.

Part I offers an introduction to a variety of critical positions concerned with the relationship between the world and the symbolic systems (such as words, visual images, social codes and conventions) through which a culture unrelentingly endeavours to 'make sense' of its world. Part II concentrates on the cultural strategies through which people and their environments are constructed, both physically and psychologically, in ideological, political, sexual and racial terms. Part III explores some of the ways in which critical theory and cultural theory have engaged with issues of perception and knowledge, with reference to art, popular culture, science and technology. The sequential movement from Part I through Part II to Part III could be summarized as follows. The symbolic systems through which the world is encoded and understood (*Language and Interpretation*) underpin all cultural formations, their power structures and their intersubjective relations (*Social Identities*); a society's makeup, in turn, both produces and is produced by systems of *Knowledge* designed to relate individual experiences to collective concerns, objectives and desires. The linear progression just described constitutes only one aspect of *Critical and Cultural Theory: Thematic Variations*. Indeed, the book also aims at offering a multi-dimensional and interactive map which allows for non-linear excursions through the book.

ii. Non-linear route

The book invites the reader – with the aid of cross-references highlighted in its footnotes – to peruse the text in a non-sequential mode. In the synopsis of the book's principal arguments offered below, some possible interconnections are suggested. (The capitalized words are meant to foreground the titles of the chapters in which specific issues are addressed.)

The MEANING we attribute to a living creature, object or idea does not result from their intrinsic properties but rather from the ways in which we read them. READING is not exclusively the act in which we engage when we peruse a written text. In fact, it is a process in which human beings are unremittingly involved as they go about the world trying to account for both their physical and their mental situations. Nor does reading consist of unearthing stable truths inherent in reality, for truths, like meanings themselves, are only ever a product of the cultural tools we employ to give shapes and names to otherwise amorphous experiences. Furthermore, the strategies which people adopt in order to interpret the world are neither timeless nor universal. They are, in fact, inevitably bound to specific social, political and economic contexts. Such contexts are predicated upon an IDEOLOGY: namely, a set of cultural practices, discourses, beliefs and rituals that aim at fashioning both single individuals and entire communities on the basis of dominant world views. In instructing us to interpret the world in certain ways, ideology concurrently constructs our SUBJECTIVITY: our social identities as components of interrelated structures of power and knowledge. The political and psychological socialization of individual subjects is instrumental to the maintenance of an ideology, to the perpetuation of its ways of reading and seeing the world, and to the attribution of particular meanings to the things we read and see.

The procedures through which ideologies and their world views are preserved are not uniform. In fact, they rely on multifarious SIGN systems: the written word, the spoken word, the visual arts, the media, codes of behaviour and ritualized conventions. What these diverse systems share is a desire to give a culture a distinctive identity, and a parallel determination to protect it against anything OTHER. The Other is anyone and anything deemed capable of disrupting the social fabric and the integrity of its imaginary identity: strangers, foreigners, intruders and so-called racial and ethnic minorities, for example. Strategies meant to keep the Other under control (by either repressing or incorporating it) have often targeted the areas of GENDER AND SEXUALITY. Sexual desire has insistently been associated with humanity's most unruly and transgressive drives. Accordingly, the regulation of people's sexual behaviour has repeatedly provided a model for keeping at bay all potentially subversive activities.

Dominant ideologies are also committed to the promotion of a culture's AESTHETIC values as a guarentee of its excellence. Indeed, a culture's appreciation of beauty, its notions of taste and refinement, and its attitudes to art are supposed to mirror its ethical and moral worth. These agendas are never neutral or innocent. They actually conform to social and political imperatives, and are intended to govern the REPRESENTATION of our cultural existence. Everything, ultimately, is of the order of a representation, because we can never know things and ideas except insofar as they are encoded through accepted systems of signification. Concomitantly, human subjects and their experiences become functions of TEXTUALITY: what we are and how we act is inevitably affected (or indeed determined) by endless chains of narratives told both by us and about us. The validity of the messages conveyed by these narratives is hard to ascertain. This is because they are structured through language, and language always contains a figurative dimension, RHETORIC, which tends to distort and displace even the apparently most straightforward messages. The statements proffered by any narrative may – but equally well may not – conform to an actual state of affairs. Hence, the representations and texts that make up our worlds tend to undermine conventional distinctions between the real and the unreal, the natural and the simulated, the world and its SIMULACRUM.

Neither the MIND nor the BODY are in a position to supply incontrovertible proof of the world's existence. This is largely due to the fact that both the mind and the body are themselves elusive entities, which refer simultaneously to a material and physical reality, and to abstract concepts. Mind and body give us the coordinates – most notably, SPACE and TIME – within which we may map out our experiences. However, the maps we draw, guided by both psychological and biological processes, are always open to redefinition. In giving shape to their surroundings, mind and body follow supposedly natural laws. However, they are also governed by mechanical principles. The rapid expansion of technology (especially in its electronic applications) has thrown this into relief by showing that the dividing-line between the organic and the artificial is becoming more and more uncertain. In any case, it is undeniable that mind and body have always operated as parts of a composite MACHINE. This cannot be regarded as the exclusive possession of an individual. Indeed, individuals never see the world through purely personal lenses. They are, in fact, constantly implicated in intersubjective networks of perception. Our cultural existence is a product of how we look at the world but it is also, ineluctably, a product of how the world looks at us: of how it constructs us through its unremitting GAZE.

The non-linear route outlined above is by no means the only possible way of reading this book *across* its three Parts, rather than sequentially, chapter by chapter. In fact, it is intended to supply just one example (as limited as an example of this kind is bound to be) of the potentially limitless number of journeys which a reader may take through the kaleidoscopic worlds of critical and cultural theory. Ultimately, the book wishes to emphasize that several disciplines influenced by critical and cultural theory have proposed stimulating variations on a wide range of themes and, more importantly, to suggest that any moderately curious reader may move on to formulate her or his own variations.

PART I

LANGUAGE AND INTERPRETATION

INTRODUCTION

Nothing means simply by virtue of existing. People, animals and objects obviously exist as material forms subject, in various degrees, to change. However, it is not their sheer physical existence that endows them with meaning. In order to carry certain meanings, people, animals and objects have to be invested with symbolic significance. Societies and cultures only ever make sense of the world (albeit tentatively and provisionally) by translating both their animate and their inanimate inhabitants into symbolic entities. The symbols employed are diverse and their import varies from one society to another, one culture to another. Such symbols include words, visual images and the codes and conventions that shape the value systems and patterns of behaviour of particular communities. It is at the point where people, animals and objects are related to the symbols which a community has been trained to recognize that they become meaningful, or significant.

Concomitantly, no physical form holds a final or stable meaning. In fact, its significance will inevitably alter according to the changes undergone by the cultural or social formation of which it is part. If this applies to concrete entities, it is no less relevant to abstract concepts. Indeed, the extent to which meaning depends on symbolic transactions and is, as a result, variable is clearly demonstrated by the shifting nature of the words used to designate abstract ideas – such as 'culture', 'society', 'value' and 'community', for example. Such ideas do not point to universal categories. Rather, they embody context-specific meanings, determined by the symbols employed to define them.

The sum total, most probably incalculable, of the symbols used to give meaning to a world constitutes language. The means by

which the symbols are grasped and processed constitutes interpretation. Just as no entity or idea has a meaning independently of
the symbols with which it is associated, so no symbol means independently of someone or something capable of interpreting it. The
essays contained in Part I elucidate the relationship between
language and interpretation as the mechanisms through which
cultures produce and consume meanings. These meanings,
moreover, define our social identities (see Part II) and approaches
to knowledge (see Part III).

Chapter 1, 'Meaning', examines some of the ways in which the
relationship between language and reality has been assessed by a
representative cross-section of philosophers and linguists. Chapter
2, 'The Sign', focuses on the impact of structuralist and poststructuralist theories on cultural and literary studies. In Chapter 3,
'Rhetoric', the interplay of language and interpretation is explored
in terms of the tension between literal and figurative modes of
signification. Chapter 4, 'Representation', concentrates on the idea
that reality is an effect of the media and techniques via which it is
symbolized. In Chapter 5, 'Reading', the focus is on the active role
played by readers – both as individuals and as communities – in
the production of a text's meanings. Chapter 6, 'Textuality', highlights the extended meaning of the term 'text' advocated by
contemporary critical and cultural theory.

MEANING

What is the relationship between language and reality? Between words and things? Between words and ideas? How do words come to convey certain meanings or concepts? Does language embody universal principles? Does it express what the world 'is' or what we 'take' it to be? Can we mean something without saying it? Can we say something without meaning it? These and several other related questions have haunted philosophers and linguists for centuries. Many possible answers have been offered and, more or less widely, accepted or rejected. The sheer diversity of such questions and of the responses they have elicited shows that the issue of meaning is the object of ongoing debates. Just what meaning is or how it comes about are, to a considerable extent, moot points. Arguably, the search for meaning consists of the incalculably large number of operations through which humans attempt to make the world intelligible. The search, therefore, is virtually endless, for it could only come to a halt if the very desire to know were to be terminated.

This chapter does not aim at supplying answers to the questions presented above. Its objective is to examine a representative selection of approaches to the issue of meaning put forward by Philosophy of Language and Linguistics. The first part of the chapter describes a range of philosophical positions spanning Classical times to the twentieth century. The second part looks at the principal goals and methodologies of Linguistics.

Let us first of all consider a cross-section of approaches to the relationship between words and concepts. Thought about language is intertwined with thought about all the major philosophical categories: knowledge, truth, meaning, reason. Its central concern is: what is the relationship between a statement and the state of affairs that it describes? Relatedly: is a sentence for which there is no such state of affairs necessarily meaningless? The two most influential positions in the history of Western Philosophy of Language are realism and nominalism. The first believes in the existence of universal concepts in a realm separate from material reality and maintains that the universal properties shared by particular things are abstract and unchanging. The second rejects the existence of transcendental universals and asserts that objects and their properties are just names and that everything that exists is particular.

The Greek Sophists (fifth century BC) were among the first to examine the relationships which need to exist between words and things if language is to convey knowledge. Gorgias, one of their principal figures, speculated that when we give one another words, that is *all* we give one another: there is no direct transfer of shared ideas or concepts from one mind to another. Even if there were, there would always be a disparity between ideas and the ways in which these are used and interpreted in particular contexts and by particular individuals. In the *Cratylus* (c. 390 BC), Plato sought to counter the Sophists' relativism, by arguing that although the words we use may be purely arbitrary and conventional, concepts are not: they are a matter of truth or falsehood. It is therefore vital, according to Plato, to arrive at ideal names conforming to the true nature of reality. This coincides with an otherworld of immaterial and eternal Ideas, or Pure Forms, that transcend the physical world. Only a correctly structured and furnished language is capable of accessing those universal, unchanging abstractions and thus communicating knowledge.[1] Aristotle (384–322 BC), by contrast, opted for a naturalistic approach. He argued that universal principles are immanent in things, and can be discovered by identifying the common properties of particular objects. Language must be able to grasp and articulate those universals. In different ways, both the Platonic and the Aristotelian models were concerned with language's ability to *represent* objects or ideas. This position was drastically challenged by the Sceptic philosopher Sextus Empiricus (c. 200 AD), who argued that words can neither

---

[1] ☞ For further discussion of Plato's theories, see Part III, Chapter 6, 'The Simulacrum'.

express nor manifest actual things. Words are radically divorced from things.[2]

Aristotle's views were later revamped by Empiricism, the philosophical tradition commonly associated with Francis Bacon (1561 –1626), Thomas Hobbes (1588–1679), John Locke (1632–1704), George Berkeley (1685–1753) and David Hume (1711–76). Empiricism followed Aristotle in believing that words name ideas and that ideas refer to things. Language is a distorting medium, for words are potentially obfuscating substitutes for ideas. Ideas are understood and shared concepts and words must embody such concepts unequivocally. If they do not, they are empty and misleading (Locke). Words that do not correspond to ideas are unscientific and unreliable. Berkeley, however, believed that words without ideas may still have a function – for example, in affecting people's behaviour, passions and emotions. Even if a word does not unproblematically correspond to an idea, it may still produce certain effects and hence certain meanings. Immanuel Kant (1724–1804) refuted the Empiricist approach by asserting the importance of *judgment*. This faculty enables human beings to bridge the gap between the phenomenal world (the natural world as we perceive it) and the noumenal world (the world of ideas). According to Kant, we never know things as they truly are – as things-in-themselves – but only in terms of how they appear to us – as phenomena. In the phenomenal world, we perceive objects but cannot truly know them because we are only confronted with their surface appearances, not with their intrinsic essences. When we exercise judgment (particularly *aesthetic* judgment), we are still tied to appearances but are also able to detect a pattern in them which gives us a glimpse of the noumenal world.[3] Judgment is also the mediating factor between words and things, language and reality.

Kant's theories were redefined by the nineteenth-century philosophical movement known as German Idealism and associated with the writings of Johann Gottlieb Fichte (1762–1814), Friedrich Wilhelm Joseph von Schelling (1775–1854) and Georg Wilhelm

[2] ☞ This concept plays a key role in poststructuralist approaches to language, as shown in Part I, Chapter 3, 'Rhetoric'.
[3] ☞ Kant's theories are discussed further in Part III, Chapter 2, 'The Aesthetic'.

Friedrich Hegel (1770-1831), Idealism denied the very existence of *things-in-themselves*. It argued that we create the world by perceiving it (like idea and ideology, idealism comes from the Greek *idein*, 'to see'). As a result, the connection between language and the world is radically severed: language and thought are self-contained and the perceiver plays an active role in constructing a/ the world. Truth, moreover, can no longer be based on a corre-·spondence between language and the world. These positions influenced deeply subsequent perspectives on the function of truth in language. From these, two major theories originated: the *coherence theory of truth*, according to which a statement is true if it 'coheres' or 'is consistent with' other statements, and the *pragmatic theory of truth*, according to which the validity of a statement depends on its practical relevance to experiences and actions. Gottlob Frege (1848–1925), the founder of modern mathematical logic, reestablished a link between language and truth by arguing that sentences are not justified by either their connection with ideas (Empiricism) or their connection with judgments (Kantianism) but by their *truth-conditions*. A systematic theory of meaning should classify the expressions contained by a language and describe in a methodical fashion the ways in which the truth-conditions of sentences are determined.

The following is a brief description of some of the principal approaches to language that developed in the course of the twentieth century. Logical Positivism, the approach formulated by Alfred Jules Ayer (1910–89), argues that there are two sorts of meaningful statements: those which can be empirically confirmed and those which are true by virtue of linguistic rules. The former are scientific statements and statements of common facts, while the latter pertain to mathematic and logic. Religious and metaphysical statements do not belong to either category and are, therefore, considered meaningless. Ethical statements are also meaningless from a factual point of view but are capable of carrying affective meanings. Pragmatism, the philosophical approach descending from the writings of Charles Sanders Peirce (1839–1914), maintains that the truth of statements can only be ascertained with reference to practice. For Peirce, in particular, the meaning of a concept is based on the relationship between the practical circumstances in which it is used and the practical consequences of its use. The meaning of a statement, accordingly, is determined by its practical effects. If ideas are effective, they can be expected to yield successful outcomes for their users. The effectiveness of ideas can be tested against the various degrees of success or failure met by a community when it applies such ideas in practical circumstances. Peirce's successors go even further, by suggesting that the effectiveness of ideas results from their very adoption by a community, not from their successful application. William James (1842–1910) offers a more subjective version of pragmatism than Peirce's. In order to test the efficacy and success of ideas, James proposes a shift from the idea of an abstract community to the notions held by particular people. Truth, relatedly, is what individuals are impelled or compelled to believe: it is a matter of what pays by way of belief. Neopragmatism maintains that meaning is inevitably bound to a context, thus negating the possibility of universal notions of truth and reality. Philosophical attempts to distinguish between the universal and the historical, the necessary and the contingent, truth and fiction have invariably failed. This suggests that meaning and truth should be regarded as nothing but effects of specific cultural circumstances.

Ludwig Wittgenstein (1889–1951), in his *Tractatus Logico-Philosophicus* (1921), is concerned with establishing a correspondence between language and the world. The world is seen as a totality of facts, or states of affairs, not of things, for things are meaningless outside their surroundings and cannot be analysed in themselves. Meaning emerges only through configurations or ensembles of things. A representation of a state of affairs is a *picture* Analogously, language contains simple names (atoms which cannot be analysed in themselves) and these names combine with others to produce propositions. Propositions are made up of simple signs whose meanings can only be elucidated in the actual use of language. A name is not a tag attached to an object but rather an element subject to rules of combination with other names. Names only function in the context of propositions. Both states of affairs and propositions are bipolar: they either obtain or do not; they are either true or false. A proposition is a linguistic correlate of a worldly state of affairs: if the state of affairs obtains, the proposition is accordingly true. Propositions must therefore be able to picture facts or states of affairs. However, we must also be able to picture to ourselves facts that are not realized but might have been.

Is it possible to draw a clear line between factual and non-factual language, science and nonscience? Logical Positivism thought that it was: theories are legitimate if they can be classified as scientific. The *Tractatus* follows this approach in arguing that philosophical statements are nonscientific and therefore unreliable. However, it also states that this does not imply that nonscience should be condemned – rather, it means that it cannot be adequately articulated through language. Wittgenstein states: 'The whole sense of the book might be summed up in the following words: what can be said at all can be said clearly, and what we cannot talk about we must pass over in silence' (Wittgenstein 1975: 6.53). This leads to a paradox: truly important things must remain unsaid, yet one must be able to convey their importance by not talking about them.

The sayable and the unsayable also impinge on the question of the self. The knowing self sees the world but cannot see itself seeing it: I can say 'I see a blue tiger' but cannot see the 'I' that sees the blue tiger. Analogously, when I look in a mirror, I can see my eyes but cannot see the 'I' that sees them. There is no I, ego or subject able to confer meaning to what it sees and thinks. 'I' is a linguistic point of reference, not a personal possession.

Establishing the conditions for the existence of a precisely meaningful language is an arduous task. The grammatical correctness of a sentence is no reliable guarantee: an utterance may be correctly shaped, yet illogical. This is documented in *How To Do Things With Words* by J. L. Austin (1911–60), the founder of Speech-Act Theory. Austin argues that in order to be meaningful, sentences must fulfil certain 'happiness conditions': they must refer to something/someone that really exists, must be honest and must be consistent (Austin 1962). However, these conditions are not guaranteed by grammatical correctness. Properly structured sentences can be meaningless if they fail due to lack of reference ('John's children are bald but John has no children'); dishonesty ('I say "I'll be there" but have no intention of being there'); or *inconsistency* ('I say "I welcome you" but then treat you as an intruder')[4].

In the *Tractatus*, Wittgenstein seems to be saying that meaningful propositions are scientific and well-formed and that meaning-

---

[4] ☞ The relationship between grammar and logic is also addressed in Part III, Chapter 3, 'Rhetoric'.

less ones are *pseudopropositions* – quite typical of philosophy – that appear well-formed but are not actually so. Meaningful propositions are divided into *atomic* and *molecular* ones. Atomic propositions are elementary statements whose meanings are directly related to the world and cannot be analysed (i.e. transformed into something more basic still). An atomic proposition pictures a possible state of affairs: if this obtains, the proposition is meaningful and if it does not, the proposition is meaningless. Molecular propositions are compounds of atomic propositions and can be broken down into their constituents. A proposition such as 'The sun is the centre of the universe' could be described as atomic: it pictures an elementary state of affairs. A proposition such as 'We owe the discovery that the sun, not the earth, is the centre of the universe to the Polish astronomer Nicolaus Copernicus' is molecular. It can be broken down into atomic units that picture various states of affairs: 1. 'Nicolaus Copernicus was a Polish astronomer'; 2. 'He discovered that the sun is the centre of the universe'; 3. 'The earth is not the centre of the universe'; and so on.

In his later writings, Wittgenstein questions quite radically the value of atomic propositions by arguing that they are not necessary to meaningful communication. He no longer maintains that a sentence must have a definite sense. Meanings, in other words, can be blurred and still function as meanings. In *Philosophical Investigations* (1953), Wittgenstein argues that it is pointless to look for the *essence* of meaning, since linguistic phenomena do not share universal principles. Language takes many forms. In each, the same words may be used. However, different uses of the same word do not make the word itself the same in all forms of language.Wittgenstein explains this by recourse to the idea of family resemblances. Words uniform in appearance are not uniform in application: only certain overlapping traits (comparable to the ones joining members of the same family) connect their different usages. All we have is a multiplicity of diverse and interacting language games, each governed by specific rules and linked – by analogy – to other games (Wittgenstein 1973). In this perspective, words and meanings are not, ultimately, judged according to their correctness or incorrectness but according to their usefulness. Meaning is the product of *contingent* situations.

The contingency of meaning constitutes a major aspect of the work of Richard Rorty (b. 1931), where it is argued that nothing carries meaning as a result of its intrinsic nature. To say that *there is a world out there* cannot coincide with saying that *there is a truth out there*. The world in and by itself is neither true nor false; only sentences can be true or false. If truth is a property of sentences, it follows that truth is not a metaphysical given. Sentences are fundamentally human inventions and depend on vocabularies, i.e. artificial constructs in the process of constant making, unmaking and remaking. The human self, too, is the product of certain vocabularies and of their cultural usages. Rorty has little faith in the idea of linguistic evolution or in the notion that there is a fixed task for language to execute. Language is about the ongoing creation of new vocabularies which do not correspond to the discovery of truer realities, but rather to the realization that reality has to be incessantly redescribed as a result of contingent mutations. These are produced by the ensemble of disciplines (philosophy, literary studies, science, etc.) which constitute a culture (Rorty 1989).

Let us now move to the field of Linguistics. The study of language as a system as carried out by this discipline comprises five main areas: grammar; syntax; hermeneutics; pragmatics; semantics. Grammar deals with the rules concerning the ways in which words can be put together for the purpose of constructing sentences. Syntax focuses on the logical principles underlying the grammatical arrangement of words or grammatical rules. Both grammar and syntax are concerned with the structural features of language. Grammar defines words as parts of speech (e.g. nouns, verbs, adjectives, adverbs) while syntax defines words or clusters of words according to the roles they play within sentences (e.g. subject, object, predicate). Hermeneutics deals with theories of interpretation.[5] Pragmatics and Semantics examine the nature and genesis of meaning. In pragmatics, the focus is on the relationship between language and ourselves, that is, on the ways in which we are able to invest certain words or sentences with meanings. Semantics concentrates on the relationship between language and the world, namely the ways in which words relate to the objects or facts they refer to.

The main models used in the study of language are the *prescrip-*

---

[5] ☞ These theories are discussed in Part I, Chapter 5, 'Reading'.

tive and the *descriptive* approaches. The first is concerned with establishing the rules that underpin a correct use of language. The second concentrates on the ways in which people actually speak and write, regardless of their correctness. Whereas traditional grammarians – from Classical Greece onwards – focused on written texts and on literary language in order to prescribe certain principles of correctness, modern linguists concentrate on speech and stress the importance of informal and colloquial language usages, as well as of dialects, as no less systematic than the standard language taught in schools. What has been marginalized as incorrect or substandard nonetheless forms a system amenable to scientific analysis and description. The same applies to so-called primitive languages, which have often been seen as shapeless and inferior purely on the basis of ideological and racial prejudices.

The two principal features of language are its dual structure and its creativity. The structure of language is dual because it comprises syntax (the study of sentences as combinations of units of meaning) and phonology (the study of sentences as combinations of units of sound). Creativity refers to a language user's ability to utter and grasp a virtually limitless series of sentences which s/he has not actually heard or read before – and which, indeed, may never have been uttered or written before.

A crucial contribution to modern linguistics in the American context was made by Franz Boas (1858–1942). He supplied a detailed investigation of American Indian languages so as to demonstrate that all languages have their own unique structures and that the linguist's task is to identify the most precise ways of describing those structures. No less important were the theories put forward by Edward Sapir (1884–1939). Sapir viewed language as a fundamentally human endowment, connected with reason rather than thought. While pursuing this humanist argument, Sapir also laid the foundations of American structural linguistics by maintaining that languages function on the basis of structuring criteria which native speakers often rely upon unconsciously. Sounds play a crucial part, in this respect. Sapir drew an important distinction (also emphasized by Saussure) between *phonemic* and *phonetic* differences. Phonemic differences are central to the structure of a language and native speakers recognize them as meaningful, or productive of meaning. Phonetic differences, by contrast, are hardly recognized. Thus, the phonetic difference between the sound |p| in the word 'pot' and in the word 'spot' is something which a native speaker does not consciously register. Phonemic differences, conversely, are picked up because they determine how certain sounds enable the recognition of the meaning of a word. Phonemes (minimal units of sound) produce meaning through contrasts: 'mat' and 'rat', for instance, are differentiated by the phonemes that go with their opening consonants.

Another influential figure associated with modern American linguistics is Leonard Bloomfield (1887-1949), the father of behaviourism. According to Bloomfield, meaning depends on the practical context in which an utterance is produced and responded to. He believed that the meanings of words cannot be precisely defined because humans do not have a total knowledge of the things or ideas to which words refer. In various specialist fields, it can be assumed that certain words are meaningful because they can be associated with scientifically classified objects (e.g. animals, plants, minerals). But when we enter the sphere of abstract concepts, such as 'love' and 'hate', our knowledge is far too hazy to allow for precise definitions of their meanings. Noam Chomsky's first book, *Syntactic Structures* (1957), was influenced by Bloomfield and his followers. However, it rejects the behaviourist framework, according to which language is a product of habits developed in relation to our environment and to how it conditions us. This model, argues Chomsky, is unsatisfactory because it does nothing to explain language's creativity – the faculty, as we have seen, that enables human beings (and even relatively young ones) to produce and understand a potentially infinite number of sentences which they have never come across before and which cannot, therefore, constitute obvious responses to environmental stimuli. According to Chomsky, we do not learn how to handle language purely as a result of environmental influences, for children actually have an innate knowledge of the universal principles that govern the structure of human language. The basic principles that determine the grammatical rules of disparate languages are, to a great extent, common to all languages, they are biologically intrinsic to humans and can therefore be genetically transmitted from generation to generation.

Echoing Saussure's distinction between *langue* and *parole*,[6]

---

[6] ☛ See Part I, Chapter 2, 'The Sign.'

Chomsky maintains that language comprises two faculties: *competence*, the system or structure of language, and *performance*, a contingent utterance or set of utterances. Competence precedes and indeed generates performance. Individual utterances are generated through the transformation of basic rules ('deep structures') into specific sentences and syntactical arrangements ('surface structures'). Competence is based on a grasp of the fundamental rules on the basis of which sentences are formed. Only a relatively small proportion of the indefinite quantity of sentences that a language can potentially produce are actually uttered (Chomsky 1965).

One of the most intriguing aspects of Chomsky's writings is their emphasis on certain vital links between linguistics and psychology. Linguistics may ultimately gain little from exploring language as an abstract system. It should, in fact, look at how language is used by different speakers and at how the use of language is related to mental processes which cause people to speak and write in the ways they do. Memory, attention and concentration all play important roles. The psychological makeup of the individual language user should also be taken into consideration. For example, the tendency to use particular syntactical forms (active, passive, declarative, interrogative, etc.) says a lot about a person. No less telling are so-called mistakes such as mispronunciations, unfinished utterances, pauses, and shifts in the construction of a sentence. As amply documented by Freudian psychoanalysis, mistakes have deep psychological roots and are therefore not easily reducible to poor grammatical training. Meaning, ultimately, is no less an effect of haphazardly constructed utterances, slips of the tongue and of the pen, misreadings and blunders than it is a product of precisely formulated sentences.

CHAPTER 2

THE SIGN

Many important developments in critical and cultural theory have been triggered by the study of language as a system of signs.[1] The discipline concerned with the analysis of this system is known as semiotics (or semiology), a term derived from the Greek word *semeion*, namely 'sign'. In examining the ways in which signs operate within a culture, semiotics proceeds from the premise that all aspects of that culture can be regarded as systems of signs: verbal and visual languages, movements, postures and gestures, buildings and furniture, clothes, accessories and menus are equally open to semiotic decoding. Understanding a culture means detecting and interpreting its sign systems. Signs do not embody specific meanings or concepts. Rather, they give us *clues* which only lead to meanings through interpretation. Signs become meaningful when they are decoded according to cultural conventions and rules which people employ both consciously and unconsciously.

The idea of language as a system of signs was introduced by the Swiss linguist Ferdinand de Saussure (1857–1913). His *Course in General Linguistics* was compiled after his death with the assistance of notes based on lectures delivered by Saussure in Geneva between 1906 and 1911. The *Course* was published in Paris in 1915, and its first English translation appeared in 1959. Prior to Saussure, the study of language had been subsumed to the discipline of philology, which consisted of tracing the historical (diachronic) development of individual languages and clusters of languages. Saussure revolutionized the study of language by

---

[1] ☞ Part I, Chapter 1, 'Meaning' supplies a useful companion piece to this chapter.

turning it into an autonomous discipline concerned with describing the state of a linguistic system at any given point in time (synchronic approach) and by drawing a distinction between *langue*, the system of language as a whole, and *parole*, a specific utterance. Above all, Saussure's theories are centred on the concept of the *sign*.

Saussure's sign consists of two elements: the *signifier*, or sound-image, and the *signified*, or the concept referred to. For example, the sounds I utter when I say 'leopard' and the letters l-e-o-p-a-r-d I put down on paper when I write the word 'leopard' constitute the signifier. The concept of a four-legged, fierce and furry feline conveyed by those sounds or letters constitutes the signified. It is the relationship between the signifier and the signified that invests a sign with meaning: neither signifies anything on its own. Saussure emphasizes that there is no natural connection between the signifier and the signified. The link is always arbitrary and conventional. Language does not reflect a pre-existing reality; nor does it name universal concepts shared by all cultures. In fact, it creates reality by chopping up the continuum of space and time into categories that vary hugely from one culture to another insofar as they are produced in relation to widely diverse environments. (It is well known, for instance, that Eskimos have several words for 'snow' whereas many other cultures deem one word sufficient to describe this particular entity.) Saussure also stresses that what makes a sign meaningful is not some intrinsic quality. Meaning is the product of a sign's difference from and relation to other signs. Sounds play a crucial part in endowing signs with meanings on the basis of differences. For example, the difference between the initial sound of the word 'dog' and the initial sound of the word 'fog' is what enables us to give each word a different meaning. These basic differences in sound are known as phonemic oppositions (*phonemes* are basic units of sound). Any two words (like 'dog' and 'fog') differentiated by a single phoneme are termed minimal pairs.[2]

In arguing that we can only grasp signs in the context of other signs, Saussure compares language to the game of chess: the pieces on the board do not mean anything outside the rules of the game.

---

[2] ☞ The relationship between sound and meaning is discussed in Part I, Chapter 1, 'Meaning'.

Each piece only acquires meaning in relation to all the other pieces and their moves, just as each sign only acquires meaning in relation to all the other signs in a language. This is shown by the operations through which sentences are constructed: selection and combination. In forming sentences, we select a certain number of words from the whole vocabulary potentially available in a language and then combine them into a meaningful sequence. Selection and combination constitute the two axes of language. Selection is associated with the paradigmatic axis ('paradigm' refers to the selection of words) and combination with the syntagmatic axis ('syntagm' refers to the combination of words). The actual words that are present in a sentence always refer, implicitly, to all the absent words that could have been used instead. They are only meaningful in virtue of their relationship with the broad system of language from which they have been picked.

Beside Saussure, the other founding father of modern semiotics is Charles Sanders Peirce (1839–1914). Peirce identifies three types of signs: the icon, a sign based on a resemblance between signifier and signified (such as a portrait); the index, a sign in which signifier and signified are causally related (e.g. smoke means fire); the sign proper, the sign in which (as argued by Saussure) the relationship between signifier and signified is utterly arbitrary. According to Peirce, a sign is only capable of conveying a meaning by virtue of an interpreter who is in a position to recognize it *as a sign* and to connect it to some relevant aspect of the world. At the same time, anything can be taken as a sign as long as there is an interpreter inclined to perceive it as such. The interpreter her/himself is a sign. S/he is able to interpret signs insofar as s/he has been equipped by a culture with the means of doing so – namely codes and conventions decreeing what may be considered meaningful. These define the interpreter no less than they enable her/him to define what s/he perceives.

In conceiving of language as a system, semiotics has encouraged the emergence of critical approaches that view individual texts as manifestations of a broader narrative system. Saussure's aversion to the historical study of language has sustained forms of criticism that steer away from the historical assessment of texts. At the same time, Saussure's emphasis on the arbitrary character of the sign and his rejection of the notion of language as a reflection of reality have contributed to a radical questioning of the ethos of realism. This is borne out by developments in the fields of formalist and structuralist criticism.

Formalism was primarily concerned with literariness: that is, with isolating the specific devices that make a particular work a literary work. Texts are autonomous and material entities: they should not be regarded as embodiments of abstract ideas or reflections of a social environment. In divorcing literature from politics, Formalism entered into conflict with Marxist theories according to which all ideological products result from social and economic relations and texts can be read as reflections of a cultural reality. Yet, the separation between literature and politics proposed by Formalism is not always total. Roman Jakobson (1896–1982), for example, argues that though autonomous, literature interrelates with other parts of the social structure, and Mikhail Bakhtin (1895–1975) argues that literary language has a crucially social dimension. This is demonstrated by polyphonic texts that challenge dominant ideologies by articulating diverse discourses and thus resisting the notion of a unified viewpoint. Formalism's central assumption is that literary texts are not mirrors held up to nature but rather organizations of signs. The effectiveness of a text stems from its ability to foreground or lay bare the devices by which it is constituted – i.e. to advertize its constructed status – and to make reality strange through the strategy of *defamiliarization*. These ideas are formulated by Viktor Shklovsky in 'Art as Technique' (1917), a text often regarded as the manifesto of Russian Formalism. Shklovsky argues that poetry does not use images (as is often assumed) for the purpose of expressing economically and thus clarifying life's complexities but rather as a means of unsettling habitual and automatic perceptions. 'The technique of art', Shklovsky states, 'is to make objects "unfamiliar", to make forms difficult, to increase the difficulty and length of perception" (Shklovsky 1988: 20). As a semiotic structure, the literary text truly works only insofar as it is capable of frustrating conventional expectations.

If literature is meant to have defamiliarizing effects, what exactly are we meant to be defamiliarized from? In order to answer this question, several Formalist critics sought to identify the basic ingredients and codes of particular textual forms. Especially influential, in this respect, was Vladimir Propp's *Morphology of the Folk Tale* (1928). Propp maintains that the traditional tale, as a prototype of all narrative forms, is based on a fixed number of components. There are seven spheres of action, associated with the characters and roles of the 'Villain', the 'Donor', the 'Helper', the 'Princess and Her Father', the 'Dispatcher', the 'Hero' and the 'False Hero', and thirty-one functions, associated with key moments in the action, e.g. 'Preparation', 'Complication', 'Struggle', 'Return and Recognition'. No tale contains all thirty-one functions. However, the ones it does contain occur in the same order in all tales. What is most intriguing about the folk tale is its duplicity: its basic form is repetitive, yet it is capable of producing a limitless number of imaginative and colourful variations. For Propp, what makes a tale ultimately appealing is not its unchanging skeleton but the changing features of its characters and settings. Later critics attempted to identify the semiotic links connecting various texts by working out elementary structures of signification. A. J. Greimas's *Semantique Structurale* (1966), for example, proposes a model based on the principle of opposition. The world only takes shape insofar as differences can be perceived in its fabric. Thus, a tale's elementary structure may lie in oppositions such as 'subject versus object' or 'sender versus receiver'.

The writings of Roman Jakobson are sometimes regarded as a bridge between Formalism and Structuralism and their discussion is here accordingly positioned. Following Saussure, Jakobson argues that language is based on processes of selection and combination: 'the given utterance (message) is a combination of constituent parts (sentences, words, phonemes, etc.) selected from the repository of all possible constituent parts (the code)' (Jakobson and Halle 1956: 75). One of Jakobson's most innovative contributions consists of the idea that selection and combination are underpinned by the principles of metaphor and metonymy. These are not understood merely as rhetorical figures but actually as the most fundamental ways of organizing signs in all forms of cultural production. Metonymy is based on contiguity. An attribute of a thing that is contiguous to it (next to it) is substituted for the thing itself ('Crown' metonymically signifies the monarchy). Contiguity also sustains the syntagmatic process of combination, whereby words are placed next to one another in sentences. Thus, combination is related to the metonymic mode. Metaphor is based on similarity. A thing is described in terms of another thing comparable to it ('life is a beach'). Similarity is also at the basis of the paradigmatic process of selection, whereby a word is chosen out of a pool of analogous words. Thus, selection is related to the metaphoric mode.

Jakobson arrived at this conclusion through his study of the linguistic disturbance known as *aphasia*. Jakobson distinguishes between two forms of aphasia: the contiguity disorder, consisting of a difficulty in combining words and hence of a tendency to produce metaphors; and the similarity disorder, consisting of a difficulty in selecting words and hence of a tendency to produce metonymies. In literary terms, the contiguity disorder is associated with metaphor and poetry, and the similarity disorder with metonymy and prose. Both metaphor and metonymy are figures of equivalence. In ordinary language, equivalence applies essentially to the axis of selection: we select certain signs from a range of equivalent signs. In poetic language, equivalence is also applied to the axis of combination: signs are strung together on the basis of similarities in pattern and sound: 'the metrical parallelisms of lines, or the phonic equivalence of rhyming words' (Jakobson and Halle 1956: 95).

For Jakobson, as for Saussure, all forms of language are based on relationships between signifiers and signifieds. However, a distinction must be drawn between prose and poetry. Prose subordinates the signifier to the interests of the signified; that is, it is more concerned with the content of an utterance and the message it conveys than with the form of the utterance, how the message is conveyed. Poetry, by contrast, foregrounds the signifier: it places great emphasis on the shapes and sounds of words as means of evoking meaning, rather than subordinating them to the concepts they stand for. The forms through which a message is articulated contribute to the message itself: 'the poetic function is defined as a specialized use of language in which the signifier intensifies the message' (Easthope 1983: 15). The poetic function is not exclusive to poetry. It also features in various aspects of ordinary language, such as political slogans. 'I like Ike', for example, uses a basic poetic form which makes it more striking than 'Ike is great' or 'I respect Ike'.

Structuralism develops some of the positions outlined above. It seeks for universal patterns of signs and, while conceding that the particular signs employed by any given culture are context bound, it also maintains that all cultures orchestrate their signs into strucmres that are fundamentally similar. A central idea deployed by Structuralism is that of binary oppositions: pairs of contrasting signs (light/dark, good/bad, active/passive, etc.) which suggest that things can be defined in relation to what they are not. The first term of a binary opposition is generally privileged as a positive concept, whilst the second is marginalized as negative. Structuralism takes as its fundamental assumption the primacy of the linguistic model, whereby all cultural systems are analysable as languages. Thus, the strategies used to explore verbal language have been applied by several critics to the study of non-verbal sign systems, most notably by Roland Barthes. In Barthes's writings inspired by semiotics and Structuralism, the tools of structural linguistics are employed to decode systems such as fashion, architecture and cuisine.[3]

Structuralism looks for reality in the relationships amongst things rather than in individual things. In the field of literary criticism, for example, it studies a text's structural properties in order to relate it to a larger cluster of texts which share comparable features and, ultimately, to culture as a whole: 'literature is not only a collection of autonomous works, which may "influence" one another by a series of fortuitous and isolated encounters; it is a coherent whole, a homogeneous space, within which works touch and penetrate one another; it is also, in turn, a part linked to other parts in the wider space of "culture", in which its own value is a function of the whole' (Genette 1988: 73). In all areas, Structuralism aims at establishing systems to which particular items could be connected: a system of literature embracing individual works with common characteristics; or an anthropological system based on universal principles which give rise to various laws, rituals and prohibitions.

Claude Levi-Strauss (b. 1908) was the first to apply Structuralism to anthropology by defining this discipline as a broad theory of cultural relationships, analysable according to the universal laws that guide mental processes and, in particular, the human tendency to articulate experiences symbolically. Amongst the many symbolic systems used by cultures to define themselves, mythology plays an especially prominent role. Myths are an

---

[3] ☞ Barthes's work is examined in detail in Part I, Chapter 6, 'Textuality'.

elemental form of poetic wisdom through which humans endeavour to understand the world through the mediation of stories. Levi-Strauss believes that in order to grasp the complexity of myths, a methodical analysis of their structure is required. Mythological stories can be read diachronically, in the order they actually present certain events and situations. But they should also be read synchronically, in terms of the specific relevance of any one of their items at any one moment in the narrative. This is achieved by breaking the story down into minimal units (*mythemes*) and reorganizing them in terms of relationships and oppositions.

According to Levi-Strauss, the very systems of kinship on which all cultures varyingly hinge constitute a language enabling communication amongst the members of a community. While in verbal language, messages are based on the circulation of words, in the language of kinship, messages depend on the circulation of women, for all societies tend to contain rules and taboos concerning who one is allowed to marry or be sexually associated with. In Levi-Strauss's theories of kinship, woman is fundamentally a sign. The system of food also constitutes a language. Although shopping lists vary hugely from one culture to another, in all societies, the gathering, processing and consumption of food form a code. This is because all cultures rely on conventional decisions regarding what can and cannot be eaten, when, by whom, with whom, and in combination with what else. Levi-Strauss uses the binary opposition Nature versus Culture to construct a culinary triangle which differentiates, structurally and semiotically, between the transformation of food by natural means ('raw' → 'rotten') and the transformation of food by cultural means ('raw' → 'cooked'):

raw

△

cooked   rotten

It is undeniable that Structuralism has played a key role in unsettling conventional ideas about language, in showing that meaning is not a given but rather a cultural construct, in inviting people to question where the meanings they tend to take for granted actually come from and how signs are socially produced. Yet, Structuralism is impaired by its pursuit of a fantasy of universality, by its determination to unite disparate forms of knowledge and signification under the banner of language, and by the idea that immutable principles can be detected beneath the tangled skein of contingent cultural codes and conventions. This has made it increasingly unsatisfactory for writers and thinkers inclined to suspect that life is never quite so neat. In 'Structuralism and Literary Criticism'(1964), Gerard Genette (b. 1930) argues that the problem with Structuralism lies in its faith in the universal explanatory power of structures. This faith does not take adequately into account the constant displacement of meaning in language: meaning changes across time and space. The structuralist model is not, Genette maintains, universally applicable to all texts. What he proposes, as an alternative, is a critical scene in which different approaches are adopted to suit the specific requirements of different types of texts, and in which the relationship between the past and the present is assiduously taken into consideration.

Genette suggests that the study of signs comprises two main critical approaches. One possible approach hinges on the separation of the present from the past, and accordingly proposes different reading modalities for the texts of the present and those of the past. Living literature is the object of ongoing interpretation and its signs are read by engaging directly with texts as experienced in the here-and-now (hermeneutic model). Remote literature is the object of a methodical analysis of forms, narrative systems and sign structures (structuralist model). The second approach described by Genette promotes a dialogue between past and present. Its fundamental premise is that the present does not merely encompass signs and texts produced in the present but also past signs and texts perceived as relevant to the present. Language and interpretation have to do with how we consume the signs of the past no less than with the signs we construct in the present. Structuralism, Genette intimates, is bound to fail as long as it tries to anchor the unanchorable, to arrest the constant slippage of signs. This slippage inevitably occurs when we realize that a word or sentence we use always begs comparison to other words and sentences that could have been employed in their place. The words and sentences we actually use displace myriad alternatives and their own value as signs is concurrently displaced. This critique of Structuralism has been developed, since the mid-1970s, by a cluster of theoretical positions commonly grouped under the heading of Poststructuralism.

Poststructuralism embraces the structuralist idea that meanings are constructed by language but suggests that language itself is not a reliable model. Language does not deliver universal structures or presences but rather traces, barely legible yet daunting imprints of an absent other which simply cannot be fixed. All structures are transient and all meanings inconclusive, for signifiers and signifieds have a knack of pulling apart and reuniting in ever new and often unforeseen combinations. Poststructuralism deems the notion of a universal system sustained by binary oppositions an act of violence bent on arresting the endless play of signs. At the same time, it emphasizes the remainders which language seems to ignore and yet which play a crucial part in all people's lives: silences, gaps, inexpressible ideas and feelings, things we mean but cannot say and things we say without actually meaning them. Language is incapable of representing a stable order. It is, rather, an ongoing process in which a sign can evoke multiple meanings, and in which a single meaning can be evoked by legion signs.

The field of poststructuralist theory termed *deconstruction*, principally associated with the work of Jacques Derrida (b. 1930), has challenged the structuralist dream of producing scientific accounts of culture by discovering its underlying sign systems.[4] These accounts are based on the assumption that there are stable points of reference outside the systems themselves – a centre, a transcendental signified – which secure their intelligibility. For Derrida, these points of reference are fictions. Even if they did exist, they would not be reliable – for how could something stable be trusted to sanction the intelligibility of systems which, as Structuralism itself concedes, undergo constant mutations? In rejecting the possibility of systematic analyses of culture, Derrida also questions the

---

[4] ☞ Derrida's deconstructionist theories are discussed further in Part I, Chapter 3, 'Rhetoric'. Other thinkers whose theories are commonly classified as poststructuralist are examined in Part II, Chapter 1, 'Ideology'; Part II, Chapter 2, 'Subjectivity'; and Part III, Chapter 6, 'The Simulacrum'.

view that certain texts (scientific, philosophical, or historical) are more reputable than stories and fictions. All texts, he maintains, are equally questionable because all texts inevitably provide subjective, partial and fragmentary versions of reality. No text, however objective it may claim to be, depicts the world as it is. All texts, moreover, are riven by internal contradictions: a piece of writing intended to prove a certain truth always contains elements which contradict its main argument. Deconstructing a text consists of recognizing and highlighting its internal incongruities. Although the verb 'to deconstruct' is often colloquially employed as if it meant 'to pull apart', this usage is incorrect. Derrida is not encouraging us to pull texts apart but actually inviting us to identify ways in which texts dismantle themselves through their own inconsistencies, ambiguities, paradoxes, silences and gaps. Deconstruction is not something one does to a text. Rather, it is something which the text has always already done to itself.

In conclusion, Structuralism could be described as a unifying system which seeks to map out scientifically a broad spectrum of cultural phenomena according to the model of language. It acknowledges the arbitrariness of the processes through which signs acquire their meanings, yet believes that fundamental linguistic rules are universal and universally applicable. In the context of Poststructuralism, reality is not only a linguistic construct but also an unstable concept. Language incessantly shapes and reshapes the world in a baffling variety of ways, which indicate that the signs through which history, philosophy, literature and human subjectivity itself are constructed are always open to freeplay.

CHAPTER 3

RHETORIC

If addressing questions to do with language and interpretation is always, to some extent, a case of facing the imponderable, this is especially apposite for the issue of rhetoric. Many critical texts explain rhetoric away as the art of expression and persuasion. However, there is a wide diversity of opinion as to what ultimately constitutes this art. The moment one begins to delve beneath superficial definitions of rhetoric as the knack of using verbal devices in sophisticated ways, a veritable can of linguistic worms gets open. It soon becomes clear that rhetoric is not merely a matter of being clever with words or being able to handle complex devices in a convincing and entertaining fashion. Rhetoric may, indeed, be the art of expression and persuasion – an art whose currency consists of figures of speech, images and tropes. Yet, these elements are not mere embellishments of ordinary language used exclusively by orators, poets and fiction writers. In fact, they pervade language in its entirety.

Language as a system of signs and symbols[1] is always based on figures of some kind – namely, conventional elements that define things in their absence. If a poem or song tells you that 'life is a long road', you may instantly take the proposition as an image, a piece of rhetoric. You know that an association has been made between two ideas in ways which you are not expected to take literally. If, in unfamiliar surroundings, you ask for directions to your destination and you are told 'this road will take you there', you will probably not register the statement as a piece of rhetoric.

---

[1] ☞ Refer to Part I, Chapter 1, 'Meaning' and Part I, Chapter 2, 'The Sign' for a detailed discussion of this theme.

Yet, upon closer inspection, you will realize that no 'road' can actually 'take' you anywhere, for you have to do the travelling yourself. Besides, 'road' is a word – not a thing – and cannot aid your journey any more than the word 'bread' could satisfy your hunger or need of money, or the word 'water' could quench your thirst on a hot day. Isn't this rhetoric, too?

The present chapter examines some definitions of rhetoric, drawing attention to its stylistic, philosophical and ideological connotations as a phenomenon that does not simply adorn meaning but actually shapes it. The central argument pursued in this chapter proceeds from the premise that rhetoric should not be viewed as a specialized and somewhat deviant form of language because rhetorical mechanisms pervade the whole of language. This can be demonstrated on two levels. Firstly, the devices associated with rhetoric, and often thought of as poetic or fictional tricks, do not only feature in poetry and fiction but also in everyday sign systems such as advertising and political slogans. Moreover, virtually any utterance could be read rhetorically as well as literally. This has largely to do with the fact that, given some ingenuity and linguistic curiosity, even the most referential sentence may become ambiguous. What is an advertisement offering accommodation for a 'professional non-smoker' really telling you about the type of tenant required? Is s/he supposed to be someone who holds a profession and also does not smoke? Or is s/he supposed to be someone who has made not smoking into a profession? 'Supervise children while using this bag'; 'Please ask if you need assistance'; 'Prams must be carried on the escalator'; and 'I like Indians without reservations' are also worth playing around with. A favourite is the case of the jogger who, training in the vicinity of Regent's Park, London, was asked by a man sporting a ginger bob, pea-green blazer, scarlet leather pants and leopard-patterned loafers if he was 'all right for the Zoo'.

Secondly, rhetoric is based on the displacement of referential meaning through images. This is true, in a basic sense, of language at large, for words never refer in transparent ways to objects and ideas but rather displace them by translating them into abstract and arbitrary signs. All words, after all, are metaphors. What lends them a certain referential solidity, argued Friedrich Nietzsche, is our tendency to forget that they are indeed metaphors. The pages that follow explore the theme of rhetoric with reference to: (1) approaches to rhetoric developed within an illustrative range of historical and cultural contexts; (2) the role played by rhetoric in the deconstructionist theories of Jacques Derrida and Paul de Man.

The idea that rhetorical devices are a distinctive feature of literary texts (especially poetry) was central to the programme of New Criticism: a critical trend inspired by T. S. Eliot and pursued by critics such as Cleanth Brooks, R. P. Blackmur, Allen Tate, W. K. Wimsatt, M. C. Beardsley and R. Penn Warren in the 1940s and 1950s. The New Critics saw the text as a complex structure of meaning, or organization of language, to be analysed with close reference to its rhetorical devices and specifically with a focus on irony, paradox, tension and ambiguity. They wanted literary criticism to develop into an autonomous science, capable of studying texts as specialized constructs and in specialized ways. They rejected Positivism, the philosophical doctrine that sought to subsume all disciplines to the laws of physics and viewed language as a neutral medium for the transcription of facts, by stressing that literature manipulates language through special (rhetorical) techniques that render it far from transparent. The critic's task, in this context, consists of isolating the devices through which a text is constructed and on the effects these produce, independently of the author's intentions and of the reader's emotions. To evaluate a text according to either of these functions, argue Wimsatt and Beardsley in *The Verbal Icon* (1954), means confusing the text and its *origins* 'Intentional Fallacy' – or the text and its *results* – 'Affective Fallacy' – (Wimsatt and Beardsley 1972). Texts, in this programme, must be assessed in terms of whether or not they work – i.e. whether or not they possess internal coherence and are able to handle their rhetorical devices satisfactorily.

New Criticism anticipates later developments in critical theory by emphasizing the importance of the text itself rather than peripheral speculations about its origins and its results. However, New Criticism proposes a somewhat limited approach to rhetoric by advocating that: (1) a text's obscurities and contradictions, produced by its rhetorical structure, must be clarified and resolved – rhetoric, in other words, must be domesticated; (2) rhetorical language is seen as peculiar to literary texts and hence divorced from ordinary language. An important reassessment of rhetorical language comes with the writings of the Formalist critic and linguist Roman Jakobson (1896-1982)[2] Jakobson believes that poetic devices (both explicitly rhetorical ones, such as images and tropes, and others, such as sound, rhyme and rhythm) constitute a special kind of language rather than a superficial decoration of so-called ordinary language: 'poeticalness is not a supplementation of discourse with rhetorical adornment but a total re-evaluation of the discourse and of all its components whatsoever' (Jakobson 1960: 377). Most importantly, the linguistic devices commonly associated with poetry are shown to be very much at work in everyday aspects of expression and signification: the 'poetic function' features in all forms of discourse and 'is not just a special set of "tricks" that poets perform' (Hawkes 1977: 81).

Rhetoric and ideology are inextricably intertwined. This is because rhetorical language often serves eminently ideological objectives, as shown by the collusion of rhetoric and politics in ancient Greece and Rome, in the courtly circles of the Western Renaissance and, of course, in contemporary societies, where a party's agenda is often encapsulated in memorable snippets of rhetoric. Classical theorists were eager to define the codes and conventions of rhetoric very thoroughly, for a command of this art was deemed essential to successful outcomes in the manipulation of language, often for political purposes. This is borne out by a number of influential textbooks produced by Greek and Roman writers: Aristotle's *Rhetoric*; Quintilian's *Institutio Oratoria*; Cicero's *De Inventione*; *De Optimo Genere Oratorum* and *De Oratore*. The rules for oral and written composition prescribed by Cicero comprised five processes: *invention* (the discovery of appropriate verbal material); *arrangement* (its cogent organization into a structure); *style* (the formulation of the mode of delivery relevant to the occasion); *memory* (the ability to store and recycle utterances and images); *delivery* (the elaboration of complex techniques for producing a successful rhetorical package).

A culture's understanding of rhetoric tends to mirror its dominant ideology. Consider the following example. Renaissance writers, keen on reviving the principles upheld by the Classics as the fountainhead of civilization and enlightenment, were particularly intrigued by the art of rhetoric and by the figure of the orator as a skilful speaker and performer well-versed in a variety

---

[2] ☛ Jakobson's theories are discussed in Part I, Chapter 2, 'The Sign'.

of disciplines and registers. However, the Renaissance could not adopt Classical ideals without somehow modifying them so that they would be compatible with its own cultural and ideological circumstances. Thus, in incorporating the lessons of ancient Greece and Rome into its own fabric, the Renaissance had to make certain adjustments. In the field of rhetoric, specifically, this meant that the qualities of the Classical orator must be retained, and that a truly accomplished person must be no less eclectic, persuasive and artful than his/her Greek and Roman predecessors. Nevertheless, certain crucial differences between Classical and Renaissance milieus must be taken into account. The Classical orator was very much a *public* figure – performing in open spaces for the benefit of varied and often non-specialist audiences – and rhetoric was, accordingly, a public art. (Indeed, the term *rhetor* refers to a 'speaker in the assembly'.) The Renaissance type expected to excel at rhetoric, by contrast, was the courtier – the product of elaborate rituals dictated by etiquette handbooks no less than by academic training. Unlike Classical orators, Renaissance courtiers deployed their rhetorical skills within private circles of experts and connoisseurs. Moreover, this private world was, more often than not, a nest of intrigue and deception.

Whereas in Classical times the orator was praised for his *claritas* – i.e. the ability to convey complicated arguments lucidly and persuasively so as to enlighten his audience – in the Renaissance adaptation of Classical rhetoric, illumination was to be achieved by circuitous means, by enveloping the message in as many layers of verbal complexity and in as many dark conceits as humanly possible. Furthermore, the courtier had to exhibit the virtue of *sprezzatura* (from the Italian 'sprezzare' or 'disprezzare', namely 'to scorn', 'to dismiss'). That is, he had to appear not to care about his rhetorical skills and was required to come across as artless even as he was exploiting his talent to the highest degree. The courtier must be a good orator, master many arts, display polished social manners and know how to handle diplomatically the court's personal and political plots. The main quality he was expected to develop was dissimulation. Living in an environment given to subterfuge and backstabbing, he had to learn how to establish prudential relationships with both princes and peers. Dissimulation became a principal rhetorical skill: it meant being able to produce complex images and to convey them in tantalizing ways to audiences averse to plain words and fond of riddles.

Both Classical and Renaissance approaches to rhetoric indicate that rhetorical language is an important aspect of human behaviour because it defines and affects people's actions. Recent developments in philosophy of language have sought to show that speech is indeed a species of action. Moving from the study of *performative utterances* (namely, utterances that coincide with something being 'done' rather than merely 'stated'), J. L. Austin (1911–60)[3] has argued that in any use of language, a speaker performs several acts. For example, if I say 'It's five o'clock', I may be performing the following acts: (1) stating the time of day; (2) reminding Louise that her favourite TV programme will be starting soon; (3) warning Barney that he may be late for work. There are three main types of speech act. A *locutionary* act is the act of saying something. An *illocutionary* act is an act done *in* saying something. A *perlocutionary* act is an act done *by* saying something. In the example presented above, (1) (stating) is a locutionary act; (2) (reminding) is an illocutionary act; and (3) (warning) is a perlocutionary act (Austin 1962).

Shifting approaches to the relationship between speech and action show that even as the lessons and models of rhetoric are carried over from one culture to another, their persistence depends on their adaptability to different ideological contexts. Rhetoric's rubber resilience cannot, however, be explained simply as a concomitant of its invaluable ideological function. In fact, it has to do with the fact that rhetoric inhabits language in all its manifestations and that, insofar as language constructs reality, without rhetoric there may be no reality for us to speak or write about. Language, as we have seen, displaces reality by substituting disembodied and conventional signs for concrete objects. Rhetoric throws this process of displacement into relief by overtly capitalizing on *tropes*: strategies which (as indicated by the etymology of this word) turn something into something else. Two important aspects of rhetoric can be cited to illustrate this point: *irony* and *allegory*. Both are devices that produce meaning by unsettling conventional assumptions about the relationship between a sign and the concept it is supposed to stand for. 'Irony' derives from

---

[3] ☞ This philosopher is also discussed in Part I, Chapter 1, 'Meaning'.

the Greek word for 'dissimulation' and is indeed the device used to say something by seeming to say something else. In irony, therefore, apparently incompatible ideas coexist: what is affirmed is at the same time negated, what is declared is simultaneously questioned. 'Allegory' (from the Greek *allegoria* = 'speaking otherwise') is also a figure of dissimulation. It cloaks its meanings with more or less complex layers of cryptic symbolism and allusions, thus emphasizing the opacity of signs. Allegory displaces meaning by speaking otherwise – by stressing that the meanings of its signs are not inherent in the signs themselves but rather associated with something other. (The dragons of mediaeval romance are arguably less meaningful as scaly monsters with fiery breath than as incarnations of the alien and the unknown.)[4]

The idea that rhetorical figures inhabit a culture's language in its entirety is often repressed or resisted. Rhetoric is presented as a game for experts to play, whose linguistic manipulations are quite separate from the supposedly clear and literal meanings of ordinary language, so as to further the notion that certain types of discourse (e.g. non-literary language) are natural and reliable and that others (e.g. poetic language) are artificial and untrustworthy. Poststructuralism has radically challenged this view by highlighting the pervasiveness of figures of dissimulation and displacement, in the belief that these epitomize the general operations of language.

In the case of Jacques Derrida (b. 1930), the idea that all language is rhetorical, since all language is marked by the slippage of meaning, is an important part of his theory of *deconstruction*. It seems appropriate, therefore, to examine that idea in relation to its broader context. For Derrida, as for several other poststructuralist theorists, everything is a text.[5] Any set of signs can be explored and interpreted as an organization of language. To this extent, Derrida argues, *there is nothing outside the text*. Texts do not exist independently of how they are interpreted. Indeed, they are not immutable objects and do not yield immutable messages. Rather, they function as *pre*texts for an incalculably large number of readings. Most importantly, texts are self-dismantling: they

---

[4] ☞ Displacement and association are also examined in Part I, Chapter 2, 'The Sign' in the discussion of metaphor and metonymy.

[5] ☞ This idea is explored in Part I, Chapter 6, 'Textuality'.

invariably contain gaps, inconsistencies and uncertainties (*aporias*) that cause them to fall or fail by their own criteria. This is the principal bearing of 'deconstruction'. This term is often used inaccurately (sadly by academics themselves) to describe the act of pulling a text apart. In fact, deconstruction is primarily about showing how texts question themselves: how even the apparently most coherent arguments are punctured by incongruities.

Derrida's deconstructionist project challenges many conventional assumptions embedded in Western thought. It undermines the humanist notion that identity is a natural and unitary endowment and advocates instead the idea of a plural and culturally constructed subject.[6] It questions the principle of *mimesis* (according to which texts are capable of faithfully reflecting reality) by stressing that reality is always an effect of how it is represented, interpreted and distorted. When we think we are looking at a faithful reflection of reality, we are actually dealing with an interpretation – more or less biased – of reality. Hence, 'we need to interpret interpretations more than to interpret things' (Derrida 1978: 278). It is in the field of historiography that reality is most blatantly distorted and yet presented as an objective chain of facts. Derrida believes that the idea of history is quite different from actual events and processes. This is because real occurrences are shaped, in their recording, by dominant systems of values that foreground certain elements and marginalize or repress others. We should therefore realize that 'there is not one single history ... but rather histories' (Derrida 1981: 58).

In arguing that everything is a text, that texts are self-dismantling, and that approaches to identity, reality and history leave much unsaid, deconstruction points to the idea that rhetoric pervades language and the cultural structures based upon it. Western philosophy and criticism have been keen on distinguishing between dependable forms of language, supposed to give us truths unimpaired by rhetorical tricks, and fictional forms, supposed to be dubious due to their reliance on rhetorical devices. However, all texts have a figurative dimension, insofar as all texts are based on the displacement of meaning and presence: 'no element can function as a sign without relating to another element

[6] ☞ This theme is examined in detail in Part II, Chapter 2, 'Subjectivity'.

which itself is simply not present' (Derrida 1981: 26–7). Fictional texts may actually be regarded as more honest renditions of the workings of language than supposedly factual ones because they resist containment. They 'operate breaches or infractions' (Derrida 1981: 69) which remind us that language and meaning are not restrainable because they spill incessantly over borders and containers.

The slippage of meaning is epitomized by the concept of *differance*. This refers to the principle of 'difference': the mechanism whereby, as proposed by Saussure, a sign derives meaning from its phonemic difference from another sign. (Any two signs, such as 'cat' and 'rat', differentiated by a single phoneme constitute a minimal pair.)[7] But *differance* also alludes to the idea of 'deferral'. In trying to establish the meaning of a sign on the basis of difference, argues Derrida, we cannot limit ourselves to minimal pairs, for a sign leads not to one other sign but rather to legion other signs ('cat' is not 'rat', but also not 'mat', 'sat', 'can', 'cad', and so on). Western philosophy has endeavoured to arrest the deferral of meaning by subordinating the unpredictable detours of language to overarching ideas, or transcendental signifieds, such as 'reality', 'truth', 'self', 'presence', 'man', 'god', etc. The displacing character of language, typified by rhetoric, has been kept at bay by recourse to a universal concept, or *Logos*, meant to function as a unifying centre. Western thought is fundamentally *logocentric*. At the same time, in its determination to differentiate between reliable (supposedly non-rhetorical) and unreliable (rhetorical) forms of discourse, Western thought has fostered phonocentrism: the superiority of speech (*phone*) over writing. In his deconstructive analyses of Plato, Rousseau, Levi-Strauss and others, Derrida has indicated that speech has traditionally been seen as immediate, natural and a guarantee of presence, and writing as artificial, ambiguous, a sign of absence. Yet, the features that characterize writing apply to language in its entirety. Writing has been used as something of a scapegoat to conceal the ambiguity and unreliablity of any form of signification.

Paul de Man (1919–83) pursues a related argument. Writing (especially literature broadly conceived) has conventionally been regarded with suspicion because of its association with rhetorical

---

[7] ☞ These ideas are outlined in Part I, Chapter 2, 'The Sign'.

language, with devices that unsettle consistency and logic. Critical theory has accordingly been opposed because of its involvement with literature and writing in general, and because of its own use of tropes. Both literature and theory have been used as scapegoats, assumed to carry all the sins (displacement, dissimulation, the perversion of logic) which are actually relentlessly committed by language in each and every form. 'The resistance to theory', de Man states, 'is a resistance to the rhetorical or tropological dimension of language' (de Man 1988: 368). Traditional scholars resist the rhetorical side of human discourse – and hence of theories committed to exposing that side – because they wish to hold onto the myth of an undistorted and undistorting language. Yet, it cannot be denied that rhetoric enters our lives the moment we utter a word – the moment, that is, an abstract symbol comes to replace a physical object: 'It would be unfortunate ... to confuse the materiality of the signifier with the materiality of what it signifies ... no one in his right mind will try to grow grapes by the luminosity of the word "day" ' (de Man 1988: 362).

In *Allegories of Reading*, de Man focuses on the relationship between rhetoric and grammar. While it is necessary to draw a distinction between the two, it is nonetheless the case that rhetoric and grammar tend to cross over into each other. De Man's project is set against the background of previous critical approaches. Prior to Formalism and New Criticism, he observes, a text's form was seen as its superficial outside and its content as the valuable inside to be discovered. Formalism and New Criticism reversed the model by viewing content as secondary to form, the text's meaning coinciding with its handling of rhetorical devices. Here, content became the outside and form the inside. Both approaches, for de Man, reduce the text to a 'box', and 'it matters little whether we call the inside of the box the content or the form' (de Man 1979: 5). De Man is equally unhappy with the search for hidden truths and with the study of rhetoric as a body of devices. Rhetoric, in his opinion, is wherever language can be found. The role played by rhetoric, moreover, often stands out when it is assessed in relation to a text's grammatical features.

At times, sentences use a familiar grammatical structure, yet their meanings are nebulous. We cannot be sure whether they should be read literally or figuratively. Grammar defines what is acceptable as a properly formed sentence. However, it cannot tell us *how* to interpret the sentence, let alone deliver precise meanings. Rhetorical questions exemplify this state of affairs. A rhetorical question is commonly defined as a question that does not expect an answer or for which an answer is more or less obvious. Yet, strictly speaking, nothing stops us from treating it as though it were an open question and from giving it an answer. Thus, a rhetorical question is a good example of the type of sentence that combines a familiar structure with an ambiguous meaning. By and large, the context in which a question occurs and its utterer's intonation tell us whether it should be taken grammatically or rhetorically. However, these are extra-grammatical factors. Nothing in the grammatical structure itself indicates beyond doubt how it should be approached. Consider the following passage:

'Right. Well, if you want to chicken out, Bum, that's your business. I wouldn't blame you.'
'Sure you would.'
'Okay I would. What's the difference?'
Logically of course that question can be read both rhetorically and grammatically.
The rhetorical reading is 'fuck it'. The grammatical reading is 'the difference between my blaming you and not blaming you is that on the one hand I will never speak to you again and hold you in the utmost disdain whilst on the other hand I won't'.
...
'Fuck it,' Bum said, opting wisely for the rhetorical reading.
(Bostock 1999: 261–2)

Grammar and rhetoric are interlocked at all times. Once this interlocking is acknowledged, it becomes evident that rhetoric cannot be marginalized as a perversion of ordinary discourse. It is generally accepted that grammar plays a crucial part in the operations of language, by laying down the rules on the basis of which adequate propositions are formed. The part played by rhetoric is far less commonly recognized. However, the realization that grammar inevitably tends to merge with rhetoric makes the latter no less vital an underpinning of human discourse.

CHAPTER 4

REPRESENTATION

REPRESENT – to exhibit the image of: to use, or serve, as a symbol for: to exhibit, depict, personate, show an image of, by imitative art: to act: to be a substitute, agent, deputy, member of parliament, or the like, for: to correspond or be in some way equivalent or analogous to: to serve as a sample of: to present earnestly to mind: to give out, make to appear, allege (that). REPRESENTATION – act, state, or fact of representing or being represented: that which represents: an image: picture: dramatic performance: a mental image: a presentation of a view of facts or arguments: a petition, remonstrance, expostulation: assumption of succession by an heir: a body of representatives. (*Chambers Twentieth-Century Dictionary*)

These definitions are not intended to supply a prescriptive or exhaustive model of analysis. However, they seem to provide an appropriate starting point for the present discussion because they highlight the complexity and multi-accentuality of the issue of *representation*. Indeed, the main aim of this chapter is to show that the study of representation must take into account a wide variety of cultural phenomena, philosophical perspectives and ideological programmes. Why have human beings operating in disparate cultural and historical contexts felt the need to represent themselves and their environments? Why do certain cultures openly admit to the constructed and fictional status of their representations and others seek to pass them off as natural and real? What do different forms of representation tell us about the societies, communities and individuals that produce them? Who are representations addressed to or aimed at?

In 1953, M. H. Abrams summed up the development of Western attitudes to representation by recourse to the metaphors of the mirror and the lamp. The 'mirror' encapsulates the notion that the mind reflects the external world (mimetic approach). The 'lamp' embodies the idea that the mind radiates its own light on the objects it perceives (anti-mimetic approach). According to Abrams, the mirror-model was predominant up to the eighteenth century when, with the advent of Romanticism, the lamp-model began to gain momentum (Abrams 1953). The image of the mind as an essentially passive, or at best reproductive, apparatus has been gradually replaced by that of the mind as an active and creative power. Today, many important developments in critical and cultural theory are associated with a crisis in representation. Words, sentences, thoughts and pictures are all representations suggesting a relation between two things (e.g. 'x represents y'). But the existence of a relation does not automatically entail the existence of the thing represented (for example, a representation of the birth of Venus does not guarantee that such an event ever really took place). It would therefore be misleading to conceive of representations as reflections of a pre-existing reality.

Furthermore, neither pictures nor sentences nor thoughts represent intrinsically: as Wittgenstein has observed, a picture of a man walking uphill could also be a picture of a man sliding backwards downhill. There is nothing inherent in the picture which makes the first reading more valid than the second. A representation only represents by virtue of being interpreted and ultimately represents anything it is capable of suggesting – that is, it has an indefinite number of potential representational contents. The concept of representation is also intimately connected with that of repetition: it could be argued that words, for example, are representations which only acquire meaning to the extent that they may be repeated – namely, used again in different contexts. When we speak or write, we never create anything from scratch: rather, we reiterate what was already there, we literally *re*-present. Moreover, no representation is immediately and unequivocally connected with an underlying reality. The idea that we may be able to paint faithful pictures of the world is becoming more and more obsolete. This applies to visual artists and fiction writers, historians and geographers, linguists and anthropologists, sociologists and psychologists, film-makers and designers. Emphasis is increas-

ingly placed on the sense of uncertainty that pervades our percep
tion of things and, concomitantly, our articulation of what we
perceive through texts (both verbal and non-verbal). The world
cannot be represented accurately and objectively for the reason
that it is not a given but rather an effect of how it is perceived
from various viewpoints. Much recent criticism has claimed that
the real as such is unattainable. We only experience it through the
mediation of texts, images and stories. These never mirror reality
transparently and neutrally but actually represent it according to
the codes and conventions of specific societies.

Such codes and conventions are not always consciously
employed. Indeed, much of the time we resort to them semi-
consciously or even unconsciously. This is because they are so
deeply ingrained in our culture's fabric that we have forgotten
their constructed (and largely arbitrary) status. That is, we adopt
them as though they were natural tools rather than the products
of cultural decisions. The representations created through the
application of those codes and conventions are accordingly naturalized – i.e. their status as constructs is effaced. In the case of
Western cultures, the process of naturalization has been assiduously sustained by their dominant mode of representation, namely
realism.[1] Realist techniques conceal the process of production of a
text or image so as to encourage us to believe that representations
reflect the world, that they offer a keyhole view on a solid reality
shared and recognized by each member of the same culture. Such
techniques do not simply pursue an aesthetic programme. In fact,
they serve eminently ideological purposes. Representations are a
vital means of supporting a culture's ideology: the world view
invented by that culture to legitimate itself and to discipline its
subjects.[2] When realism represses the artificiality of representations, its main objective is to assert itself as an objective and transparent depiction of the world in the name of ideological stability.

The principal message it aims at conveying is that reality is
unchanging, for denying that something was made is to deny that
it could be unmade. This is what Norman Bryson terms the
'natural attitude': a suppression of 'history', of the possibility of

---

[1] ☞ Realism is further explored in Part III, Chapter 2, 'The Aesthetic'.
[2] ☞ An in-depth discussion of this topic is supplied in Part II, Chapter 1,
'Ideology'.

change, and of the particular cultural contexts in which representations are both produced and consumed. This attitude must be challenged, for 'the real ought to be understood not as a transcendent and immutable given, but as a production brought about by human activity working within specific cultural constraints' (Bryson 1983: 5). At the same time, it is necessary to question the assumption that 'visual experience' is 'universal and transhistorical' (Bryson 1983: 10), for the ways in which we perceive representations are as historically contingent as the representations themselves. A recognition of the immanently cultural and social character of all representations simultaneously entails a recognition of the historical situation of the viewing subject. As soon as we acknowledge that representations are cultural fabrications, the realist ethos is radically undermined. We gradually realize that if an image can be constructed, it can also be taken apart into its constituent elements and that each of these elements can offer precious insights into our culture's ideology and, in particular, into the connection between the control of representation and political power.

Thus, the central concern of any critical assessment of representations should consist of *denaturalizing* both the cultural images and the institutionalized responses to such images that surround us at all times. This entails questioning many of the concepts and symbols which we are generally invited to take for granted as timeless, objective and a matter of common sense. Any cultural product can be approached as a form of representation offering vital clues to a culture's belief systems, its interpretations of reality and its ways of translating both factual and fictional situations into images. Any representation, in turn, can be approached as a text, or a system of signs.[3] How such a text signifies is as important as what it signifies. Moreover, although a specific representational form may seem to be defined by techniques, devices and aims intrinsic to that form alone, we must increasingly be aware of the crucial role played by interdisciplinarity and cross-fertilization in the production of cultural images and in the dissemination of their ideological messages.

It is also important to bear in mind that the collusion of representation and ideology is not just a contemporary phenomenon,

---

[3] ☞ This theme is examined in detail in Part I, Chapter 6, 'Textuality'.

for representation has been intertwined with ideology throughout human history. In the domain of artistic representation, a good example is supplied by the law of perspective. From a technical point of view, perspective refers to the devices used to create the illusion of three-dimensionality on a two-dimensional surface. However, it is not merely a technical phenomenon, for it actually carries momentous ideological connotations. Perspectivalism aims at codifying representation and vision according to strict mathematical rules by establishing the notion of one correct way of seeing and concurrently promoting the myth of the spectator as the master of vision. The beholder is defined as a privileged geometrical point in space upon which, as long as s/he occupies an ideal viewing position, all of an image's lines converge. Thus, perspective centres representation on the eye of the viewer, metaphorically enbaling him or her to play God.

There are two main problems with this project. Firstly, perspective does not endow the spectator with an authentic sense of control but only with an illusion of control, for while God is held to be omnipresent and all-seeing, the human spectator can only be in one place at any one time. Secondly, the human eye is incapable of dominating the world because vision is always partial: the eye represents things to the mind from a particular and hence limited angle. The very notion of 'the eye' (often equated to 'the I') is dubious, for sight is normally shared by two eyes which, regardless of impairments, see differently. The idea of the single eye (monocularism) has served to divorce vision and representation from the reality of the body and from the plurality of its systems of perception. Yet, even as we acknowledge the illusory character of perspectivalism, we should not underestimate its profound ideological significance. This is testified by the fact that its laws were first established in scientific terms in the Renaissance, a time of possibly unprecedented intellectual and economic growth, marked by the emergence of capitalism and of modern notions of individual enterprise. The emplacement of the viewer as something of a God epitomizes the spirit of the age.[4] This example suggests that certain representational techniques evolve in response to a culture's ideological demands. Ways of representing space, in

---

[4] ☞ The relationship between vision and ideology is further examined in Part II, Chapter 6, 'The Gaze'.

particular, do not reflect the reality of space itself but rather cultural perceptions of it.[5]

The idea that the world may be objectively perceived and represented by establishing one correct way of seeing has recently been questioned by *digital* vision. Electronic technology often fosters multi-perspectivalism: computers frequently employ two cameras, which see differently just as human eyes do. The displacement of the single eye, moreover, goes hand in hand with the displacement of the 'I'. Indeed, the digital representation of the 'I' emphasizes its shifting and wandering nature. According to Sean Cubitt, the subject 'I' has two digital correlatives: 'the blinking cursor/insertion point that stands just ahead of every last letter' and the 'nomadic I-bar/arrow and its various metamorphoses – the pointer-tool'. Both of these functions metaphorically underscore the rootless status of the 'I': 'The cursor as perpetual tourist meanders through a landscape which is always foreign' and the pointer 'circulates', seeking 'a home from which its very freedom has exiled it'. Moreover, the movements of the digital 'I' are represented by a blind toy: a mouse that 'runs its errands tail-first' (Cubitt 1998: 88–91).

The interplay of representation and ideology described in relation to perspectivalism is further borne out by the fact that all cultures and traditions of thought have inevitably relied upon symbolic and mythical constructs which people have (implicitly or explicitly) been required to assimilate and internalize. Even cultural trends and philosophical movements apparently committed to dismantling those constructs have themselves depended on imaginary representations for the sake of advancing particular ideological agendas. This is one of the main arguments pursued by Theodor Adorno and Max Horkheimer in *Dialectic of Enlightenment* (1944). Here the two critics propose that although the objective of the Enlightenment was, ostensibly, to liberate people from irrational fears and illusions nurtured by mythology and its representations, it ultimately proved analogous to myth itself. The Enlightenment aspired to transcend explanations of life and the universe which it regarded as fictitious, in order to attain to putatively deeper and higher truths. However, it was itself caught up in a chain of ideological mystifications. No sooner is an

---

[5] ☛ See Part III, Chapter 3, 'Space'.

explanation provided than it solidifies into a myth, a dogmatic belief that people are expected to leave unexamined. Classical mythology claimed superiority over magic by presenting itself as a coherent and universal representation of the workings of the cosmos and of the relationship between the human and the divine. Yet, its somewhat dogmatic claims to truth and universality made it vulnerable to criticism.

Adorno and Horkheimer argue that the supplanting of magic by Classical mythology constitutes an attempt to suppress the plurality and fluidity of primitive belief systems and rituals, in the pursuit of unifying representations. The Enlightenment, in turn, claims to supersede mythology by dissolving illusory superstitions in the name of scientific knowledge. However, the cult of reason turns out to be yet another myth, yet another totalizing endeavour. All mythologies, whether stemming from religion or from science, ultimately amount to the repression of human diversity, to the subjugation of variety to a dominant value: unity (Adorno and Horkheimer 1986). Italo Calvino's evaluation of myth echoes the view expounded by Adorno and Horkheimer: 'Myth tends to crystallize instantly, to fall into set patterns, to pass from the phase of myth-making into that of ritual, and hence out of the hands of the narrator into those of the tribal institutions responsible for the preservation and celebration of myths' (Calvino 1987: 23). In contemporary Western cultures, the crystallizing of myth into 'set patterns' is aided by fashion and the media. The representations they incessantly churn out for mass consumption are mythological in the sense that they are laden with symbolic connotations.[6] The myths they embody are not, by and large, allowed to grow or expand in new directions. In fact, they are frozen into signifiers of identity and status by the 'tribal institutions' of corporational economies which, while promoting decentralization (most notably through the Internet), simultaneously display an addiction to unity.

The obsession with unifying agendas, which Adorno and Horkheimer associate with Classical and Enlightenment mythologies, is still rampant today and manifests itself through the cults of

---

[6] ☞ The mythological status of commodities has been exhaustively analysed by Roland Barthes, whose theories are discussed in Part I, Chapter 6, 'Textuality'.

conformity and uniformity. These, in turn, give rise to representations that promote the desirability of sameness, of all things fitting in neatly with one another. This process of homogenization, often misconstrued as a democratic move, has the effect of effacing cultural differences and of collapsing them into a specious notion of the norm. Differences, and the very right to difference, are harnessed to a corporate identity that elides the 'other'.[7] Benetton's publicity campaigns, with their more or less predictable variations on the theme of 'United Colours', bear witness to this assimilating trend. Here, as Christine Boyer points out, 'everyone is supposedly brought together under one huge multicultural banner that transcends all divisions'. Yet, this is only 'an illusion of a happy ending' that works by 'suppressing the acceptance of real differences that painfully still exist' (Boyer 1996: 121).

The coalescence of representation and ideology results in legion myths that translate identities into images. Ultimately, therefore, what the study of representation highlights is the mediated character of cultural existence. What might once have been regarded as lived experience is increasingly transferred to the realm of images. However, as Guy Debord stresses, images should not be dismissed as a flimsy and superficial spectacle for they actually embody social relations. At the same time, they ask us to reflect upon the relationship between what we perceive and what we know. The concept of representation has invariably played an important part in debates concerned with this issue – an issue that has engaged philosophers, cultural theorists, linguists and critics for as long as language and interpretation have been under scrutiny. Let us look at some of the problems raised by those debates.

Representation has been traditionally associated with concepts of resemblance and imitation. Objects are supposed to have two images: their actual images and the mental images of them produced by various individuals. The latter can be thought of in various ways: e.g. as intellectual abstractions, as ideals or as fantasies. Various questions arise from this approach. What enables us to differentiate amongst different representations? How can we account for their reality? Is a conscious representation somehow more real than a dream or hallucination? If so, why? Is there any reliable way of knowing what other people's mental representa-

---

[7] ☛ This theme is examined in Part II, Chapter 5, 'The Other'.

tions (both conscious and unconscious) are like? Could we ever assume that everybody represents the world according to analogous criteria? If so, on what basis? These and related questions have led to two main positions. On the one hand, there are critics who endeavour to distinguish reality from illusion, reliable representations from figments of the imagination, in the belief that a solid and authentic reality lies behind its representations. On the other hand, there are critics who maintain that no representation is ultimately truer or more dependable than any other and that even illusions have their own reality. Illusions, indeed, may make reality more real by exhibiting familiar situations in distorted guises and thus compelling us to reassess their conventional meanings. The ambivalent status of representations, thrown into relief by these contrasting attitudes, is comparable to the ambiguity surrounding the concept of 'imagination'. The Greek term for 'imagination', *phantasia* (from *phos* = light), posits the imagination as an enlightening faculty through which we form images of the world and from which thoughts, opinions and memories proceed. Yet, this same faculty is also associated with idle musings, fictions and visions and accordingly branded as unreliable.

The very etymology of 'representation' is ambiguous. The Latin word *repraesentatio* – from which 'representation' derives – is related to *praesens*, the participle of *praeesse*. This verb means 'to be before' in a double sense: i.e. spatially and hierarchically. It could refer to a person or object 'being ahead' or 'in front of' someone or something else in space, or to a person or object 'being superior' to someone or something else in a system of power. (By extension, what is present to us is not merely something that stands before us in a physical sense but also something that imposes itself upon us in a figurative sense as powerful and commanding.) In the field of rhetoric,[8] 'representation' refers to the ability to evoke a vivid impression of presence through words and figures of speech. According to the Roman writer Quintilian, in particular, it denotes a flair for making things bright and striking and thus stimulating an audience's imagination. The issue of a representation's relation to principles of truth and falsity

---

[8] ☞ Definitions of this discipline and an outline of its aims and methodologies are supplied in Part I, Chapter 3, 'Rhetoric'.

surfaces once more: do rhetorical images evoke mental representations of real things or are they used to make the false seem true? The empiricist approach to representation proposes a distinction between the ways in which we interpret nature (i.e. infer the laws of nature from the facts that it presents to our senses and to our minds) and the ways in which we speculate about nature (i.e. form subjective images of it). Speculations, according to this model, are misleading: they are fictions, more or less biased and selective, that misrepresent nature. When speculation comes into play, the mind does not reflect genuine facts but rather acts as a disfiguring mirror. The idea of the mind as a distorting medium has been advocated by several disciplines. Not all of them, however, have followed the empiricist line and dismissed subjective mental representations as practically useless. In fact, what is often emphasized is not the notion that the mind should be reformed so as not to misrepresent reality but rather the idea that misrepresentation is integral to human existence. Important developments in the study of subjectivity carried out in the areas of psychoanalysis and theories of ideology, for instance, have stressed that misrepresentation plays a central role in the construction of personal and collective identities: what we think we are is often a product of how our culture misrepresents us and of how we misrepresent ourselves.[9]

Most importantly, misrepresentation is an inevitable component of perception. We always relate to reality, however mediated it may be, as physical bodies. This entails that our sense impressions are bound to be affected by our material circumstances. Our individual faculties and our surroundings impact on what and how we experience, and on how we represent what we experience to our minds and possibly to others. Given that both our faculties and our environment are subject to contingent variations (to do with factors as disparate as light and climate, moods and dispositions), it would be preposterous to assume that we could represent the world uniformly and objectively. Objectivity is a myth designed to make us believe that there is one proper way of seeing and representing reality – and therefore a means of marginalizing all that is

---

[9] ☞ These concepts play an important part in Jacques Lacan's psychoanalytic theories and in Louis Althusser's writings on ideology. They are examined in detail in Part II, Chapter 1, 'Ideology' and in Part II, Chapter 2, 'Subjectivity'.

different, other, alternative. However, since we cannot dodge the fact that we always perceive and represent the world through our bodies and other people's bodies, we cannot, as a result, deny that our perceptions and representations inevitably entail an element of *distortion*. This should not, however, be a cause for panic, since intense and unexpected kinds of pleasure can be gleaned from the experience of distortion. Just consider the pleasure yielded by the utterly imaginary and impermanent, yet tantalizing, forms one can perceive in clouds, in the pattern of a carpet or in the flickering of candle-flame. Furthermore, the media through which we perceive reality tend to *misrepresent* the objects of our perception. Looking through the water of a pool at the tiles at its bottom, we do not perceive the tiles as they really are but rather as distorted by ripples of sunlight, reflections and refractions. Likewise, a landscape observed through a stained-glass window will inevitably be modified by the colours and shapes of the window's pattern. Distortion and misrepresentation are not secondary or accidental aspects of human experience. We do not perceive the world as it is but rather as mediated by various filters and channels: forms of language and forms of interpretation that do not mirror the world but actually construct it, thereby perpetuating or challenging its ideologies.

CHAPTER 5

READING

One of the most important contributions made by critical and cultural theory to the fields of language and interpretation consists of its redefinition of the concept of reading. Reading is increasingly regarded as a widespread cultural phenomenon. It is not simply the act in which we engage when we peruse a written text. In fact, reading is a process in which we are involved all the time, as we go about the world trying to understand or decode the signs that surround us. In this perspective, reading is one of the most vital mechanisms on which our social existence pivots. We can only make sense (however tentatively and provisionally) of our lives and surroundings by incessantly reading the texts supplied by our spaces and places, by our historical circumstances, by the political systems we inhabit, by psychological processes (both conscious and unconscious) and, of course, by the plethora of images unleashed by the media, literature and art.[1]

Our existence in the world and the act of reading are inextricably intertwined, arguably, for the reason that the world in its entirety can be metaphorically conceived as a text. This is not a linear text with a clearly identifiable beginning–middle–end narrative structure. Rather, it is a tangle of stories in which any one strand constantly loops back upon itself. Nor is it a text that conveys its plots and themes transparently: some of the most intriguing aspects of the stories it tells lie with what remains untold, or is told elliptically from the periphery of the narrative, in its interstices, or through its silences. According to George Santayana:

---

[1] ☞ This expansive notion of the text is examined in Part I, Chapter 6, 'Textuality'.

'There are books in which the footnotes, or the comments
scrawled by some reader's hand in the margin, are more interest-
ing than the text. The world is one of these books' (Santayana
1940: 56).

The leading thread of many influential approaches to reading is
the idea that a text has no autonomous existence apart from its
reader. It is up to the reader to fulfil or actualize the messages
which the text itself only contains in a virtual or potential state.
Without a reader prepared to interpret the text, the text would
remain pretty meaningless. At the same time, a reader's interpretations depend on her/his historical and cultural context: the available reading tools (i.e. dominant ways of understanding the world)
vary according to the circumstances in which the reading takes
place. This applies to all sorts of objects: from poems to commer-
cials, from news programmes to paintings, from historical docu-
ments to geographical maps, from the concert hall to the catwalk.
Developments in the theory of reading show how the meaning of
a text depends on the frame of reference which the reader brings
to bear upon it. In examining these developments, we should
always bear in mind that theories of reading do not constitute a
unified critical movement or school. Writers working in a broad
range of theoretical fields (e.g. Formalism, Structuralism, Poststructuralism, Psychoanalysis, Feminism) have variously contributed to ongoing debates about the reading process and the part it
plays in the construction of both individual and collective identities. What these writers show, despite their different disciplinary
affiliations, is an emphasis on reading as a dialogue, or transaction, between texts and their readers and a related emphasis on
the reader's creative role. In several camps, this has led to a
radical questioning of the author's power.

'Author' derives from the Latin verb *augere* which means 'to
make grow' or 'to produce'. At the same time, it is associated with
notions of authority and authoritarian behaviour. The concept of
authorship, therefore, points simultaneously to liberating and
restrictive agencies. A momentous contribution to the authorship
debate has been made by Roland Barthes's essay 'The Death of
the Author'. According to Barthes (1915–80), Western culture has
assigned inordinate value to the figure of the author, by defining
him as a kind of 'Father' or 'God' exclusively responsible for the
creation of a work and wholly in control of its meaning. Barthes

challenges this tradition of thought by giving unprecedented prominence to the text's reader, and by maintaining that the text's meaning is an effect of its reader's interpretation rather than a product of its author's intentions. Interpretation, moreover, is never definitive, for texts do not provide monolithic messages but rather vast galaxies of signs to be pursued in many directions. 'We know now', Barthes states, 'that a text is not a line of words releasing a single "theological" meaning (the "message" of the Author–God) but a multidimensional space in which a variety of writings, none of them original, blend and clash. The text is a tissue of quotations drawn from the innumerable centres of culture. ... a text is made of multiple writings ... but there is one place where this multiplicity is focused and that place is the reader, not, as was hitherto said, the author' (Barthes 1977: 142–4). Michel Foucault's essay 'What is an Author?' has also been influential in challenging conventional approaches to authorship. Foucault (1926–84) historicizes authorship by arguing that the author is not an individual but rather a concept defined by specific cultural, ideological and historical circumstances. Foucault proposes the phrase *author-function* as more appropriate than the word author. This phrase does not denote a specific person but rather a body of works, theories and values associated with a particularly prestigious name (e.g. Freud or Marx): 'such a name permits one to group together a certain number of texts, define them, differentiate them from and contrast them to others' (Foucault 1988: 201). Critiques of authorship such as the ones initiated by Barthes and Foucault have served to explode the myth of the author as an exceptional being whose genius is supposed to transcend space and time.

The reassessment of traditional attitudes to authorship has led to major redefinitions of the reader's own role. A reader is not constrained by the formulae and devices adopted by an author in the construction of a text. According to some critics, a text – though open to an incalculable number of interpretations – is nonetheless in a position to guide the reader by means of self-interpretation. That is, a text may give the reader clues and tips suggesting how it could or should be read. Ultimately, however, nothing can contain the text except, perhaps, the grammatical conventions imposed by the language in which it is written. Even this limiting framework loosens up when a text gets translated into another language, thus revealing other possible and unforeseen meanings. Most importantly, the text cannot be contained by its author because any piece of writing 'is readable even if the moment of its production is irrevocably lost and even if I don't know what its alleged author consciously intended to say at the moment of writing it, i.e. abandoned the text to its essential drift' (Derrida 1976: 37).

The following ideas summarize some of the principal positions examined in greater detail later in this chapter. Reading is always historically located: it occurs within a specific cultural context and is shaped by the requirements of a particular community of interpreters. It is based on mental schemata which constantly produce hypotheses, project them onto the world, test them by trial and error, and assess their validity in terms of mechanisms of recognition, comparison, familiarity, etc. Reading is inscribed in culturally sanctioned ways of seeing the world (or scopic regimes) responsible for demarcating what can and what cannot be said, read, written, or seen in a given context. It is shaped by processes of socialization and by the cultural grooming of perception: what and how we read depend on what and how we are expected, made or allowed to read. We must also be able to recognize the unread: what we are unable to read because it does not fit in with the expectations of our culture.

Before looking at some representative voices in the field of Reader-Response Criticism, it is necessary to examine the principal philosophical positions that constitute their background. Most relevant, in this context, are Phenomenology and Existentialism. In both, the issues of perception and interpretation play an important part. Phenomenology maintains that philosophy should focus on the contents of our consciousness, not on things-in-the-world, for we only experience things in terms of how they appear to us – i.e. as phenomena.[2] This approach is principally associated with Edmund Husserl (1859–1938). His writings focus on the search for essential mental processes and qualities of objects. Husserl prioritizes logic over psychology, for logic deals with universal essences whereas psychology deals with particulars. Phenomenology is the descriptive analysis of essences in general: it is concerned with

---

[2] ☞ This concept is examined in detail in relation to Kant's theories in Part I, Chapter 1, 'Meaning' and Part III, Chapter 2, 'The Aesthetic'.

what is universally meant rather than with subjective perceptions. With Martin Heidegger (1889–1976), Phenomenology moves towards Existentialism, according to which subjectivity is not a given but a process of constant production. The world is a product of our projections (what we make of it) but we are also subjected to the world – we are flung down or thrown into being, in a place and time we did not choose. We are both inside and outside nature: we have a will and a consciousness but we are also animals, and hence cannot adopt a stance of detached contemplation from a mountain top, for we merge continually with the objects of our consciousnesses. Our thinking is always historically situated – not in terms of a social/collective history, but in terms of a personal history which amounts to being-towards-death. In *Being and Time* (1927), Heidegger questions the notion of Being as a pure presence, insulated from Time[3] and advocates the concept of *Dasein* (from *Da* = there + *Sein* = to be) as a form of Being which has no fixed nature. 'Being-there' can never be taken for granted: it has to be invented, legitimated and appropriated all the time.

This view anticipates the Existentialist position advocated by Jean-Paul Sartre (1905-80), according to which existence precedes essence – namely, existence is a constant performance of choices and actions which allow us to come into being, rather than the embodiment of a pre-existent metaphysical essence. ('Man is only what he makes of himself'.) The problem with *Dasein* is that it misinterprets itself and its world by regarding itself as a fixed entity or substance and is thus tempted to believe that it may transcend the contingent world: in fact, Dasein is in the world and inseparable from it, with others and inseparable from them – and this inseparability threatens its integrity. Existentialism goes on to emphasize the centrality of perception. For Maurice Merleau-Ponty (1907–61), in particular, the form of an object depends on how it is perceived, however erroneously and distortedly. He also stresses the importance of embodiment: we never perceive as pure consciousnesses, since consciousness is inevitably embroiled in a tissue of flesh and blood.

Heidegger's stress on the perceiver's historical location has a

---

[3] ☞ For an example of this notion, see the discussion of Plato's theory of Pure Forms in Part III, Chapter 6, 'The Simulacrum'.

parallel in the work of the major exponents of Reception Theory. This refers to the critical school which emerged in 1964 in association with the University of Konstanz. Hans-Georg Gadamer, in particular, asserts that the literary work never pops into the world as a finished and neatly packaged parcel of meaning, since meaning depends on the historical situation of the interpreter. For Gadamer, understanding a text or event involves a process of ongoing mediation between the present and the past. The interpreter is always historically situated and her/his present context therefore determines how s/he understands texts and events. At the same time, the interpreter's present context also affects her/his attitudes to the past. Readings of the past depend on particular assessments of history in the present. Simultaneously, our grasp of our present circumstances is influenced by what we make of the past. The temporal dimension is also emphasized by H. R. Jauss, who argues that a text is received against a collective horizon of expectations: an accepted set of cultural values that define what a text may be predicted to communicate within a particular community at a particular time. The more radically a text departs from the horizon against which it appears, the more innovative it is. The impact of the ideas we formulate and the ways in which we express them is inseparable from the historical contexts in which they occur.

In the domain of science, this point has been sustained by T. S. Kuhn whose *The Structure of Scientific Revolutions* (1962) divides the history of science into two categories: periods characterized by uniform development within an accepted paradigm and periods of drastic change in which the dominant set of concepts is displaced and a new paradigm is introduced. The replacement of one paradigm by another is not dictated by logical and predictable criteria. No obvious evolutionary trajectory can be traced in paradigm shifts. A new paradigm is adopted when a community of people working in a certain area (e.g. science) finds it necessary to formulate new ways of dealing with the data under investigation. Relatedly, a fact in science depends on the frame of reference which the observer brings to bear on the object.

Theories of reading have also been influenced by *Gestalt* psychology, according to which the human mind does not perceive things as discrete elements but rather as configurations, or organized patterns. In interpreting a text, the reader looks for such configurations. This point can be illustrated with reference to the phenomenological approach to reading proposed by Wolfgang Iser. Iser works on the assumption that all texts leave gaps and that these gaps invite readers to produce their own connections: to organize various textual components into patterns and interactions. Thus, beside the text's artistic pole (the author's creation), there is always an aesthetic pole (the reader's concretization of the text). The reader, Iser maintains, tends to unify the text by filling in its gaps. Paradoxically, this does not lead to a comforting feeling that the text can be contained but rather to an awareness of its limitlessness. Unifying readings alert us to the text's infinite richness and multiplicity, for 'one text is potentially capable of several different realizations, and no reading can ever exhaust the full potential, for each individual reader will fill in the gaps in his own way'. 'The potential text', in other words, 'is infinitely richer than any of its individual realizations' (Iser 1988: 216). Readers constantly 'oscillate' between 'the building and the breaking of illusions' (Iser 1988: 222): the creation of patterns and the recognition of their fragility.

Obviously, certain textual forms are more likely than others to stimulate a reader's imagination and flair for devising patterns. It is on this basis that Umberto Eco proposes a distinction between *closed* and *open* texts. The closed text is the one in which the structure and the style of a narrative attempt to control readers' interpretations by telling them (more or less explicitly) how to read their characters, themes and situations. The open text, by contrast, articulates its narrative so as to unleash multiple associations and interpretations: it does not presume to convey a single message and does not seek to determine what different readers will make of it (Eco 1979). Eco's views bear affinities to Roland Barthes's distinction between the *readerly* text and the *writerly* text (Barthes 1975). The readerly text assumes the existence of a fixed reality and posits itself as a means of portraying that reality: readers are passive recipients of its messages. The writerly text, conversely, encourages readers to participate in the process of its construction: it does not offer a static reality but rather invites us to produce myriad realities.[4]

[4] ☞ Barthes's theories are discussed in detail in Part I, Chapter 6, 'Textuality'.

Regardless of a text's degree of openness, however, all narratives engage the reader in a process of detection. All texts could be conceived as variations on mystery and crime fiction. The reader is not the only detective on the scene, since a text's characters are likewise intent on working out their place in a pattern and on interpreting the clues that will advance or stall the action. Thus, characters are readers. Conversely, readers can be thought of as characters. This is most obviously demonstrated by texts in which characters act as interpreters. According to J. L. Borges these scenarios are rather unsettling reminders of our own imaginary status: 'Why does it disturb us that Don Quixote be a reader of the *Quixote* and Hamlet a spectator of *Hamlet*? I believe I have found the reason: these inversions suggest that if the characters of a fictional work can be readers or spectators, we, its readers or spectators, can be fictitious' (Borges 1970: 231).

Stanley Fish corroborates the idea of the reader as a textual function (Fish 1980). *Readers are readable.* Fish emphasizes that texts are produced by their interpreters but also argues that readers themselves are produced by their cultural milieus – specifically, by the decoding procedures of the interpretive communities to which they belong. Any community adopts certain reading strategies and instils them into its members so as to guide their interpretations. The dividing-line between readers and texts collapses, as readers become texts determined by their communities. Concomitantly, texts become readers: they expect to be read in ways sanctioned by the community and thus read us as we read them, i.e. monitor our ability to employ the interpretive skills we are supposed to have developed. Alberto Manguel endorses the notion that human beings are 'books to be read' and underscores the material dimension of the reading process. Reading 'serves as a metaphor to help us understand our hesitant relationship with our body, the encounter and the touch and the deciphering of signs in another person' (Manguel 1997: 169). Hence, the idea of the reader-as-book carries eminently physical connotations.

The closing part of this chapter looks at the relationship between reading and the body. It focuses on two main ideas: (1) the symbolic link between reading and sexual desire; (2) the text's status as a material object. How can one explain the symbolic connection between reading and sexuality? Could it be that it is the eminently private character of the reading experience that makes it akin to the erotic one? The association of reading with privacy, even secrecy, is a relatively modern phenomenon: 'reading out loud was the norm from the beginnings of the written word' and there is little doubt that in the ancient libraries, scholars 'must have worked in the midst of a rumbling din' (Manguel 1997: 43). Silent reading was mistrusted, in the conviction that it 'allowed for day-dreaming', that 'a book that can be read privately, reflected upon as the eye unravels the sense of the words, is no longer subject to immediate clarification or guidance, condemnation or censorship' (Manguel 1997: 51). The notion of intimacy is endowed with sexual undertones by the fact that private reading often takes place in bed. Italo Calvino's *If on a Winter's Night a Traveller* capitalizes on this idea by consistently equating reading and love-making. The central characters, a male reader and a female reader, use bed and book alike as means of establishing a dialogue. They read each other via the novels they both cherish, and via the senses, in the 'unrecognizable tangle' formed by their bodies 'under the rumpled sheet'. Yet, any understanding thus achieved is inevitably riddled with doubts. The male reader cannot help wondering whether the female reader is actually reading him or rather 'fragments' of his body 'detached from the context to construct for herself a ghostly partner, known to her alone'. Moreover, there is no way of ascertaining whether the readers/ lovers share sensations and thoughts in their readings or merely inhabit parallel universes. This echoes the idea that any interpretation or configuration is always tentative. Both the reading of the book and the reading of the body yield a story that 'skips, repeats itself, goes backward, insists, ramifies in simultaneous and divergent messages' (Calvino 1993: 149–51). Its voice is that of a 'silent nobody made of ink and typographical spacing' (Calvino 1993: 143) which anyone can appropriate because, ultimately, it does not belong to anyone.

The erotic metaphor is one way of understanding the relationship between reading and the body. At the same time, we should bear in mind that reading is affected by our physical environment. When we pick up a book, we do not relate to it in purely intellectual ways. Thus, Calvino's narrator urges the reader to 'find the most comfortable position', whilst reminding him that 'of course, the ideal position for reading is something [one] can never find' (Calvino 1993: 3). Furthermore, books themselves are/have bodies and gain their individual identities from the ways in which they are handled. Surely, the body of a book going through the hands of a reader inclined to break its spine, write into its margins, pig-ear its pages, is substantially different from the anatomy of a book whose reader would regard these habits as unforgivable violations. Ultimately, reading is about communing with an object. As Manguel points out: 'books declare themselves through their titles, their authors, their places in a catalogue or on a bookshelf, the illustrations on their jackets; books also declare themselves through their size. ... I judge a book by its cover; I judge a book by its shape' (Manguel 1997: 125). An intriguing dramatization of the idea of the book-as-object is supplied by the experimental art form devised by Calvino's character Irnerio. For him, a book is 'not for reading. It's for making. I make things with books. I make objects. Yes, artworks: statues, pictures, whatever you want to call them. I even had a show. I fix the books with mastic, and they stay as they were. Shut, or open, or else I give them forms, I carve them, I make holes in them. A book is a good material to work with; *you can make all sorts of things with it*' (Calvino 1993: 144; emphasis in original). Calvino's novel also stresses the text's materiality by suggesting that books form a 'thick barricade', made daunting by the fact that the books you have read are inevitably outnumbered by the 'Books You Haven't Read' – ranging from 'Books You Needn't Read ... Books Read Even Before You Open Them Since They Belong To The Category Of Books Read Before Being Written ... Books That If You Had More Than One Life You Would Certainly Read Also But Unfortunately Your Days Are Numbered ... Books That Everybody's Read So It's As If You Had Read Them, Too'. These 'troops' of unread or unwanted volumes, moreover, are not inanimate objects but sentient entities, capable of looking at their potential readers 'with the bewildered gaze of dogs who, from their cages in the city pound, see a former companion go off on the leash of his master, come to rescue him' (Calvino 1993: 5–6). Arguably, the shelves of the unread (like of those of the unwritten) will always constitute the world's largest library.

CHAPTER 6

TEXTUALITY

Recent theoretical developments have substantially redefined the concept of language (by emphasizing that all sorts of signs and symbols – not merely 'words' – can be thought of as language) and the concept of reading (by showing that what we read is not just books, newspapers, etc. but our cultural environment as a whole).[1] The text has undergone a comparable reassessment. Everything can be regarded as a text: plays and platters, billboards and blackboards, guns and gowns, statistics and statues are all, in different ways, texts: namely, objects and data that are always open to varying readings and interpretations. This openness entails that a text cannot be viewed as the sealed and self-contained product of a single author. Texts are not so much fixed entities as processes: they keep changing and gaining novel connotations according to how they are received and perceived by their readers and to the cultural circumstances in which they are produced and consumed. Etymologically, 'text' is associated with weaving (from the Latin *texere* = 'to weave'). The idea that a text is neither closed nor the exclusive possession of one maker underscores the idea that its 'fabric' can be endlessly made and unmade.

This chapter examines the theme of textuality with reference to relevant aspects of the writings of Roland Barthes and Julia Kristeva. These two critics have been selected on the grounds that they constitute apt illustrations of contemporary approaches to textuality as an expansive and multi-faceted phenomenon. Both Barthes and Kristeva have contributed to the extension of the concept of the text. They have done so on various levels. Firstly,

---

[1] ☛ This idea is discussed in *Part I*, Chapter 5, 'Reading'.

they have engaged with materials drawn from a wide range of fields (e.g. literature, the media, popular culture, fashion, art) and shown that such materials, in spite of their diversity, can all be regarded as texts. Secondly, they have addressed the question of textuality in the light of a broad spectrum of disciplines (literary criticism, cultural studies, semiotics, art history, politics, psychoanalysis, gender studies), thereby advancing the cause for interdisciplinarity. This plurality of approaches suggests that if it is the case that any cultural product can be treated as a text, it is also the case that any such text can be examined by recourse to all the interpretive tools available in a culture. It should no longer be a matter of making one particular text the exclusive object of study of one particular discipline but rather a matter of showing how disparate disciplines criss-cross in a culture and in the decoding of its products.

Thirdly, both Barthes and Kristeva have experimented with a variety of textual forms, thus releasing the concept of the theoretical text from conventional generic constraints. Indeed, they have challenged traditional distinctions between critical and creative writing by producing critical texts that read very much like fictional texts, like stories, and – in Kristeva's case – novels that are also vehicles for articulating theoretical issues. In both writers, interdisciplinarity is corroborated by intertextuality. Kristeva coined this term in 1966 to describe the interdependence of disparate texts. No text is wholly autonomous and self-contained. In fact, texts always absorb and transform other texts. They are built from traces and echoes left by other stories and voices. To this extent, any text can be thought of as a tapestry of quotations, a mosaic of allusions. If texts are intertextual, subjective (i.e. personal or individual) responses to texts are intersubjective: that is, dependent on how each person's interpretation of the world interacts with the interpretations proposed by other people within the codes and conventions of a community, and is accordingly endorsed or rejected. The operations of intertextuality are exemplified by some of Barthes's writings: a text like *A Lover's Discourse*, for example, is a veritable palimpsest in which many texts drawn from various historical and generic contexts come together. Finally, both critics have speculated about the relationship between textuality and the body, suggesting that texts and bodies are analogous. Bodies can be read, for our experiences are invariably written on the body. Concurrently, eminently physical and erotic drives come into play in both the reading and the writing of texts.

The earlier phases of Barthes's theoretical career deploy semiotic and structuralist methodologies as a means of examining the codes and conventions of both verbal and non-verbal systems of signs. One of Barthes's main aims is to expose the *doxa*, the body of unexamined opinions and assumptions that govern cultures and societies, and thus show that reality is never transparent. Barthes approaches the text as a multi-layered, onion-like construct articulating various (often conflicting) meanings, which lends itself to a critical process of disentanglement but never leads to a solid core of truth. The reader's identity is accordingly pluralized in a patently anti-humanist fashion.

Writing Degree Zero (1953) deconstructs the claims to universality made by *écriture classique* (the form of writing endorsed by dominant traditions) by suggesting that writing is never timeless but actually always committed to the legitimation of specific ideologies. It is in the interest of bourgeois ideology, for example, that realism has traditionally passed itself off as an objective reflection of reality capable of conveying immutable truths about a supposedly stable human nature.[2] Experimental texts may subvert the codes of realism and demonstrate that there is nothing natural about its particular approach to reality. Yet, no style of writing remains revolutionary for ever (however disruptive its inital impact may be) due to ideology's remorseless strategies of appropriation, assimilation and colonization of anything which threatens its fabric – hence, the necessity for continual experiment. The most transgressive text is the writerly text (*scriptible*): this offers no clear solutions and requires the reader's constant and active participation in its construction. By contrast, the readerly text (*lisible*) offers a comfortable frame of reference, consolidates the status quo and thus allows readers to take refuge in a sober sense of conventionality.[3] A parallel dichotomy is proposed between the *écrivant*, the fundamentally realist writer committed to the recording of reality and eager to treat the text merely as a vehicle for the

---

[2] ☞ Realism is also discussed in Part I, Chapter 4, 'Representation' and in Part III, Chapter 2, 'The Aesthetic'.

[3] ☞ This theme is also addressed in Part I, Chapter 5, 'Reading'.

transcription of facts, and the *écrivain*, the writer concerned with the act of writing and with language themselves and inclined to view the text as an autonomous object of interest independent of any external referents. The *écrivant* writes transitively (s/he writes a record of reality) while the *écrivain* writes intransitively: s/he writes – full stop (Barthes 1967a).

In *Mythologies* (1957), Barthes extends his analysis of cultural encoding to non-verbal texts and posits a double order of meaning based on the distinction between *denotation* (the literal level) and *connotation* (the mythical level). By bringing out a text's latent connotations, it can be shown that even the ostensibly most literal and innocent images are implicated in ideological processes and in the consolidation of a culture's myths (Barthes 1972a). *Critical Essays* (1964) corroborates this idea by outlining what Barthes sees as the principal function of criticism. While it has often been assumed that criticism must aim at expressing and elucidating a text's meaning, for Barthes the critic's task actually lies in *unexpressing* the text: unravelling its superficial denotational dimension and exposing its mythical character (Barthes 1972b). The investigation of non-verbal sign systems is also the objective of *Elements of Semiology* (1964). Here, Barthes applies Saussure's distinction between the *paradigm* and the *syntagm*[4] to disparate languages, such as the discourses of food, architecture, furniture and clothing, and shows that any specific menu, building, interior arrangement or outfit can be treated as a syntagmatic combination of elements selected from the whole paradigm of the language to which it belongs (Barthes 1967b).

Vestimentary and sartorial conventions are further investigated in *The Fashion System* (1967), where Barthes decodes clothes both in terms of their material and formal qualities and in terms of their representation in fashion photography. On both levels, clothes are treated and analysed as texts. Indeed, the tools available to literary criticism can also be used to explore fashion's stylistic features:

Fashion has three styles at its disposal. One is objective, literal; travel is a woman bending over a road map ... motherhood is

---

[4] ☞ These terms are described in detail in Part I, Chapter 2, 'The Sign'.

picking up a little girl and hugging her. The second style is romantic, it turns the scene into a painted tableau: ... night is a woman in a white evening gown clasping a bronze statue in her arms. Here life receives the guarantee of Art. ... The third style of the experienced scene is mockery; the woman is caught in an amusing attitude, or better still, a comic one; her pose, her expression are excessive, caricatural.
(Barthes 1990c: 302)

Barthes also stresses that there are affinities between the promotion of fashionable products and the realist mode: both capitalize on texts designed to make the implausible seem probable through their obsessive insistence on details.

S/Z (1970) is often regarded as the culmination of Barthes's experiment with structuralist techniques. In this work, Barthes analyses Balzac's short story 'Sarrasine' by dissecting it into 561 *lexias*, or units of reading, and by devising five *codes*. The *hermeneutic code* refers to the strategies through which the story sets up certain enigmas and varyingly resolves or complicates them. The *code of signifiers* refers to the ways in which important clues can be gleaned from apparently insignificant words or bits of words. The *symbolic code* refers to recurring patterns in the text. The *proairetic code* refers to the actions presented in the text. The *cultural code*, finally, refers to the accepted body of knowledge or opinion against which the story is told. This complex decoding method may justify an interpretation of *S/Z* as a fundamentally structuralist project. However, Barthes's handling of structural analysis also points to a radical departure from Structuralism. This is made evident by his use of a linear (rather than spatial) style of textual interpretation. While Structuralism was keen on isolating the text's main components and reorganizing them into a map or diagram able to reveal central relationships and oppositions, Barthes's reading of 'Sarrasine' along the line of writing refuses to arrest the flow of the narrative. The adoption of a linear reading allows the text to work on its readers and to modify their expectations and interpretations through shifts, gaps and changes of direction – the way in which Barthes reads Balzac's text typifies the process of reading as open and discontinuous (Barthes 1975).

The Pleasure of the Text (1975) develops the approach alluded to in *S/Z*, not only through its content but also through its form: indeed, it is an emblematic example of the type of text that continuously skips, meanders, redefines itself and simultaneously invites the reader to do the same. Here, Barthes develops the readerly/writerly opposition with a focus on textuality and the body. The text of *pleasure* affords a comfortable read and vicarious satisfaction. The text of *bliss*, conversely, unsettles us through its formal subversiveness and semantic anarchy and yields a pleasure akin to orgasm (*jouissance*). The body of this transgressive text is not uniform but lacunary. It is riddled with gaps that stoke our desire to fill them and which concurrently hold sexual appeal: 'Is not the most erotic portion of the body *where the garment gapes*? ... it is intermittence which is erotic' (Barthes 1990a: 9–10; emphasis in original). Gaps are produced not only by texts but also by readers, as they allow their pleasure to 'take the form of a drift' that does not 'respect the whole' (Barthes 1990a: 18). What readers derive pleasure from is not the text's 'content or even its structure, but rather the abrasions [they] impose upon the fine surface' (Barthes 1990a: 12). In suggesting that the intercourse between readers and texts is erotic, Barthes also emphasizes that this relationship does not hinge on proprietorial forms of penetration/possession but rather on play: on a polymorphous sexuality that defies the regulation of pleasure according to any rigid rules.

In *A Lover's Discourse* (1977), Barthes opens up the text's body by simulating the discourse he examines instead of explaining it from a detached critical stand point. The discourse of love is random, incoherent and fragmentary, and Barthes's text is accordingly structured on the basis of fragments which the reader may recognize and configure into a pattern, yet remain partial and incomplete. The discourse is always in motion, confirming the original meaning of *discursus*: 'the action of running here and there, comings and goings' (Barthes 1990b: 3). This mobility is underscored by the collapse of conventional distinctions between the categories of writer, reader, critic and character. Barthes's narrator is simultaneously a writer, a critic, a fictional persona, the reader of other texts and of his own text. Western culture has endeavoured to discipline the disjointed discourse of love by turning it into a unified body: the '*love story*, subjugated to the great narrative Other' (Barthes 1990b: 7; emphasis in original).

When love is not thus colonized, it is rejected as an absurd body of delusions: it becomes 'atopic', placeless (Barthes 1990b: 35). Barthes responds to this state of affairs through a circular text that acknowledges no hierarchies and roams indefinitely, thus mirroring the 'errantry' of love's 'Ghost Ship': 'Though each love is experienced as unique and though the subject rejects the notion of repeating it elsewhere later on', he soon 'realizes that he is doomed to wander until he dies, from love to love' (Barthes 1990b: 101) – just as texts are adrift in a sea of interpretations that never fully grasp their textures.

In her early writings, Kristeva – like Barthes – focuses on the ways in which texts are shaped by cultural codes and conventions, and argues that texts embody certain ideologies, yet are capable of subverting them through linguistic experimentation. Kristeva uses semiotics to show that the idea of a stable sign is a myth which serves the illusion of cultural stability. Readers should learn to recognize the lacunae and gaps in texts where meaning collapses and the dominant system of signs can no longer be treated as a guarantee of order. In *Semeiotike*, Kristeva proposes a shift from the analysis of meaning to the analysis of the signifying process. This project is based on the idea that signs do not hold permanent meanings but rather aquire significance by being strung together and by being decoded in particular ways. The process of production of meaning is termed *signifiance* and the method which explores this process is termed *semanalysis* (Kristeva 1974). One of the keywords employed in *Semeiotike* is *ideologeme*: a textual formation produced within specific cultural and historical circumstances. Epic, myth and the folktale pivot on the ideologeme of the symbol: they are closed because the ideas they present are supposed to be decodable according to a fixed repertoire of images. The modern novel, conversely, pivots on the ideologeme of the sign: it is open insofar as there is no agreed method for interpreting its signs. Certain textual formations are more likely to be supportive of the dominant ideology than others. The monological text (the text that promotes a uniform ideology) aims at depicting a stable reality. The dialogical text (the text committed to polyphony) transgresses the law and stresses that reality is always negotiable. The texts that challenge most drastically the status quo employ a form of discourse that refuses to reduce language to communication, suspends logic, and plays with the structures of grammar and syntax: *poetic language.*[5]

Like Barthes, Kristeva places increasing emphasis on the relationship between the text and the body. She is especially concerned with identifying different forms of language, characteristic of distinct stages of human development, to demonstrate how the nature of the link between textuality and physicality alters as children grow into adults. The *semiotic* is associated with the pre-linguistic moments of childhood in which the infant babbles the sounds it hears to imitate its surroundings and to interact with them. These sounds coexist with corporeal activity, through which the infant gradually discovers its own body and its place in a larger environment. There are no rigid linguistic categories or meanings in the semiotic. Accordingly, the semiotic body is a fluid entity without any clear shape or boundaries. Emotions are expressed through variable noises, movements and gestures that constitute a jumble of heterogeneous drives, or *pulsions.* Thus, the semiotic yields fundamentally physical texts. The *symbolic,* by contrast, refers to the signs prescribed by adult society.[6] It is associated with dominant symbols of power, such as state, family, god and property, and represses the body by subjugating its drives to abstract laws. Above all, the symbolic strives to mould subjectivity according to principles of separation and difference. Linguistically, it enforces the rules of grammar, syntax and logic; sexually, it establishes strict distinctions between masculinity and femininity, heterosexuality and homosexuality; culturally, it subjects individuals to political, religious, familial, legal and economic structures. Beside the semiotic and the symbolic, with their respectively open and closed texts, Kristeva posits the *thetic.* This is associated with the stage of human development in which we become aware of our autonomous existence and begin to assert ourselves as independent beings. Thus, the thetic is related to the symbolic: our awareness of our separation from others enables us to enter the adult sphere of language and the law. In becoming separate, however, the subject does not only acquire an identity: it also

---

[5] ☛ Compare this idea with Jakobson's theories on the 'poetic function' discussed in Part I, Chapter 2, 'The Sign'.
[6] ☛ The concept of the *symbolic,* introduced by Lacan, is examined further in Part II, Chapter 2, 'Subjectivity'.

discovers that it lacks something vital, that it cannot ever merge with others. This sense of loss produces desire, the insatiable longing to restore the infant's world of undifferentiation. Thus, the thetic is also related to the semiotic because it insistently draws us back into the imaginary domain of pre-linguistic wholeness. The thetic, then, is a borderline form of textuality.

The semiotic is repressed by the symbolic, yet it survives in adult discourse through bodily (non-verbal) qualities of language such as tone, rhythm, laughter and silence and through experimental texts that capitalize on rhetorical displacement, disruption and contradiction. Therefore, the semiotic retains the potential ability to defy the symbolic by creating a playful *excess* over precise meaning. Texts which bring the semiotic back onto the scene exemplify the notion of *jouissance*: a highly physical form of pleasure comparable to sexual orgasm which infiltrates the symbolic order and shakes it up: 'In cracking the socio-symbolic order, splitting it open, changing vocabulary, syntax, the word itself ... *jouissance* works its way into the social and symbolic' (Kristeva 1984: 79).

In *Powers of Horror*, Kristeva refines her approach to the relationship between textuality and the body. She argues that children develop into adults by constructing themselves as individual texts through physical processes of great intensity (Kristeva 1982). In order to enter the symbolic order, the subject must differentiate itself from others in specifically bodily ways: the budding subject is required to shed everything which culture perceives as unclean, improper, disorderly, asocial or anti-social: namely, the abject. 'Abjection' is the term used to describe the processes through which we get rid of the defiling elements that threaten our textual frame. However, the ability to develop a symbolic identity is insistently challenged by those borderline parts of the body through which abject materials pass and the materials themselves: blood, semen, urine, faeces, tears, milk, sweat, etc. These deny the body's self-containedness, for they are neither fully contained within the body nor wholly external to it. As the subject endeavours to cast off the abject so as to define itself as an autonomous text, it soon realizes that its mastery of the abject is inevitably incomplete – just as any decoding of a text and any unweaving of its fabric are always provisional. The abject ceaselessly returns, disrupting our boundaries and our identities. Thus, it is a metaphor for all sorts of states of uncertainty. In challenging the solidity of our textual frames, the abject reminds us that the possibility of loss looms large over our lives. However, living with loss – and at a loss – is not a condition of utter despair. In fact, loss is often at the root of our most imaginative efforts: the acknowledgment of our self-division and incompleteness encourages us to go on constantly redefining our textual selves and this process is immensely creative. Indeed, it is comparable to artistic production.

In *Black Sun*, Kristeva actually argues that a powerful means of giving the experience of loss a form is art. This works on two levels. On the one hand, the creation of texts is a means of plugging (albeit tentatively) the holes that riddle our lives. On the other, it can help us come to terms with loss by enabling us to relive it again and again. In the construction of texts, we are productive but simultaneously drain our bodies and minds. Thus, artistic creation is a way of re-experiencing the initial drama of loss from which all subjectivity stems. The inability to come to terms with loss would result in melancholia or depression – namely, conditions that challenge the symbolic by rejecting socially approved forms of expression and communication but also impair our ability to relate to others (Kristeva 1989). By contrast with melancholia and depression, love is posited as a means of forging intersubjective relations. Like Barthes, Kristeva rejects the popular tendency to domesticate love by turning it into a love story with a beginning, a middle and an end. There is nothing challenging or thought-provoking about such a narrative. It is just a way of making sense of love, of transforming its fluid nature into a neat parcel of more or less stereotypical meanings. Genuine love, according to Kristeva, is porous: it means openness to the other and an ability to dissolve the boundaries of the individual self (Kristeva 1987).

The text's erotic import is likewise related to themes of openness, separation and loss. As we have seen, Barthes argues that texts come across as most intensely physical and sexual when they *gape* – i.e. reveal their gaps and fissures, their divided character, what is lost to them. Kristeva's subject is one such text. In her writings, people and stories become virtually interchangeable in virtue of their common nature. Neither the text nor the self can be anchored: both unfold and branch off in disparate directions and with no obvious destinations: 'The advantage of life (or a story) in the shape of a star – in which things may move without necessarily intersecting and advance without necessarily meeting, and where every day (or chapter) is a different world pretending to forget the one before – is that it corresponds to what seems to be an essential tendency in the world itself: its tendency to expand, to dilate' (Kristeva 1992: 214–15).[7]

PART II

SOCIAL IDENTITIES

INTRODUCTION

Part I argues that human beings and their environments gain meaning from their association with symbolic constructs. This Part suggests that physical, psychological, political, ideological, sexual and racial elements play a key role in the construction of our identities. Saying that people and their worlds are constructs is not tantamount to denying their existence as parts of nature. It is, rather, a means of showing that natural forms and functions are not in themselves meaningful but only become so when they are ascribed certain social identities on the basis of factors such as the ones mentioned above. The human body, for example, does not derive meaning from its existence as a natural entity. It acquires significance only insofar as it may be shaped and understood as a cultural product or an object of cultural knowledge (see Part III).

In arguing that people and their environments are constructs, various strands of critical and cultural theory have radically challenged the doctrines of humanism and realism. Humanism's belief in the unity and stability of identity has been undermined by the claim that identity is actually the transient effect of multifarious cultural practices. Identity is not an immutable essence or substance so much as an image or series of images. Images, in turn, do not reflect the world but rather mould it according to specific requirements. While realism maintains that images mirror reality and offer a keyhole view on a solid world, there for everyone to share, the anti-humanist approach stresses that images are contingent cultural fabrications.

Images sustain a culture's ideology: namely, the image of reality created by that culture to legitimate itself and to produce certain identities for its subjects. By effacing the constructedness of identities and images, humanism and realism peddle an ideological agenda based on the notion that reality is unchanging: in denying that identities and images are 'made', they aim at disallowing the possibility of their being 'unmade' (challenged, disrupted). Conversely, embracing the idea that both personal and collective identities are constructs means accepting their openness to dislocation and change. Apparently stable and immutable identities are actually ephemeral assemblages designed to embody ideologically contingent meanings, beliefs and systems of values.

Chapter 1, 'Ideology', examines various applications of this term in the context of political philosophy. Chapter 2, 'Subjectivity', explores changing approaches to the idea of identity with a focus on psychoanalytic theory and on the discursive production of the subject. In Chapter 3, 'The Body', the construction of social identities is discussed with reference to the symbolic import of the organism. Chapter 4, 'Gender and Sexuality', investigates the constitution of gendered and sexual identities in relation to feminist theories and their collusion with issues of class and ethnicity. Chapter 5, 'The Other', focuses on the construction of racial and sexual identities through binary oppositions (e.g. self versus non-self) and on postcolonial theories. In Chapter 6, 'The Gaze', identity is assessed as a function of seeing and of the power relations associated with this act.

CHAPTER I

IDEOLOGY

The term *ideology* was coined by the French philosopher Destutt de Tracy to describe the science of ideas: that is, the discipline that would enable people to recognize their prejudices and biases. The concept of ideology can be used, as Karl Marx (1818–83) and Friederich Engels (1820–95) did in *The German Ideology*, to challenge the notion that ideas could ever develop independently of the political and economic contexts in which they are formulated. Ideology, in this respect, designates culturally determined bodies of ideas meant to advance the interests of certain social groups, often to the detriment of others (Marx and Engels 1974). This chapter examines various definitions of ideology with reference to Marxist and Post-Marxist theory. Examples are drawn from the writings of Marx and Engels, of members of the Frankfurt School (Adorno, Horkheimer, Benjamin), of Georg Lukacs and of Antonio Gramsci. The chapter then looks at theories of ideology overtly influenced by Poststructuralism, with particular attention to Louis Althusser and Michel Foucault. This part contains cross-references to the essay on 'Subjectivity' (Part II, Chapter 2), since both Althusser and Foucault have, in different ways, indicated that ideology aims primarily at the construction of individuals and collectivities as subjects.

Marxist and Post-Marxist theories investigate the issue of ideology with a focus on one fundamental question: why do people accept and internalize conditions which they know to be disadvantageous? Relatedly: why do people end up investing in their own unhappiness and put up with oppression because of the marginal pleasures this may bring with it? In seeking to answer these questions, critics and philosophers have proposed various definitions of ideology. The main ones are:

- a body of ideas, ideals, values or beliefs;
- a philosophy;
- a religion;
- false values used to keep people under control;
- a set of habits or rituals;
- the medium through which a culture shapes its world;
- ideas promoted by a specific social class, gender or racial group;
- the values that sustain dominant structures of power;
- the process whereby a culture produces meanings and roles for its subjects;
- the alliance of culture and language;
- the presentation of cultural constructs as natural facts.[1]

Thus, ideology can be defined both neutrally, as a set of ideas with no overt political connotations, and critically, as a set of ideas through which people fashion themselves and others within specific socio-historical contexts, and through which the prosperity of certain groups is promoted. The theories here examined lay emphasis on the critical interpretation, which Paul de Man sums up as follows: 'When they are ... being enlisted in the service of collective patterns of interest ... fictions become ideologies' (de Man 1990: 183). *Fictions* are not fixed and immutable entities, for they are always open to ideological manipulation. In examining fictions, therefore, there would be little point in searching for stable forms of knowledge, since their messages vary according to the ways in which ideology appropriates them. According to Raymond Williams, this makes literature, in particular, a histori-cally determined form of signification. Literature should not refer to a universal and unchanging aesthetic realm, or canon of excel-lence, but rather to a practice inextricable from the ideological circumstances of its production (Williams 1977).

Ideology can use all sorts of strategies to legitimate itself. These are not always explicitly political. In fact, some of ideology's most successful ploys rely on concepts that may at first seem to have

[1] ☞The issue of *naturalization* is explored in Part I, Chapter 4, 'Representation' and in Part III, Chapter 2, 'The Aesthetic'.

little to do with politics. One such concept, according to Terry Eagleton, is the aesthetic. The aesthetic has time and again been harnessed to ideological imperatives. It has been used to show that people can be brought together into one happy family – a harmonious realm of shared feelings – to efface the stark reality of 'the market place' and lack of 'ideological consensus' in 'actual social relations' (Eagleton 1990: 38). The social body is dominated by selfish drives. If ideology is to impose itself as a unified system of values, it must devise ways of effacing this unsavoury state of affairs. Thus, it relies on the aesthetic as a means of enlisting individual experiences to a collective paradigm of 'sentiments' and 'affections' (Eagleton 1990: 23) and hence producing a sense of community. The aesthetic, far from opposing or escaping ideology, could be said to embody it.

At the basis of most Marxist theory rests the belief that all cultural products (commodities, texts, works of art) are the resut of social and material practices, related to other social practices, within the field of history as a dialectical process. History is animated by class conflict and all intellectual production bears the traces of material struggles: both reading and writing are inscribed in a struggle over meaning and hence in relations of power and knowledge. Marx and Engels argue that all forms of social, political and intellectual life are determined by a culture's economic base: this consists of the mode of production characteristic of a certain society (e.g. ancient, feudal, capitalist) and of forces and relations of production (the power structures determined by who owns the means of production). Social change may only be effected by modifying the base. Ideology and institutions, for their part, belong to the superstructure of society and serve to ratify the material interests of the dominant classes.

Art is ultimately – though not exclusively – determined by economic factors. However, the link between artistic production and economic structures is not always obvious. Why, asks Marx, do we still enjoy ancient Greek art although it is based on an obsolete mode of production (Marx 1973)? According to the art historian Max Raphael, such a question can only be addressed by considering what could possibly have made Greek art relevant to later cultures and their own modes of production. Thus, it is not enough to look at how a particular economy determines its artefacts. It is also necessary to reflect on how such artefacts are received, enjoyed and recycled in different economic contexts (Raphael 1980: 105). Pierre Macherey corroborates this point by stressing that: 'Works of art are processes and not objects, for they are never produced once and for all, but are continually susceptible to "reproduction": in fact they only find an identity and a content in this continual process of transformation' (Macherey 1977: 45).

In emphasizing the primacy of the economic base, Marx concurrently stresses that capitalist ideology hinges on the repression of the body and of the world of the senses.[2] In promoting private property, for example, capitalist ideology reduces the potentially infinite richness of sensuous life to a single urge, the longing to own: '*all* the physical and intellectual senses have been replaced by the simple estrangement of *all* these senses – the sense of *having*' (Marx 1975: 352; emphasis in original). The division of labour intrinsic to the capitalist mode of production is largely responsible for desensualizing people's lives since, in refining individual skills, it inevitably channels them into one limited – and hence alienating – activity. The capitalist is ultimately as sensuously deprived as the labourer, for his entire existence is dominated by the desire to accumulate as an end in itself: the capitalist denies himself both intellectual and bodily pleasures to ensure that his capital will go on growing. Whatever pleasures he allows himself are thoroughly organized and mapped out, and thus take the guise of culturally sanctioned release mechanisms.

Several philosophers have attempted to transcend the economic determinism characteristic of certain strands of Marxism in the belief that it supplies a reductive interpretation of the relationship between ideology and reality. Particularly important, in this respect, is the concept of *hegemony*, as theorized by Antonio Gramsci (1891–1937). Gramsci seeks to identify the mechanisms which enable a system to preserve its hold even when it is overtly based on the rule of one class over others. Hegemony is the answer proposed by Gramsci. This form of power is not simply sustained by economic or political dominance. In fact, it thrives by persuading the subordinated social groups to accept the system of cultural and ethical values treasured by the ruling group as though these were universally valid and embedded in human

[2] See also Part II, Chapter 3, 'The Body' and Part III, Chapter 1, 'The Mind'.

nature. Power would be a flimsy thing if it were to rely on coercion or wealth alone. In fact, the dominant classes can only assert their authority in convincing ways if they are able to project their world view onto the social order and make it appear as common sense. Hegemony differs from ideology because it does not merely refer to the values of the dominant classes but rather to a whole series of processes through which those values are perceived as part of the natural order of things by those who are oppressed by them. (Gramsci 1971).

Various aspects of Marxist theory have been influenced by the writings of the Idealist philosopher G.W.F. Hegel (1770–1831). His system is based on a dialectical notion of history as the progressive unfolding of an unchanging spiritual essence.[3] The trajectory of human history can be read as a gradual revelation of the Spirit in its evolution towards self-consciousness, marked by a systematic movement towards higher and higher ends. Whilst retaining the dialectical principle, Marxism redefines this approach to history by emphasizing the material dimension of human experience. For Hegel, history is an evolutionary process that proceeds towards an identifiable goal – the full expression of the Spirit – and gains coherence from this immaterial concept. Marx's dialectical materialism, conversely, maintains that history has no predictable end or sense of direction imposed by abstract forces. Any historical change will always depend on material transformations of the base and on the ways in which class struggle manifests and resolves itself.

Hegel has also influenced Marxist aesthetics. According to the Idealist philosopher, the material and sensuous forms of artworks are only ephemeral manifestations of deep philosophical messages. Thus, a text's form should be dismissed as superficial, and its content prioritized as the reflection of an underlying reality. This notion has given rise to the approach commonly described as reflection theory. One of the most famous (and, for some, crudest) applications of this concept of art is Andrey Zhdanov's socialist realism. This style flourished in the Soviet Union under Stalin and aimed at glorifying the regime through overwhelmingly positive images of labour and of its cultural symbols. Many would readily associate it with often monumental pictures and sculptures of

[3] ☞ This idea is also discussed in Part III, Chapter 4, 'Time'.

robust workers, brimming with health and pride, rendered in a minutely naturalistic fashion. Quite a different version of reflection theory is supplied by Georg Lukacs (1885–1971), who is often cited as the principal proponent of the Hegelian approach. Lukacs is not especially interested in the formal attributes of texts but actually seeks to establish the philosophical and cultural world views they communicate. Lukacs praises the realist text as capable of mirroring the true underlying order of things, and the universal structures of history and society. Realism is superior to both Naturalism, which supplies objective yet purely random depictions of the world, and Modernism, which supplies subjective impressions of life and bleakly denies any sense of historical development: 'Man, for these writers [i.e. Modernists], is by nature solitary, asocial, unable to enter into a relationship with other human beings ... the hero is strictly confined within the limits of his own experience. There is not, for him, – and apparently not for his creator – any pre-existent reality beyond his own self ... the hero himself is without personal history. He is "thrown-into-the-world": meaninglessly, unfathomably. ... The disintegration of personality is matched by a disintegration of the outer world' (Lukacs 1972: 476–9).

Lukacs's negative assessment of Modernism is in stark contrast with the evaluation of this movement proposed by Theodor Adorno (1903–69), one of the most prominent members of the Frankfurt School. Founded by Carl Grunberg in 1923, the School wished to move beyond the crude economic determinism associated with vulgar Marxism and purely functional and pragmatic interpretations of Marx's philosophy. It aimed at developing a self-critical approach that could consistently assess the relationship between that philosophy and contemporary culture. 'Critical Theory' is the phrase used to describe the School's project and systematic investigation of mass communication in modern societies, of their technocratic culture industry and of the relationship between popular culture and art. Keen on celebrating the redemptive value of art, Adorno enthusiastically welcomes Modernism as the most realistic model available, for it depicts people as helpless and isolated and thus forcefully calls for action, for measures that would rectify their dismal situation. Writing about Kafka and Beckett, Adorno states: 'The inescapability of their work compels the change in attitude which committed works merely demand'

(Adorno 1977: 191). Kafka, moreover, is said to have 'laid bare the inhumanity of a repressive social totality' (Adorno 1984: 327).

Despite their differences, both Lukacs and Adorno associate art with the interplay of knowledge and ideology. Lukacs does so explicitly by positing Realism as a privileged means of conveying socio-historical truths. Adorno seems more concerned with the aesthetic dimension but also refers to the cognitive function – for example, when he asserts that 'art implies reality because it is a form of knowledge' (Adorno 1984: 366). As a form of knowledge, the effectiveness of art grows in direct proportion to its ability to expose hidden ideological agendas: 'The greatness of works of art lies in their power to let those things be heard which ideology conceals' (Adorno 1984: 155).

Whilst commending Modernism, Adorno is also committed to separating what he regards as authentic art from popular products that are merely capable of affording transient gratification. Adorno sees genuine art as a superior form of cognition and a foretaste of a better society, in contrast with the spurious fusion of culture and entertainment fostered by mass production and mass consumption. These practices, dubbed the pleasure or culture industry, are forced upon people by a commercial ideology which subjugates everything to the logic of the market place, thus transforming people themselves into commodified stereotypes, numbing their responses and condemning them to a destiny of endless deferral: 'The culture industry perpetually cheats its consumers of what it perpetually promises' for 'the promise ... is illusory: all it actually confirms is that the real point will never be reached, that the diner must be satisfied with the menu' (Adorno and Horkheimer 1986: 139). However, not all members of the Frankfurt School subscribe to this view of popular culture. For example, Walter Benjamin, though eager to assess the ideological purposes which popular images serve, welcomes mass production as a means of destroying the original artwork's putative uniqueness, or *aura*, and hence releasing it into wider and more accessible cultural domains.[4]

In recent years, theories of ideology have been substantially influenced by Poststructuralism. By examining the cultural

[4] ☞ Benjamin's theories are examined in some detail in Part III, Chapter 5, 'The Machine' and in Part III, Chapter 6, 'The Simulacrum'.

processes through which human beings are constructed and controlled, Poststructuralism has challenged radically certain conventional notions of identity, particularly liberal-humanist ones. Where liberal humanism saw the subject as permanent and autonomous, Poststructuralism sees it as split and unstable. For Michel Foucault (1926–84), ideology works according to one main rule: defining the difference between normal and abnormal subjects. It is on the basis of this distinction that people's behaviour is supervised and policed. Although there are no immutable criteria for establishing what is aberrant – since definitions of insanity, disability and criminality are ideologically determined and hence variable – the concept of abnormality is used in fairly consistent ways. Indeed, it is instrumental to the construction of dominant notions of identity, for the idea of normality can only be asserted against an *other* that deviates from the authorized norm. Thus, although perceptions of the abnormal alter over time, the ideological function of the deviant does not. Cultures incessantly fabricate novel versions of abnormality in order to go on legitimizing prevalent versions of normality.

Ideology's disciplinary strategies impact directly on the human body as the primary object of both the social sciences (psychology, medicine, sociology, criminology) and of the institutions through which such sciences articulate their ideologies (hospitals, schools, prisons, law courts). The body's drives are thoroughly manipulated for the purpose of producing efficient and docile subjects, and subjugated to abstract notions of propriety and usefulness that make the soul the prison of the body. The body is disciplined primarily through dividing practices designed to segregate the diseased, the insane and the lawless. Up to the eighteenth century, power relied substantially on gruesome spectacles of execution and torture as deterrents. With the development of the modern penal system, public display was superseded by confinement as the single and most effective form of punishment for practically all crimes. Concurrently, the prison system provided a model for other institutions (schools, armies, hospitals, factories) and for their own disciplinary mechanisms (Foucault 1979).[5]

Louis Althusser (1918–90) rejects economic determinism by

[5] Foucault's theories are examined at greater length in Part II, Chapter 2, 'Subjectivity'.

redefining the base/superstructure relationship: the economic base determines politics and ideology but, at the same time, it depends on politics and ideology as the very conditions of its existence. For example, the political regimes of ancient societies were the conditions of existence of the slave economy, while religion and the Church were the conditions of existence of the feudal economy in the Middle Ages. Althusser attributes fundamental significance to the notion of Ideological State Apparatuses. These are the institutions – such as educational systems, religious groupings, political parties, trade unions, the media, sport, art, the family – through which capitalism goes on reproducing its relations of production – i.e. the power structure based on the division between those who own the means of production and those who do not. Those apparatuses serve to integrate people into the system by subjecting them to the ruling ideology (Althusser 1972). Althusser has been criticized for replacing economic determinism with yet another form of determinism by positing ideology as the all-pervasive and inescapable determinant of social existence. However, Althusser also draws attention to the possibility of challenging and resisting ideology's omnipresence. Literature, amongst other forms of creative production, is deemed capable of puncturing from within the models of perception fostered by dominant ideologies. The study of texts – and of their emancipatory and transgressive potentialities – is based on an aesthetic mode that eludes categorization and thus keeps our interpretive options relatively open. Indeed, the aesthetic mode neither claims to offer scientific knowledge nor panders to the misperceptions on which ideology pivots. If it enables certain forms of understanding to emerge, these do not crystallize into scientific laws but rather provide flexible methods of inquiry. Concurrently, if it engages with fictions, this is not done in order to support ideology's obfuscation of reality but rather to encourage us to acknowledge the vital role played by image-making and story-telling at all levels of our social existence.

One of Althusser's most vital contributions to the debate on ideology lies with the assertion that ideology does not merely reflect society's economic base but has its own material existence as a practice or activity of production. Its main product is the human subject. (Subjectivity is the theme examined closely in Part II, Chapter 2. However, since Althusser's speculations on ideology are inseparable from his views on subjectivity, the latter are discussed in the present chapter.) Through its institutions and rituals, ideology transforms the individual into a social being. Such a being is a construct, yet it is encouraged to forget that this is the case and to regard itself as authentic and autonomous. Ideology thrives on misrecognition. It hails us into existence as free agents endowed with a centre and with boundaries and fosters the illusion that the world we inhabit is likewise well-defined and meaningful. The subject fashioned by ideology is imaginary, for power only pretends to value it and has no true regard for its faculties. Power is only concerned with ensuring that the subject will misrecognize its subordination as self-determination.[6] If ideology is to be opposed, its reliance on mystification must be exposed. Humans must recognize that their conditions are consistently misrepresented, that their freedom is illusory and, above all, that neither individuals nor social formations are as centred and coherent as ideology claims. Challenging ideology, arguably, means exposing the decentred character of both reality and subjectivity. The question then arises as to whether this strategy would actually undermine the status quo. This question has gained urgency in the context of debates surrounding Postmodernism.

Althusser may have commended a disunified subject as a challenge to ideology and convinced many of the desirability of this model. However, we must be aware that in postmodern cultures, subjectivity is insistently constructed on the basis of disunity. There you are: watching the World Cup Final with Vivaldi's *Four Seasons* playing softly in the background, garbed in a silk kimono over Calvin Klein's underwear, nibbling tortilla chips with the accompaniment of alternate sips of Bulgarian Chardonnay and Lavazza, a semiotic analysis of *Taxi Driver* resting in your lap, and a report on the Spice Girls' latest performance draping your knee, only partly concealing both the roof of the Stephen King best-seller perched upon it and the nose of the Rottweiler puppy curled up next to you on the Ikea couch with its pashmina loose covers.

Although there is no consensus as to the ideological import of Postmodernism,[7] most critics would probably agree that its forms

---

[6] The concepts of the *imaginary* and of *misrecognition* are discussed further in Part II, Chapter 2, 'Subjectivity' with reference to Jacques Lacan.
[7] See Part III, Chapter 2, 'The Aesthetic'.

of production and consumption have radically decentred the subject. Even if we do not read this dislocation, as Arthur Kroker does, as an omen of 'schizoid behaviour and the implosion of all signs of communication' (Kroker and Cook 1988: xvii), we must nonetheless consider its impact on humanist idealizations of the coherence of the self. Patricia Waugh sums up postmodern redefinitions of identity thus: 'If Modernism had tried to anchor in consciousness a centre which could no longer hold – the conscience of the heroic, socially alienated artist', Postmodernism has gone further by showing 'that there is nothing for consciousness to be anchored to: no universal ground of truth, justice, or reason' (Waugh 1992: 178). Whatever we make of Althusser's reflections on ideology and subjectivity in relation to debates on Postmodernism, his interrogation of economic determinism has had one undeniable effect: it has systematically exposed the fictitiousness of social identities. Whether the subject constructed by ideology is now intended to be a unitary or rather a fragmented artefact remains, at least for the time being, a moot point.

CHAPTER 2

SUBJECTIVITY

In exploring the cultural construction of both personal and collective identities, critical and cultural theory have increasingly moved away from the word 'self' and used the term 'subject'instead. This is because the word 'self' traditionally evokes the idea of identity as a private possession and a notion of the individual as unique and autonomous. 'Subject' is more ambiguous. A subject is both active and passive. For example, the subject of a sentence may denote the person that performs the act described in the sentence or the person on whom the act is performed ('Mary ate a bear'; 'Mary was eaten by a bear'). The passive side of the subject is also borne out by a phrase such as 'the Queen's subjects' and by the idea of the subject as medical patient. Poststructuralism has emphasized that the subject is not a free consciousness or a stable human essence but rather a construction of language, politics and culture. Subjectivity can only be understood by examining the ways in which people and events are *emplotted*: inscribed in the narratives that cultures relentlessly weave to fashion themselves. Drawing on this position, the present chapter offers a cross-section of viewpoints on subjectivity, with an emphasis on the decentring of identity.

In traditional epistemology (the branch of philosophy concerned with the nature and acquisition of knowledge), the term subjectivity frequently designates individual experience and thought processes defined with reference to the 'I'. Relatedly, epistemology has sought to establish whether it is possible to move from this inevitably limited perspective to objective knowledge. According to Rene Descartes (1596–1650), the 'I' denotes a free consciousness that constitutes the very essence of being human. Descartes's famous dictum – 'I think, therefore I am' – encapsulates this idea: the 'I' is an autonomous subject which, in being conscious of its ability to think, is automatically conscious of its existence. The term subject does not always refer to an individual being or mind. In the philosophical tradition of Idealism, for instance, it often indicates the universal 'I' or 'Self' that brings reality into existence by perceiving and conceptualizing it.[1] In both Descartes's system and Idealism, with obvious differences, subjectivity is thus associated with human powers – perception, reasoning, free agency. These approaches have been drastically challenged by anti-Rationalist and anti-Idealist positions that reject the notion of the subject as an autonomous consciousness, and stress instead the determined character of subjectivity. Especially important, in this respect, are the writings of Soren Kierkegaard, Arthur Schopenhauer and Friedrich Nietzsche.

Kierkegaard (1813–55) rejects both Rationalist and Idealist conceptions of the subject as a self-governing consciousness. He sees no evidence for the existence of a free thinking substance of the kind posited by Descartes. Neither does he subscribe to the Idealist notion of the individual subject as a manifestation of a universal principle supposed to endow each being with a unique identity and to validate its existence as a component of a total pattern of things. In fact, Kierkegaard's subject is a vulnerable and insecure creature, compelled to define and redefine itself endlessly through actions and decisions whose validity can be rescinded anytime. Inaugurating Existentialism,[2] Kierkegaard maintains that any attempt on the subject's part to assert itself will only force it to recognize its absurdity and flimsiness in the face of God's absolute infinity (Kierkegaard 1974).

Schopenhauer (1788 1860) likewise argues that the subject is neither free nor able to achieve objective knowledge. Knowledge is based on mere facades and the subject itself is knowable only in terms of its appearance, as a physical body and as muscular activity. Beside these physical dimensions, what defines subjectivity is the will: a blind, unconscious, and indomitable will-to-live. It is through the concept of the will that Schopenhauer denies most

---

[1] ☞ This approach is examined in Part I, Chapter 1, 'Meaning' and in Part III, Chapter 2, 'The Aesthetic'.

[2] ☞ See Part I, Chapter 5, 'Reading'.

explicitly the idea of individual value, the will is an impersonal force that comes to be incarnated in a finite number of beings without any of them ever exhausting the will's potentialities. To this extent, the death of a particular subject is practically irrelevant, for such a subject is only ever a transient manifestation of the will, whereas the will itself is immortal and indestructible. This conception of individual life sets Schopenhauer's philosophy in stark opposition to Idealism, especially in its formulation by G.W.F. Hegel (1770–1831). According to Hegel, the subject is free: it gives expression to a universal principle (the Spirit) and, concurrently, this principle forms the core of its unique identity. Like Hegel, Schopenhauer posits a universal metaphysical dimension as the basis from which individual subjects ensue. But unlike Hegel's Spirit, Schopenhauer's will is totally indifferent to the subject's individual identity and to its prospects of self-realization. Moreover, there is nothing noble about the 'I': the best the subject can do is endure the burden of its existence – a grotesque farce that oscillates endlessly between pain and boredom (Schopenhauer 1969).

If Schopenhauer conceives the subject as an illusory and pathetic figment of the philosophical imagination, Nietzsche (1844–1900) takes the project further by stressing that subjectivity is the product of repressive value systems. People are trained to cherish abstract concepts such as reason, truth, morality, logic and identity to conceal the fact that all these ideas are actually functions of biology, of the structure of our bodies and senses. There is nothing inevitable about these structures and therefore, had our biological and physiological systems been different from what they are, so would our conceptions of the subject and its world. Developing Schopenhauer's speculations on the will, Nietzsche sees life as a creative will-to-power which requires at all times the confrontation of danger and suffering (Nietzsche 1967). This will-to-power is not reducible to a desire to wield authority over other people, since the sheer urge to dominate lacks the dimension of creativeness. Genuine will-to-power entails the discovery and actualization of humankind's boundless potentialities, including those which are methodically crushed by the dominant cultural paradigm. Will-to-power comprises both active and reactive energies, life-asserting and life-denying forces. Nietzsche posits the figure of the *Ubermensch* ('overman' is one approximate translation of the term) as the type of subject who, through unending creative efforts, is capable of reinventing existence and of accepting life's random contingency, in opposition to all forms of classification, dogmatism and hypocrisy. The *Ubermensch*'s energy has been continually repressed throughout human history. Indeed history, for Nietzsche, traces the ascendancy of reactive forces, bent on subjugating the creative impulse to moral, religious and scientific laws established by the *herd* of the weak and the enslaved to mask their own impotence.The subject that challenges those laws is branded as an immoral transgressor. Thus, the whole tradition of Western thought amounts to a celebration of nihilism – meaning, by this term, a reduction and eventually a negation of life itself.

Nietzsche's critique of conventional morality points to the status of the subject as an artefact of dominant ideologies, systematically trained into a masochistic internalization of constraining values. The subject is an incomplete biological entity that does not unproblematically feel at home in nature and therefore needs the protective shield of cultural codes and institutions. Yet, these only increase its subjection and alienation. Rationalist and Idealist configurations of the subject as an autonomous and universal entity carry no objective validity. Descartes' system, specifically, is exposed by Nietzsche as specious. The Rationalist philosopher's assumption that the thinking subject exists by virtue of its awareness of its ability to think rests on rickety foundations. Indeed, the existence of thinking cannot be proved beyond doubt. And even if it could, it would be hard to demonstrate that thought proceeds from the 'I' and that the 'I' is, in turn, validated by its ability to think. This is because there is no final evidence for the existence of the 'I' as a stable substance or essence.

The positions just outlined anticipate Poststructuralist approaches to subjectivity. Foucault and Lacan are examined next as illustrative case studies. Michel Foucault (1926–84) is primarily concerned with investigating the processes through which the subject is constructed within specific historical and ideological contexts. To begin with, Foucault's approach is archaeological, in that it seeks to unearth significant historical changes which mainstream historiography has left unheeded (Foucault 1973a). Central to this stage of Foucault's theorizing is the concept of episteme (from the Greek *epistomai* – 'to know', 'to believe'). This term refers to the system of knowledge that dominates a particular historical period and establishes crucial distinctions between what is legitimate and what is illegitimate, what a culture should embrace and what it should exclude. Foucault's approach is archaeological in a further sense: like the discipline of archaeology, it focuses on the material dimension of history in order to show that subjects are not abstract entities but embodied beings. From the mid-1970s onwards, Foucault moves from the archaeological approach to what he calls the genealogy of knowledge/power, to show that knowledge and power are interdependent and mutually sustaining forms of control and means of organizing subjectivity. The eighteenth century is an era to which Foucault attributes particular importance, since it is at this point in history that structures of knowledge and power begin to define systematically the difference between normality and abnormality and to use this distinction to discipline behaviour. It is at this time, moreover, that many societies begin to exclude and confine the subjects they deem abnormal (such as the insane, the sick and the disabled), and to use the abnormal as the yardstick against which to assert their notion of the normal.[3] In his exploration of changing attitudes to mental illness, specifically, Foucault points out that when madness comes to be perceived as shameful, hiding it becomes a cultural imperative. At the same time, by confining and concealing the mentally sick, cultures define their ideal of a rational/reasonable – and hence normal – subject (Foucault 1973b).

The structures through which subjects are fashioned, as both minds and bodies, are termed by Foucault *discourses*. A discourse could be described as a set of recurring statements that define a particular cultural object (e.g. madness, criminality, sexuality) and provide the concepts and terms through which such an object can be studied and discussed. Discourses produce distinctions between what can and what cannot be said about an object and establish who has the right to say whatever can be said. The fact that statements occur with regularity in a culture does not mean that they constitute a logical or coherent system. Indeed, Foucault rejects conventional notions of history as a linear chronology of facts and emphasizes instead its incongruities and ruptures. Discourses,

[3] Foucault's positions on this issue are also discussed in Part II, Chapter 1, 'Ideology'.

accordingly, are characterized by discontinuity and do not evolve according to a predictable temporal trajectory. This is borne out by the Latin etymology of the term discourse: *dis* = 'in different directions' + *currere* = 'to run'. Each era produces different discourses through which the subject may be objectified according to the ruling values, beliefs and interests of its society. Whatever we may call the *truth* is always embodied in historically contingent discourses. Indeed, Foucault denies the existence of any reality outside or beyond discourse.

The human body is very much at the centre of Foucault's exploration of the complex processes through which human beings are constructed by culture and ideology (Foucault 1979). Among the various strategies through which the subject's body is policed and monitored, dividing practices play a particularly important part. One such practice, already mentioned, is the confinement of the mentally sick to asylums – the same shelters, ominously, earlier used to keep lepers out of sight. Another is the subjection of medical patients to psychiatric probing and to the omnipotent gaze of professionals literally able to penetrate their bodies. Another still is the solitary imprisonment of criminals. Foucault draws attention to the transition from forms of social control based on the public display of pain and the spectacle of execution to the modern penal system which is based on imprisonment.[4] He also stresses that the same disciplinary mechanisms employed by the prison system govern the daily functioning of factories, hospitals, armies and schools. All these structures rely on strict hierarchies, normalizing judgments, repetitive tasks, the minute control of activities through rigid timetables and spatialization, i.e. the principle that each subject has an appointed place. The inherently carceral character of virtually all social structures is epitomized by the architectural configuration of the *Panopticon* (which Foucault derives from Jeremy Bentham). In this ideal prison, each subject is confined to a small cell and continually observed by the invisible, yet all-seeing, gaze of a single person reminiscent of Orwell's Big Brother. The same model is applicable to schools, lunatic asylums, barracks, factories, hospitals, etc. The Panopticon's main aim, argues Foucault, is 'to induce in the inmate a state of consciousness and permanent visibility that assures the automatic function-

---

[4] This shift is discussed further in Part II, Chapter 6, 'The Gaze'.

ing of power' whereby each subject becomes its own jailer (Foucault 1979: 201).

In *The History of Sexuality*, Foucault focuses on forms of disciplinary control related to the regulation of sexual activities, instincts and desires. One of his points of departure is a typically Victorian double-bind mentality, whose repression of sexuality is actually a defensive cover for a compulsive obsession with sex. Foucault argues that since the Victorian age, four main strategies have been employed in order to regulate sexuality. The 'hysterization of women's bodies' is the strategy that disciplines femininity by constructing women as 'thoroughly saturated with sexuality' and hence in need of rigorous control. This practice is meant to guarantee women's docility and social usefulness within the family. The 'pedagogization of children's sex' constructs children as sexual beings 'prone to indulge in sexual activity' that is branded as dangerous and immoral. This legitimizes the strategies through which 'parents, families, doctors, and eventually psychologists' repress children's sexuality: 'this pedagogization was especially evident in the war against onanism, which in the West lasted nearly two centuries'. The 'socialization of procreative behaviour' encompasses the practices through which fertility, conception and birth are policed not merely as aspects of individual lives but rather as instrumental to the functionings of the social body in its entirety. Finally, the 'Psychiatrization of perverse pleasure' focuses on 'the sexual instinct' so as to establish what should be regarded as normal drives and what as 'anomalies' and hence develop 'a corrective technology' for so-called deviant behaviour (Foucault 1990: 104–5).

In the domain of psychoanalysis, sexuality is likewise ascribed central significance in the development of the subject. In showing that the self is an unstable constellation split into conscious and unconscious forces, Sigmund Freud (1856–1939) emphasizes the importance of sexual drives in the processes through which the infant grows into an adult. According to Freud, human beings develop a gendered identity through two complexes: the Oedipus complex and the castration complex. Male children are supposed to feel sexual desire for the mother and resentment towards the father, and to relinquish these feelings out of the fear of castration: they interpret the absence of the penis in women as a sign of their having been castrated, and suspect that the same injury may

92

be inflicted upon them. The female counterpart of the Oedipus complex is the Electra complex, whereby the female child is supposed to be sexually attracted to the father and jealous of the mother. Here Freud posits a dissymmetry in the formation of male and female subjects: while in boys the Oedipus complex is resolved by the fear of castration, girls cannot experience this fear, for they have already been castrated. As a result, Freud maintains, women's sense of morality and the law tends to be weaker than men's for they are unable to fear any major injury or punishment. (This is one of the aspects of Freudian theory that has given rise to most intense dissatisfaction amongst feminist critics.)

Jacques Lacan (1901–81) rereads Freud by making language central to psychosexual development. Indeed, he argues that subjectivity is a product of language and that there is nothing outside language. Reassessing the Oedipus complex in this light, Lacan maintains that what the child is required to renounce is not the desire for a physical mother or father figure but rather a primordial realm of apparent fullness, not yet subjected to the categories of language and its dividing grids. The order of early childhood prior to the acquisition of language is termed the *Imaginary*[5] and is characterized by undifferentiation, since it does not acknowledge any separation between self and other, infant and mother, inside and outside, male and female. At the age of six-to-eighteen months, the infant goes through the so-called mirror phase (Lacan 1977: 1–7). At this juncture, the infant – still physically uncoordinated and dependent on others for sustenance and support – perceives its reflection in the mirror as an autonomous and unified body-image and identifies with it, drawing pleasure from this gratifying illusion of coherence and wholeness. The Imaginary state of plenitude is shattered when we enter the world of adult language, laws and institutions, which is termed the *Symbolic*.[6] The unity of self and other – infant and mother – is disrupted by the emergence of a third figure, the father. The terms 'mother' and 'father' are not to be taken literally in this context: 'mother' refers to the figure (any figure) to whom the infant is

---

[5]☞Compare Althusser's use of the term *imaginary* in Part II, Chapter 1, 'Ideology'.
[6]☞This concept is also discussed in relation to Julia Kristeva's theories in Part I, Chapter 6, 'Textuality'.

physically and emotionally closest in the early stages of its devel opment, while 'father' indicates the social and cultural forces to which the child must adjust in order to develop into a subject. Beyond both the Imaginary and the Symbolic lies what Lacan calls the *Real*, namely what neither language nor culture are capable of naming and representing.

Within both the Imaginary and the Symbolic, the emergence of subjectivity is predicated upon four factors: division, alienation, fiction and misrecognition. The first division occurs in the mirror phase in the form of a split between the 'I' that watches and the 'I' that is watched. Here the subject identifies with something other than itself (its reflection in the mirror), and the image of itself it constructs therefore hinges on alienation, on self-displacement onto another. At the same time, the image is fictional for it does not consist of a flesh-and-bone body but of a transient apparition. Finally, the image is a product of misrecognition: the subject finds its reflection alluring insofar as it yields a coherent picture of the self, when the child's real body is actually a jumble of disjointed drives. Analogous mechanisms characterize the emergence of subjectivity in the Symbolic. Indeed, a second division takes place when the subject enters the order of language and the law, this time in the form of a split between the 'I' that speaks and the 'I' that is spoken about. Here the subject is alienated from its physical roots by its integration into an impersonal order of abstract, disembodied signs which will never adequately articulate its thoughts and emotions. The Symbolic subject is also fictional, for in entering language, we become akin to characters in a story: namely, the narrative which language relentlessly goes on telling without any regard for individual aspirations or desires. Finally, the subject of the Symbolic is a product of misrecognition: the subject misrecognizes itself as the independent author of its utterances when in fact it is spoken by language.

The subject's integration in the Symbolic also marks the advent of sexual difference. This, according to Lacan, is not physiologically ingrained in the body but constructed by language as its systems of signs designate the subject as male or female. Sexual difference is an arbitrary construction built around the Phallus. This is not a physical attribute (the penis) but rather an abstract signifier which no subject – male or female – can possess: the Phallus denotes an absolute power which the Symbolic categorically denies for all its subjects. Indeed, the entry into the Symbolic order precludes the possibility of us possessing anything. It incorporates us into a chain of signs which were there well before our birth and will go on existing long after our death. This entails that we are generally powerless to express our deepest feelings, fears, needs and fantasies. We can only say what language allows us to say, what conforms to a cultural set of codes and conventions designed to give the world an intelligible form. Thus, our insertion in the Symbolic produces a profound sense of loss or lack: the loss of the Imaginary world of plenitude, on the one hand, and the lack of adequate means of expressing ourselves, on the other. From this loss/lack ensues desire, which Lacan posits as the motivating principle of human life: just as meaning in language is constantly deferred, so is the satisfaction of desire. Moreover, language has an independent life of its own, for its signifying chains cannot be unproblematically fastened to a world of objects. This is confirmed by the fact that the relationship between the signifier and the signified is unstable since two separate signifiers, such as 'Ladies' and 'Gentlemen', may refer to the same signified (WC) or be interpreted as contrasting place names.

All the materials for which language allows no expression and all aspects of our being which refuse to be formalized according to dominant rules are repressed and go to constitute the unconscious. To this extent, the unconscious can be described as a product of language, as the domain of the unrepresentable, the unspeakable, the unnameable. While for Freud the unconscious is chaotic and primitive, Lacan argues that it has its own language and is indeed structured like a language. Glimpses of the unconscious at work can be caught in ambiguous aspects of language such as slips of the tongue and of the pen, dreams, jokes, puns and nonsense. Above all, the unconscious manifests itself as an assault on conventional meaning and logic, and on the possibility of exhaustive interpretations of reality. Lacan accords the unconscious a vital role but argues that power ultimately resides with the Symbolic as the system which gives rise to the unconscious in the first place by marginalizing the subject's unspeakable desire for wholeness.

The Symbolic cannot and should not be resisted since its structures are instrumental to the constitution of subjectivity. However, we must also be aware that such structures entangle us in a net from which it is virtually impossible to escape. Therefore, the absorption into the Symbolic order simultaneously releases the subject to the possibility of social intercourse and condemns it to a forever divided status. Thus, subjectivity both underpins our existence as socialized creatures and epitomizes our instability. In Lacan's own words: 'life is something which goes, as we say in French, *à la dérive*. Life goes down the river, from time to time touching a bank, staying for a while here and there, without understanding anything .... The idea of the unifying unity of the human condition has always had on me the effect of a scandalous lie' (Lacan 1970: 190).

CHAPTER 3

THE BODY

Since the latter part of the twentieth century, the body has been
the focus of increasing attention in a wide range of disciplines and
media. Some critics attribute this growing interest in a subject
which Western thought has traditionally tended to marginalize[1] as
merely fashionable. Others argue that the body has become especially prominent as a result of intimations of its disappearance.
These are primarily related to the culture of disembodiment
brought about by computer technology and by its substitution of
telepresence for physical contact. In this perspective, growing
interest in the body is attributed not so much to a fashion as to a
recognition of the body's changing significance in a rapidly
mutating socio-economic scenario. According to W. A. Ewing, for
example, 'what puts the body squarely in the centre of debate is
not fashion, but urgency. The body is being rethought and recon-
sidered by artists and writers because it is being restructured and
reconstituted by scientists and engineers' (Ewing 1994: 9).

This chapter's central argument is that in recent years, the body
has been radically reassessed by both science and philosophy.
Science has shown that it can be disassembled and restructured.
Philosophy has challenged the traditional superiority of the mind
over the body by stressing that corporeality is central to our
experience and knowledge of the world. This can be exemplified
with reference to a number of discourses, from psychology to
medicine, from art to fashion. Above all, the body has been redefined by the claim that the physical form is not only a natural
reality, but also a cultural concept: a means of encoding a society's

[1] See Part III, Chapter 1, 'The Mind'.

97

values through its shape, size and ornamental attributes. Images of the body pervade the structures of signification through which a culture constructs meanings and positions for its subjects: 'The body is ... both an object represented ... and an organism that is organized to represent concepts and desires. Two systems of representation intertwine and overlap. Language is a system of signs[2] produced in a particular set of historical circumstances and involving repetitions and encodings of the kind to which societies attribute specific meanings either consciously or unconsciously' (Adler and Pointon 1993: 125). All societies create images of the ideal body to define themselves: social identities have a lot to do with how we perceive our own and other people's bodies. This may explain why different cultures have regularly tried, through a variety of laws and rituals, to delimit the body: to erect clear boundaries around it. Framing the body is a vital means of establishing structures of power, knowledge, meaning and desire. Yet, the body has a knack of breaking the frame. Its boundaries often turn out to be unstable, for how can we confidently establish where the body 'begins' and where it 'ends'?

It remains difficult to define – let alone contain – the body due to its composite and multi-layered nature. On both the biological and the figurative planes, the body goes on exhibiting levels of complexity that elude even the most obdurate attempts to frame it. In the domain of science, this is attested to by the Human Genome Project: the area of research concerned with mappping out the totality of an organism's genes. (This, so far, is estimated to consist of three billion base pairs based on 100,000 genes on the DNA of our forty-six chromosomes.) The Project stands out as something of an ultimate frontier. Its expected findings are deemed capable of strengthening the body, particularly through the identification of the causes of fatal diseases and hereditary conditions. Yet, the Project has also triggered anxious speculations about the ultimate nature and integrity of the organism. These have been fuelled by the issue of genetic engineering, for example, as well as by the viability of copyrighting genomes. Thus, genetic research may well be able to provide a map of the body but it is not in a position to demarcate its limits.

Not only does the body frustrate our attempts to contain it: it is

[2] This concept is discussed in Part I, Chapter 2, 'The Sign'.

also, in itself, a proverbially leaky container. On the figurative level, this is shown by idiomatic expressions that emphasize the instability of its boundaries. The body holds myriad substances and emotions but it has relatively little control over their coming in and spilling out: it may be 'filled with anger' and 'brimming with tears' at one and the same time, for example (Lakoff 1987: 271–81). Despite its instability, the body plays a crucial role in our interpretations of the world, our assumption of social identities, and our acquisition of knowledge for, as Francisco J. Varela points out, 'the proper units of knowledge are primarily *concrete*, embodied, incorporated, lived' (Varela 1992: 320; emphasis in original). Experience and knowledge are inevitably embodied. This is emphasized by Phenomenological and Existentialist approaches[3] to the relationship between the body and the mind. The Existentialist philosopher Maurice Merleau-Ponty, in particular, stresses that the world derives its meanings not from fixed and intrinsic attributes but from how it is perceived and acted upon by an embodied consciousness (Merleau-Ponty 1962). Roger Poole corroborates this position: 'Consciousness is not "pure", but exists within a membrane of flesh and blood'; this indicates that 'the body actually lives a world, and thus projects "its" values over a world' (Poole 1990: 264–5).

Both philosophy and science have been increasingly stressing the crucial part played by the body in the acquisition of knowledge. Babies develop an understanding of their surroundings through their bodies well before they learn how to communicate verbally. They imitate facial expressions practically from birth and come to associate different expressions with different tones of voice. At three months, they begin to understand cause and effect – again, through their bodies: for example, if one end of a ribbon is tied to an infant's toe and the other to a mobile, s/he will learn to move the mobile by moving the relevant part of her/his body. At six months, babies begin to understand objects, although they are not necessarily aware that such objects are separate from their own bodies or indeed that other people are distinct from them. This understanding coincides with the acquisition of adult language.[4]

---

[3] ☞ See Part I, Chapter 5, 'Reading' and Part II, Chapter 6, 'The Gaze'.
[4] ☞ For a related account of psycho-physical development, see the discussion of Lacan's theories in Part II, Chapter 2, 'Subjectivity'.

By the age of eighteen months, most babies will have come to perceive other people as separate and to understand that not everybody feels the same as they do. Small children learn to cope with their environment by adjusting their movements, postures and expressions to what they perceive around them. This often entails mimicking older people: imitation enables children to relate to others without direct physical contact. Accordingly, it helps them realize that things exist even if they cannot be touched. This understanding subsequently extends to the recognition that things exist even if they cannot be seen, especially in the case of other people's thoughts, emotions and desires.

In assessing the role played by the body in the acquisition of knowledge, a distinction must be drawn between the *body schema*, which refers to an instinctive and nonconscious attunement to one's environment, and the *body image*, which refers to bodily actions performed consciously and intentionally. The body schema prevails in the learning stages which precede a child's conscious awareness of owning a body. The body image evolves from the child's recognition that s/he possesses a body, that such a body is capable of performing certain acts deliberately and that these acts can affect other people's feelings and conduct. However, it would be incorrect to associate the body schema exclusively with childhood and the body image exclusively with adulthood, for both are present in adult life. Which modality is at work depends on whether physical movements are enacted consciously or instinctively. For example, if I raise my hand to request permission to speak in a formal context, I am projecting a body image, since I am doing so intentionally. If, on the other hand, I shift my posture to keep my balance while standing in a bus, I am projecting a body schema, since I am doing so automatically. The concept of the body image was elaborated in the 1930s by Paul Schilder, who argues that body and body image are not necessarily one and the same thing. For example, while the boundaries of the body as an organism could be said to coincide with the skin, the boundaries of the body as a cultural image are far more variable. Indeed, the body image includes the space which surrounds the body, and any one individual is bound to produce different body images depending on the distance s/he places between her/himself and other people (Schilder 1935).

The vital part played by the body in the learning curve confirms the proposition that knowledge is inevitably embodied. Our material reality is inescapable. Therefore, as Ewing stresses, the ultimate lesson yielded by the body is 'a certain knowledge of eventual death' (Ewing 1994: 238). Closely related to the concept of embodiment is the term *incorporation*. 'Incorporation' derives from the Latin *corpus* ('body') and is indeed the Latinate version of 'embodiment': in one available usage, it can refer to the process through which something (often an abstract concept) acquires a body or takes on a bodily form. 'To incorporate', accordingly, is often synonymous with the verb 'to embody' or even the verb 'to incarnate' (from the Latin *carnis* = 'flesh'), i.e. to take on a fleshly identity. However, 'incorporation' also refers (more frequently, in everyday language) to the integration or absorption of human beings, objects and ideas into cultural, political and economic structures.[5] In this usage, 'incorporation' designates an ensemble of ideological practices meant to organize diverse entities into a coherent whole – by and large, for the purpose of cultural stability. One meaning of incorporation highlights the physical dimension: the extent to which knowledge depends on abstract concepts becoming embodied and thus participating in a material reality. The other meaning marginalizes the body by treating people, objects and ideas as free-floating data to be efficiently patterned into an abstract network of social relations. The tension between materiality and abstraction is amply documented by artistic and aesthetic approaches to the body.

As the most frequently represented object (at least in Western art), the body has often been considered a means of celebrating human strength, energy and beauty. Yet, the body has concurrently been dematerialized by various strands of Western art, insofar as its symbolic significance has been prioritized over its physical existence. This has largely been accomplished through stylization, especially in the realm of portraiture: much of the time, portraits do not depict real bodies but rather idealized versions of their sitters. Moreover, it is not uncommon for the portrayed body to be overwhelmed to the point of insignificance by clothes, accessories and props designed to convey the sitter's prosperity or intellectual worth. Despite these strategies of symbolic transfiguration, however, the material dimension cannot

[5] ☞For example, through colonization: see Part II, Chapter 5, 'The Other'.

be fully repressed. Indeed, the work of art itself is a body, a physical object susceptible to change and deterioration. Pictures, for example, may be physically modified by a number of factors. As Homan Potterton points out, they may be 'maliciously damaged', 'affected by the environment' and 'altered by the efforts of past restorers' – not to mention by 'improvements' such as 'the application of judicious draperies and fig-leaves in areas that were at one time considered indecent' (Potterton 1977: 15).

While art and aesthetics[6] ultimately fail to contain the body's materiality, science and medicine are no more successful in their attempts to rationalize it. Indeed, medical and scientific approaches to the body are saturated with mythical metaphors. This is exhaustively demonstrated by Cecil Helman's *The Body of Frankenstein's Monster*, which argues that science in general and medicine in particular, far from being at odds with the ancient discourses of myth, magic and fantasy, are heavily indebted to their imagery and symbolism. This is attributable to the eminently narrative character of the medical experience: 'to be a doctor', Helman argues, is 'to live in a world of narratives', since 'telling a story' (as emblematically dramatized by the *One Thousand and One Nights*) is a 'basic human way of organizing experience' and of 'shaping suffering into a form' (Helman 1992: 8–9). Moreover, medicine, like story-telling, is based on an ongoing dialogue between physical and symbolic realities: 'Just as medical diagnosis involves the constant process of turning the body from flesh into metaphor, so medical treatment seems to consist partly of turning metaphor back into flesh' (Helman 1992: 10). As Jean-Francois Lyotard argues, the operations of science are inextricable from fictional discourse and imagery, for scientific findings can only be articulated, ultimately, by recourse to narratives (Lyotard 1987).[7] The collusion of medical and mythological discourses is also testified by popular attitudes to surgery, and particularly transplants, as responsible for the dissolution of corporeal boundaries. This same theme has featured for time immemorial in the narrative domain: the invasion of the individual body by spirits, demons, vampires and, more recently, aliens is a theme to which the imagi-

---

[6] ☞ See Part III, Chapter 2, 'The Aesthetic'.
[7] ☞ See the discussion of Postmodernism in Part III, Chapter 2, 'The Aesthetic' for further detail on this topic.

nation insistently returns to dramatize human anxieties about the precariousness of the physical frame. The body subjected to prosthetic surgery is not only an invaded body: it is also a patchwork body, vividly reminiscent of Mary Shelley's famous creature and indeed of contemporary cyborg figures.

An area to which recent writings on the relationship between the body and science have devoted considerable attention is that of food-related cultural attitudes. In this context, the discourses of health and fitness, fashion and status symbolism intersect with specifically medical debates surrounding eating disorders, their detection and their treatment. In his historical survey of eating habits, Stephen Mennell shows how changing attitudes to the body are inseparable from crucial shifts in a culture's approach to food. In the Middle Ages, for example, it was common for all social classes to alternate between frugality and feasting, fasting and gorging: this oscillation, caused by precarious living conditions, frequent famines and high mortality rates, was paralleled by emotional volatility as a typical trait of the average mediaeval personality. In the Renaissance, the ability to literally stuff oneself came to be read as a marker of power and wealth, sophistication and etiquette being regarded as practically irrelevant concepts. There is evidence, for example, that Catherine de Medici was admired for her gargantuan appetitie and frequent indigestion. In the eighteenth century, the precept that gluttony is shameful made its first serious appearance (Louis XVI's eating habits were accordingly deemed scandalous). This civilizing of appetite coincided with increasing economic security and a shift from the value of quantity to the value of quality. The body was accordingly disciplined through the introduction of table manners, the elaboration of refined culinary skills and the rapidly spreading belief that delicacy and taste require self-restraint. This model, first promoted within courtly circles, gradually reached the bourgeoisie (Mennell 1991). An analogy can be observed between the discourse of food and vestimentary fashions. In the Renaissance, for example, overeating as a signifier of power was paralleled by the display of ostentatious clothing. The emphasis was on physical bulk and layers upon layers of richly decorated garments, which made dress hardly distinguishable from theatrical costume. Paradoxically, although the padding out of the body through dress was designed to convey physical solidity (and hence power), it often had the opposite effect: the body tended to appear frail and insubstantial in comparison with its artificial casing. The refinement of culinary habits in the eighteenth century was likewise accompanied by changes in fashion: here, too, propriety came to be associated with the avoidance of excess, and sartorial extravagance with foppery. In the nineteenth century, it was common to associate the bulging bellies of politicians and businessmen with material wealth, and the aristocrat's slim body with a disdain of the bourgeoisie. As power came to be equated with the control of other people's labour rather than with sheer accumulation, and food supplies became more evenly distributed across society, corpulence went gradually out of vogue and was eventually superseded by the ideal of the slender figure. This is the ancestor of one of today's most treasured fetishes: the slender body.

Susan Bordo likewise traces the historical roots of contemporary attitudes to food and physical size, by focusing on the evolution of the discourse of dieting. For the ancient Greeks and the Christians, dieting was fundamentally the concern of a male elite preoccupied with the state of the inner self or soul, and aimed at either self-mastery or the domination of carnal desire. From the late nineteenth century onwards, dieting has been mainly a middle-class concern and has concentrated on the body itself and on outer appearances. The discourse of dieting and the ideal of slenderness have operated as normalizing strategies and hence ways of producing what Michel Foucault (1926–84) terms the *docile body*: that is, an ideologically useful and economically efficient mechanism.[8] According to Bordo, the individual body is a microcosm reproducing the anxieties and vulnerabilities of the macrocosm, namely the social body. Contemporary politics of corporeality mirror the contradictions of capitalism and consumer culture: their simultaneous glorification of autonomous selfhood and relentless commodification of human beings. The body images by which we are bombarded today are likewise contradictory. For example, the boyish female ideal could be read as a rejection of stereotypical notions of femininity that associate woman with reproductive faculties, but it is also an indicator of fragility and defencelessness which serves to perpetuate another stereotype: that of woman as the weaker vessel. Furthermore, capitalism fosters a

[8] Foucault's theories are examined in detail in Part II, Chapter 2, 'Subjectivity'.

split mentality, whereby the producer self is expected to cultivate a work ethic of thrift and efficiency, at the same time as the consumer self is encouraged to indulge. This duplicity is amply documented by women's magazines that repeatedly juxtapose pictures of delicious dishes and low-calorie diets.

Bulimia is the extreme incarnation of this schizophrenic attitude, since it combines unrestrained consumption and drastic cleaning-up acts. Anorexia, on the other hand, reflects self-disciplining work ethics, whilst obesity signifies ultimate self-indulgence. To some extent, therefore, both anorexia and obesity constitute forms of resistance to dominant cultural paradigms that require the coexistence of self-restraint and self-indulgence. However, whereas obesity rejects the values upon which mainstream, mass-produced images are founded, anorexia pays homage to their compulsive promotion of the myth of thinness-as-beauty. Indeed, it could be argued that anorexia throws into relief the equation between the individual microcosm and the social macrocosm by articulating, at the level of the singular body, problems that afflict the collective body (Bordo 1990). Eating disorders indicate that personal and social maladies are inextricably interconnected. Anorexia, for example, is a social problem to the extent that it is largely occasioned by the pursuit of body ideals set by advertising and the fashion industry. At the same time, it is often triggered by an individual's dissatisfaction with personal and familial relationships. On both the social and personal planes, notions of success and failure play a vital role as self denial ultimately points to a tragic parody of the imperative to prove oneself. Food-related disorders are largely associated with women. This association perpetuates the stereotypical pairing of femininity and hunger as a metaphor for a putatively voracious sexuality. Paradoxically, however, anorexia also comes across as an anti-feminine syndrome, exhibiting a virile capacity for self-management. Anxieties about fat as the eruption of unwanted flesh are counteracted by framing the body: the minimalist look and the athletic/muscular look seem to be the most fashionable options. Not infrequently (as shown by cases of anorexic subjects who are also addicted to physical exercise), the framing of the flesh is accomplished through a somewhat unholy marriage of the two looks.[9]

[9] ☛ The discourse of 'framing' is also addressed in Part II, Chapter 6, 'The Gaze'.

While in biological and anatomical terms the word 'organism' refers to the physical apparatus as an ensemble of organs and related functions, in figurative terms the same word carries complex ideological connotations. Indeed, it aims at conveying the image of the body as a unified structure whose various parts harmoniously interrelate with one another. These parts, moreover, form a hierarchy that attributes different degrees of power and importance to distinct organs and functions. The image of the body as a coherent whole has repeatedly been used to lend stability to the human organism as the supreme expression of the marvels of Creation. At the same time, it has served political purposes. Indeed, the notion of the individual body as a unified structure has been employed as a metaphor for the idea of the nation as a bounded territory delimited by inviolable borders. The analogy between the physical body and the body politic underscores the multiplicity of meanings and interpretations to which a seemingly innocent word is open. Thus, whilst the body can be conceived of as singular (i.e. as a manifestation of individual identity), it can simultaneously be thought of as collective (i.e. as a manifestation of corporate identity). A corporate identity, in turn, refers both to a material body (such as a nation state's geographical location) and to an immaterial body: namely, the body of beliefs, myths, laws and rituals through which ideologies assert and consolidate themselves. It is worth noting, in this respect, that the Latin word *corpus* is still used in modern English precisely to describe a body of texts: narratives and legends that contribute to a society's view of its history.

The ideological connotations of the term 'organism' have been highlighted by Gilles Deleueze and Felix Guattari, who argue that the image of a monolithic and watertight body is a myth promoted by capitalist ideology. Indeed, it mirrors the urge to accumulate and to preserve property within a sealed domain. The real body, by contrast, is fluid and sprawling. It is also fragmentary, as testified by people's tendency to experience their bodies in terms of parts rather than as totalities. The bodily model proposed by Deleuze and Guattari is a body-without-organs: a body that is not subjected to constraining definitions of its various organs, of their functions and interrelations. If the unified organism symbolizes a bounded national territory, the body-without-organs is, by contrast, deterritorialized (Deleuze and Guattari 1988). It has no definitive form or meaning. Therefore, it serves to remind us that life is a complex structure irreducible to an organic whole, and that all embodied creatures are born, grow and perish by mingling all the time with other nascent, developing or dying bodies.

CHAPTER 4

GENDER AND SEXUALITY

This chapter examines the impact of issues of gender and sexuality on the fashioning of social identities, with reference to various strands of feminist thought and to sexual politics. The term 'sex' has traditionally referred to the difference between males and females with regard to their reproductive functions and, by extension, to activity leading to reproduction. The reduction of sex to a purely biological phenomenon crudely underplays the role played by culture in producing sexual preferences and, concurrently, multifold forms of sexual activity. The introduction of the term 'gender' into the vocabularies of critical and cultural theory has been motivated primarily by the necessity of surpassing reductionist accounts of femininity and masculinity as coterminous with an individual's biological sex, and of stressing their socio-political determination. 'Sexuality' generally refers to a person's sexual proclivities, and the practices in which s/he accordingly engages.

Especially influential, in the redefinition of traditional approaches to gender and sexuality, has been the work of Judith Butler, who argues that gender is performative.[1] This implies that a person's gendered identity is produced through performance and role-playing. Repetition plays a vital part in this process, for it is by performing certain acts repeatedly that the individual acquires an apparently coherent identity. Repetition, moreover, is dictated by what a particular culture expects of its members: by dominant ideologies and ways of organizing sexual behaviour. 'Gender performativity', Butler maintains, hinges on the 'reiterative

---

[1] ☞Performativity as an aspect of language is discussed in Part I, Chapter 3, 'Rhetoric'.

practice of regulatory sexual regimes' (Butler 1993: 15). A gender role, therefore, is neither natural nor optional: in fact, it is constructed by various cultural discourses,[2] and particularly by language. Even simple statements which may be uttered upon a person's birth or prior to it (such as 'it's a girl', 'it's a boy') contribute crucially to the social construction of gendered identities (of 'girlness', of 'boyness') and to the enforcement of performative acts associated with them. However, any identity acquired through the repetition of expected acts is not truly coherent, let alone stable. Coherence and stability are illusory. Like all constructs, they can be deconstructed. This is demonstrated by the fact that there are many performative acts that undermine, more or less drastically, normative conceptions of sexual and gendered identity: for example, cross-dressing, the adoption of ambiguous names and the assumption of alternative personas. This indicates that although our identities may be limited by our societies, there is scope for combining and recombining certain markers of gender and sexuality. Thus, discordant and ironical images can be produced through which the myth of biological determinism is exploded.

In recent years, increasing emphasis has been placed on the need to conceive of gender and sexuality in the plural: there are many genders and many sexualities. Social identities are not centred on fixed properties acquired at birth and bound to remain stable thereafter. In fact, they result from multiple and shifting roles which people are required to play in both private and public contexts on the basis of their genders and sexualities. Despite a growing recognition of the plural and culturally determined character of gender and sexuality, there is still a tendency to normalize them. This is often accomplished through binary oppositions that distinguish between normality and deviance. These oppositions are dangerously reductive, for they fail to take into adequate consideration the diversity of sexual desires and activities that take place within the spheres of heterosexuality, homosexuality and bisexuality. Normalizing strategies are largely a result of the heavy legacy of sexual morality: the subfield of ethical philosophy concerned with establishing the principles of moral behaviour in sexual matters and with clarifying the means by which the observance of

[2] ☞See Part II, Chapter 1, 'Ideology' and Part II, Chapter 2, 'Subjectivity'.

such principles may be secured. It seeks to define what sexual activities are permissible, and who is ethically or legally entitled to take part in them. However, activities deemed morally wrong in one camp may seem morally justifiable in another. Sadism is a case in point. Often condemned as harmful and perverse, sadistic acts were actually regarded by the Marquis de Sade (1740–1814) himself as less deleterious than the acts which can be occasioned by their repression. Angela Carter corroborates this point by arguing that Sade is actually a 'moral pornographer' whose texts do not encourage brutality but actually provide a 'critique of current relations between the sexes' (Carter 1979: 19), and show that these hinge on 'the infliction and the tolerance of extreme pain' (Carter 1979: 26).

One criterion put forward by sexual morality for establishing what practices are legitimate hinges on the distinction between natural and unnatural acts. This criterion is founded on the premise that natural sexual acts should fulfil reproductive purposes. Yet, there is no final way of demonstrating that acts that do not lead to reproduction violate the laws of human nature (whatever these might be). Furthermore, a sexual act only becomes culpable as a result of ideological moves intent on making it so – such as the Roman Catholic interdiction against non-repoductive sex as incompatible with God's will. Another position within sexual morality advocates that sexual acts are reprehensible if they pivot on the objectification of one party by another. In the context of debates on pornography, for example, several critics maintain that what makes pornography questionable is not so much its representational content as its tendency to capitalize on exploitative power structures. Andrea Dworkin, for example, stresses that 'In the male system, women are sex; sex is the whore. The whore is *porne*, the lowest whore, the whore who belongs to all male citizens: the slut, the cunt. Buying her is buying pornography. Having her is having pornography' (Dworkin 1981: 202; emphasis in original). While the view that a sexual partner should be treated as a person rather than an object is relatively widespread (though not necessarily translated into practice), there is still considerable diversity of opinion as to who such a partner should be. Many communities restrict sexual relations to the domain of institutionalized contracts, such as marriage. Others allow sexual intercourse between partners engaged in a stable (albeit non-ratified) relationship but put a ban on casual sex. Sexual relations amongst children, between adults and children, and between humans and other animals are almost universally censored. Various measures taken by cultures to regulate sexuality by defining with whom one may have morally sound relationships stem largely from the view of sex as an unruly appetite hell-bent on loosening the social fabric.

Discourses committed to the policing of sexuality affect all subjects. However, their repressive effects are most glaringly obvious in the context of two histories of exclusion. One history traces the practices through which sexual morality has benefitted men at the expense of women. The other history outlines the processes that have defined lawful sexual conduct by demonizing homosexuals. Let us consider each of these histories in further detail.

Discrimination against women based on prejudices associated with gender difference has been the central preoccupation of feminism. It is crucial to realize, in this regard, that there are many feminisms within feminist thought and practice, and that a recognition of their different approaches and methodologies is essential to an understanding of feminism itself. Nonetheless, various strands of feminism share an ongoing commitment to the advocacy of women's rights to social, political and economic equality; the enhancement of their educational and professional opportunities; the assertion of their sexual autonomy and reproductive rights; their protection from physical and psychological abuse; the rejection of male-dominated forms of language; and the deconstruction of denigrating representations of femininity.[3] 'Feminism' derives from the French word *feminisme*, coined by the utopian socialist philosopher Charles Fourier in the nineteenth century. It was first used in its English form in the 1890s to refer to women's fight for equal opportunities. Although sustained defences of women's rights can be traced back to mediaeval and Renaissance Europe, the birth of modern feminism is often associated with the publication of Mary Wollstonecraft's *A Vindication of the Rights of Woman* in 1792. Inspired by the American Revolution (1776) and by the French Revolution (1789) to apply democratic principles to

---

[3] ☞ The construction of gender stereotypes in the visual filed is discussed in detail in Part II, Chapter 6, 'The Gaze'.

women's struggle for emancipation, this treatise opposes women's intellectual subordination and claims equality between men and women in the educational sphere. However, *A Vindication* does not extend the demand for equality to the political domain, thus suggesting that women can fulfil their duties as citizens from within boundaries of domestic life (Wollstonecraft 1986).

Histories (or rather *herstories*) of feminism tend to distinguish between First-Wave and Second-Wave feminisms. The first developed between 1830 and 1920, and its political programme revolved around campaigns for enfranchisement and the extension of civil rights. The second emerged in the 1960s in connection with women's increasing access to the worlds of work and education, the availability of birth control, and the establishment of legislation on the right to abortion and on equal-pay policies. Four major texts are commonly associated with Second-Wave feminism. Betty Friedan's *The Feminine Mystique* (1963) played a vital role in encouraging the constitution of various consciousness-raising networks for women. Simone de Beauvoir's *The Second Sex* (first published in 1949 and translated into English in 1953) was especially influential in advocating that the construction of woman as man's Other has affected all forms of social and cultural existence. In proclaiming that 'One is not born a woman; one becomes one', Beauvoir uncompromisingly rejects the idea of a female essence or nature. Kate Millett's *Sexual Politics* (1969) asserts that power relations between the sexes are shaped by a repressive ideology based on a male conspiracy that keeps women in a state of false consciousness: women remain subjugated to patriarchy because they are incapable of discerning the nature and causes of their subordination. Millett's notion of ideology is rather inflexible and does not pay sufficient attention to the histories of women who have been consciously aware of their predicament and opposed patriarchal values (Millett 1977). Like *The Second Sex*, Germaine Greer's *The Female Eunuch* (1970) maintains that women's presumed inferiority is a cultural fabrication sustained by institutions such as the nuclear family and the educational system and by the capitalist division of labour. *The Female Eunuch* develops this idea with reference to various aspects of history, literature and popular culture, thus demonstrating that an evaluation of the contexts in which women's psychological castration takes place is of vital importance.

Since the late 1980s, the objectives of feminism have been complicated by the emergence of the term 'postfeminism'. This is a highly controversial term. Some critics use it to indicate that feminism has fulfilled its mission: women have gained full equality, are no longer tied to domestic chores, enjoy good educational and professional opportunities, and have full choice when it comes to marriage and motherhood. This interpretation of postfeminism as the *after* of feminism is called radically into question by critics who do not see emancipation as a universal achievement and stress that, in fact, many women across the globe are still fighting for their most basic rights. These critics also emphasize that women who hold fulfilling and well-paid jobs, have cooperative partners and can afford to be professionals and mothers at the same time are still in the minority. Moreover, despite legislation on equal wages, many women still earn up to 20 per cent less than men, and only about 16 per cent of successful women in executive jobs are also mothers. Julia Kristeva[4] argues that many women's identities are actually split as a result of their having to perform a balancing act between professional commitments and familial responsibilities: 'Women's sexual and material independence has helped them by creating an image of autonomy, performance, and social value.' Nevertheless, there is 'a very striking split in the discourse of postfeminist women. We see a joyful liberation ("our life is our own", "our body is our own"), but at the same time we hear women express deep feelings of pain ... The media talk a great deal about staying home, but this home often seems empty once the husband and the children are gone' (Kristeva 1996: 71). In *The Whole Woman*, Germaine Greer likewise argues that although women have come a long way in the last thirty years, the battle is not yet over and that there is a danger of women becoming complacent about what has been achieved and settling for false forms of equality (Greer 1999).

However, another interpretation of postfeminism (influenced by Poststructuralism) is also available: according to this position, postfeminism does not point to the demise of feminism but rather to a redirection of feminism's concerns. Particularly important is the move away from the assumption that 'woman' and 'femininity' are natural categories, towards an understanding of the discourses

[4] Kristeva's theories are examined in detail in Part I, Chapter 6, 'Textuality'.

through which gender differences are encoded as cultural signs. This understanding is only attainable by ensuring that the theories and practices used to interrogate naturalized ideas do not simply protect the interests of privileged women. One of the shortcomings of both the First Wave and the Second Wave was that their agendas embodied primarily white, Western and middle-class values. Women tended to seek the opportunities already available to men of their own ethnic and class background. Recent feminist thought has departed from Westernized, white and heterosexual 'norms' and increasingly addressed issues of gender equality in conjunction with issues of race and ethnicity. It has sought to expose the racial specificity of the stereotypes governing representations of black women as seen through colonial and imperial eyes (e.g. the images of oversexed and mysterious predators).

Whilst it is undeniable that both black and white feminists have challenged sexism, we must nonetheless acknowledge that black feminists have also had to confront the racism inherent in certain facets of white feminism. This has frequently been difficult to recognize because it has not taken the form of explicit discrimination. Rather, it has resulted from the tendency of much feminist scholarship to *incorporate* black women and their distinctive concerns into Western paradigms. Black feminists have shown that although the aims of black and white feminists often converge, black women's otherness must be addressed as a specific issue: it should not be absorbed into a general notion of otherness based on white women's experiences. Freud notoriously described femininity as a *Dark Continent*. This definition was not meant to apply specifically to black women, since for Freud *all* women were mysterious territories not yet penetrated by the light of male Reason. However, we should consider what that image may entail in racial terms, and differentiate between the concept of darkness associated with women generally and the concept of darkness associated specifically with black women – as the Other not only of man but also of all those who feel authorized to use white skin as a protective mask.[5]

Feminist theories can be described by recourse to two principal categories: essentialist feminism, which maintains that there is a

---

[5] ☞ See Part II, Chapter 5, 'The Other'.

natural essence at the core of femininity, and anti-essentialist feminism, according to which femininity is neither natural nor essential but rather the product of culture and politics. Essentialist feminism comprises three interrelated approaches. Humanist feminism argues that there is a 'deep self' common to all women that unites individuals from disparate backgrounds on the basis of universal characteristics. Experiential feminism elaborates this idea to demonstrate that women share not only certain fundamental attributes but also material experiences, such as motherhood. Radical feminism contends that dominant ideologies hinge on principles of inclusion and exclusion which dictate that certain categories of people must be treated as outsiders. This is the fate met by women in patriarchy and can be taken as the model upon which countless other forms of oppression are constructed.

Anti-essentialist feminism focuses on the practices through which sexual difference is culturally constructed, and through which people's biological and anatomical characteristics are invested with mythical meanings. In this context, the term 'mythical' is meant to suggest that images and stereotypes of masculinity and femininity (such as the association of men with reason and science, and of women with emotions and nature) are not really based on natural distinctions. In fact, they stem from contingent decisions laden with ideological connotations.[6] Accordingly, anti-essentialist feminism stresses the need to denaturalize the stereotypes promoted by ideology by highlighting their artificial status.[7] Anti-essentialists do not deny that men and women are biologically and anatomically different. However, they argue that masculinity and femininity are not timeless realities grounded in natural laws but actually cultural concepts that change significantly through time and space. Gender relations, with their inequitable distribution of power between women and men, are sociopolitical fabrications erected on the premise that men are intellectually, politically and linguistically superior to women. These relations (and underlying definitions of sexual difference) are always

---

[6] ☛This meaning of myth is examined in *Part I*, Chapter 6, 'Textuality', in relation to Barthes's theories.
[7] ☛*Naturalization* and *denaturalization* are also discussed in Part I, Chapter 4, 'Representation' and Part III, Chapter 2, 'The Aesthetic' in relation to the ethos of realism.

contextual. This point is persuasively argued by Thomas Laqueur in *Making Sex* (Laqueur 1992).

Both essentialist and anti-essentialist approaches have addressed the issue of the relationship between women and nature – either to suggest that femininity enjoys a special relation to the natural world or to highlight the artificiality of this assumption. Some critics embrace the pairing of femininity and nature as a means of opposing the alliance of patriarchy and science. Others reject that connection, on the grounds that it has traditionally justified the domination of a female nature by a male technocracy. These arguments have gained momentum in the context of *ecofeminism*. Central to this position is the idea that the Earth is a living, nurturing and all-embracing force, animated by specifically female and maternal elements. Ecofeminism argues that there are fundamental analogies between the oppression of women and the patriarchal control of the environment, and that this makes nature a feminist issue. It also shows that patriarchal language has often used the connection between femininity and nature to denigrate both. At times, femininity is 'animalized' through the association of women with supposedly inferior creatures: 'pets, cows, sows, foxes, chicks, serpents, bitches, beavers, old bats, old hens, mother hens, pussycats, cats, cheetahs, birdbrains, and harebrains'. At others, nature is devalued through its metaphorical description as a female body available for male consumption: as a 'virgin' land to be penetrated, for example (Warren 1997: 12).

The cult of penetration relies on a specious valorization of phallic sexuality. However, the recognition that sexuality is plural has increasingly undermined the idea that any one sexual practice is preferable to any other, or indeed that its meaning is stable. Heterosexuality and homosexuality, for example, are concepts endowed with different meanings in different contexts. Let us briefly consider these and some related terms. The term 'homosexuality' (from the Greek *homo* = 'same' and the Latin *sexus* = 'sex') was coined in 1869 by the Hungarian writer Benkert, in contradistinction to 'heterosexuality' (*heteros* meaning 'other' in Greek). The noun 'homosexual', though originally intended to apply to both men and women, has come to refer primarily to men. Homosexual women have increasingly been designated as 'lesbians' (from *Lesbos*, the place of origin of the sixth-century BC poet Sappho, whose writings often refer to erotic relations amongst women). A related term is 'homosocial': this refers to feelings fostered by institutions such as armies and single-sex schools that lead to bonding amongst people of the same sex. It also alludes to the expression (in art, literature, etc.) of latent homosexual contents. 'Heterosexism', finally, is the term often used to describe forms of language and behaviour that convey explicit hostility against lesbians and gay men, and may even degenerate into obsessive aversion: 'homophobia'.

Broadly defined as erotic intercourse involving people of the same sex, homosexuality has encountered fierce opposition in Western history. Nevertheless, the moral and legal condemnation of homosexuality is surrounded by ambiguties. This is famously exemplified by the writings of the Greek philosopher Plato (fifth century BC), who both commends homosexual intercourse as spiritually superior to heterosexual relationships (e.g. in the *Symposium*) and condemns it as unnatural on the grounds that non-human animals do not engage in it (e.g. in the *Laws*). The Christian philosopher St. Thomas Aquinas (1224/5–74) is so averse to homosexual intercourse as to state that it is more opprobrious than rape: while rape 'merely' violates another person, homosexuality contravenes a natural law. However, homosexuality is not a deviant or indeed peripheral form of sexuality. Sex surveys (such as the Kinsey Report, 1948–53, and the Wolfenden Report, 1957) have indicated that it is actually widespread, and that its ethical and political demonization as a perversion is far from tenable. Developments in biology and psychoanalysis have further confirmed the preposterousness of philosophical and religious agendas keen on presenting homosexuality as a bizarre and marginal occurrence. No consensus has been reached, however, as to whether homosexual preferences should be attributed to innate dispositions or rather to environmental causes. Michel Foucault (1926–84) has contributed significantly to this debate by arguing that homosexuality is a social construction used by dominant ideologies to differentiate between normality and abnormality.

The notion that definitions of homosexuality are culturally determined is central to gay politics. This phrase loosely refers to both lesbian politics and gay men's politics. This could be partly explained on the grounds that since the early 1970s, there have been many instances of cooperation between lesbians and gay men. These include hugely popular information switchboards, websites, bulletins and periodicals which are concerned with encouraging a recognition of gay people's often unacknowledged roles, and with practical issues to do with equal opportunities, health, welfare and safe sex. Lesbian politics and gay men's politics are not, however, identical in their aims and concerns. Certain strands of lesbian feminism actually argue that, in different ways, both heterosexuality and male homosexuality value men above women and that lesbian relationships are the only way of asserting women's rights – to the point that separatism (maximum withdrawal from patriarchal power structures) may be the only revolutionary option available.

The debate has acquired further levels of complexity in virtue of the emergence of movements committed to the exploration of sexual diversity, such as *Queer Theory*. A determination to highlight the pleasure of multiple sexualities is central to this approach. The assertion of plurality and diversity aims at dissolving conventional identity categories and at encouraging a recognition of pleasures not previously acknowledged (Bristow and Wilson 1993). A plurisexual individual may ultimately not 'bother', as Kate Woolfe puts it, 'to figure the gender of the people [s/he is] attracted to' (Woolfe 1998: 90). The notion of *transgender* is especially important, in this respect. A transgenderist is neither a transvestite nor a transsexual: s/he is not defined by cross-dressing or by a literal change of sex effected by medical technology. Rather, s/he is someone who moves across conventional gender boundaries (even regardless of sexual preferences) and performs multiple parts through diverse identity narratives.

Cherry Smyth argues that in patriarchal societies, the binary opposition hetero/homo has been imposed as a means of 'annihilating the spectrum of sexualities that exist' (Smyth 1992: 20). Radical feminism has advocated no less restrictive oppositions, such as the one between lesbian sex as supposedly 'loving and monogamous' and gay male sex as 'exploitative and promiscuous' (Smyth 1992: 36). According to Smyth, it is preposterous to talk of one kind of homosexuality, one kind of lesbianism, or one kind of lesbian pleasure. Since sexual practices never occur in a vacuum but are actually implicated at all times with political and social issues such as racism, economic exploitation and censorship, sexualities can only be adequately evaluated in relation to their broader cultural contexts. The desires and pleasures associated with any one form of sexuality are likewise inseparable from the cultural circumstances in which they are experienced. The cultural specificity of sexual preferences and of related activities is confirmed by the fact that both homosexuality and heterosexuality encompass diverse practices. Radical feminism has often presented heterosexuality as a unified phenomenon, and accused it of sustaining patriarchal institutions by exposing women to defenceless exploitation. Homosexuality, by contrast, has been presented as a liberating option. This idea has been questioned by anti-essentialist critics who argue that not all heterosexuals live their heterosexuality in the same way. Analogously, talking about homosexuality as a uniform category is spurious. According to Smyth, this is borne out by the sheer diversity of 'queer' sexualities: 'there are straight queers, biqueers, tranny queers, lez queers, fag queers, SM queers, fisting queers' (Smyth 1992: 17).

If it is vital to acknowledge and respect these differences, it is no less important to prevent them from crystallizing into labels. Indeed, as Mary McIntosh argues, when differences become fixed tags, they inevitably prove divisive. This happens, for example, when people maintain that 'feminism is only for women, anti-racism only for black people, and so on'. In fact, we should examine the 'interrelationships' between various forms of both oppression and pleasure (McIntosh 1993: 30). Oppression and emancipation do not always consist of practical and obvious actions with practical and obvious consequences. In fact, they are often articulated through cultural representations, images and symbols which embody disparate fantasies and ideals. We must learn to read these cultural products as narratives – stories that frequently perpetuate disabling gender stereotypes but also, at the same time, invite us to question where the stereotypes come from, whose interests they serve, and under what circumstances: 'Culture itself is the limit of our knowledge; there is no available truth outside culture with which we can challenge injustice. But culture is also contradictory, the location of resistances as well as oppressions, and it is therefore ultimately unstable. It too is in consequence a site of political struggle' (Belsey and Moore 1997: 8).

CHAPTER 5

THE OTHER

This chapter examines a cross-section of philosophical approaches to the idea of the Other and then proceeds to discuss its relevance to the fashioning of social identities and subject positions. The concept of the Other was used by G.W.F. Hegel (1770–1831) to argue that human consciousness is incapable of perceiving itself without recognition by others. This point is illustrated through the parable of Master and Slave. Hegel maintains that these two figures are mutually defining. On the surface, the Master appears to be all-powerful but he actually requires recognition from the Slave: his chances of attaining self-awareness depend on the existence of the Slave. The Master forces the Slave to labour in unfavourable conditions so as to fulfil his own needs and desires. The Slave, in turn, may only satisfy the master's requirements by repressing his own urges: he has to 'overcome' himself (Kojeve 1969: 228). In so doing, the Slave develops an ability to transform both himself and the natural world on which his labour is bestowed. The Master, by contrast, is trapped in a state of total dependence upon his subjugated Other. Unable to transform nature through work, he remains locked within a static self that is not truly his. As Madan Sarup points out, work is the primary means through which the enslaved subject may transcend his situation: 'It is because work is an auto-creative act that it can raise him from slavery to freedom. The future and history hence belong not to the warlike Master, who either dies or preserves himself indefinitely in "identity to himself", but to the working Slave' (Sarup 1988: 22).

In the philosophical traditions of Phenomenology and Existentialism,[1] the Other is the factor that enables the subject to build up a self-image. The Other is the person or group that confers meaning upon the subject by either helping it or forcing it to adopt a particular world view and to define its position therein. Moreover, the concept of the Other is used to take perception and knowledge beyond the limited perspective of the individual. This entails a radical questioning of the doctrine of *solipsism*, according to which nothing exists except me and my thoughts and feelings. What Phenomenology and Existentialism propose, by contrast, is a world of intersubjectivity, in which any one individual's interpretations of reality always interact with those of countless other people and are always, as a result, open to redefinition. The Existentialist thinker Jean-Paul Sartre (1905–80), in particular, contends that our sense of self depends on our being the object of another's gaze.[2] The picture painted by Sartre is based on a paradox. On the one hand, we enjoy a sense of wholeness and control over our environment as long as we feel that we are the subjects of the gaze – namely, as long as we feel that we can look undisturbed at the world around us and take it all in without anybody else interfering with our vision. On the other hand, it is only when we ourselves become objects of another person's gaze that we really come into being. Our existence is an effect of some Other's recognition of us, even though, ironically, the Other's gaze is also what ultimately deprives us of any real sense of autonomy and mastery (Sartre 1956).

In the domain of psychoanalysis, analogous views have been put forward by Jacques Lacan (1901–81), who argues that our existence as subjects is a function of our relationship with the Other. In Lacan's writings, this term holds several complementary meanings, three of which are especially relevant to the present context. The Other is everything which we must learn to separate ourselves from in order to develop into adult individuals (parents, for example). It is a fictional image of ourselves (such as a mirror image) which we tend to identify with, and yet must learn to conceive of as separate from the physical body. Above all, it is the

---

[1] ☞See Part I, Chapter 5, 'Reading' for an evaluation of these doctrines.
[2] ☞See also Part II, Chapter 6, 'The Gaze'.

realm of language, laws and institutions in which we are required to live as socialized creatures.[3]

In philosophy, the Other is also related to the problem in the theory of knowledge known as 'other minds'. This is concerned with three principal issues: whether we can know that other beings have thoughts and feelings and, if so, how we can know it; whether, assuming we could establish beyond doubt that other beings indeed have mental lives, we could know that they resembled our own; whether we could interpret other beings' behaviour (physical, cultural, linguistic) as a reliable reflection of how they think and feel. These are crucial questions, for many assumptions and prejudices surrounding others stem precisely from an inability to grasp how they function. This inability, moreover, often gives rise to repressive strategies of incorporation. In *Totality and Infinity* (1961), Emmanuel Levinas (b. 1906) advocates this point by emphasizing that Western philosophy has insistently repressed the Other by striving to give it a definite place. In fact, the Other transcends all structures and any attempt to categorize it amounts to domesticating – and, by extension, colonizing – its intrinsic alterity. If other people's conduct strikes us as somewhat unfamiliar, an easy way of dealing with them is to assume that their thoughts and feelings are incompatible with our own mental lives. Masters, rulers and colonizers of various sorts have traditionally relied on this assumption and used it to draw a sinister conclusion: the notion that the Other's thoughts and feelings are not merely different but also crude and inferior.

It can hardly be denied that in Western culture, dominant ideologies have time and again defined themselves in relation to a subordinated Other. Self and Other are inextricably connected. This notion has been gaining increasing popularity since the advent of Poststructuralism and its emphasis on the ways in which Western culture has coded so-called *marginal* groups as the Other. Women, gays and people of colour, for example, have recurringly been seen to deviate from the norms of patriarchal, heterosexual and white society. In the sphere of gender politics,[4] alterity has manifested itself in one basic form: the construction of woman as Other. Woman has traditionally been regarded as everything

[3] ☞See also Part II, Chapter 2, 'Subjectivity'.
[4] ☞See Part II, Chapter 4, 'Gender and Sexuality'.

which man is not *supposed* to be, and man as everything which woman is not *able* to be. However, there are many different ways of encoding and interpreting alterity in the context of gender relations and related forms of discrimination. If *all* women have been constructed as man's Other, it is nonetheless crucial to realize that there are various versions and degrees of otherness. The ways in which a particular woman experiences her alterity relate not only to her biological sex and her gender position within a culture but also to her ethnic background, education, profession, social class, and both physical and psychological abilities and disabilities. These variations must be consistently taken into consideration, so as to avoid producing universalizing and homogenizing definitions of otherness which efface the distinctive concerns and predicaments of women within particular racial and social groups.

Western culture has also insistently marginalized disabled people as Other. As Len Barton points out, the 'consistent bias against disabled people throughout recorded history' is 'clustered around the myth of the "body perfect"' (Barton 1996: 1), and results in a series of stock responses that encompass 'horror, fear, anxiety, hostility, distrust, pity, over-protection and patronizing behaviour' (Barton 1996: 8). Mainstream sociologists have shown scarce interest in disability as a social phenomenon, preferring to see it as a medical or psychological issue. This neglect stems from the tendency to take the rational and whole individual as sociology's central object of study, and to deem anyone who departs from this assumed norm as either irrelevant or as an instance of 'exotic behaviour' (Barton 1996: 6). Relatedly, disabled people's social productivity is generally ignored. Medically, disability is inequitably regarded as a form of either biological or psychological inferiority. The medical definition has traditionally influenced popular interpretations of disability which almost invariably result in discrimination, disempowerment, oppression and abuse. These views have coloured dominant responses to the disabled-as-Other throughout Western history. Obsessed with fitness as the index of moral (as well as physical) excellence, the Greeks condemned disability – as shown by the relegation of the god Hephaestes to the underworld as a result of his lameness. The Romans favoured the practice of infanticide in the case of frail babies, and often treated disability as a form of entertainment (as in the case of staged fights between dwarfs and female slaves). In the Middle

Ages, disabled bodies were often taken as evidence of the workings of Satan, and unhealthy infants, in particular, regarded as changelings. Tudor and Stuart England continued to consider physical impairment as a spectacle (as evinced by its passion for Courtly fools and trips to Bedlam), and as a visible manifestation of evil (as in the famous case of King Richard III). Although attitudes to disability have obviously altered since the Renaissance, contemporary idealizations of the 'body perfect' and the pursuit of the 'beauty myth' suggest that disability is still surrounded by fantasies.

In assessing contemporary responses to the disabled body, it is vital to realize that more is needed than merely a widening of resources and opportunities for citizens with disabilities. For one thing, a more adequate understanding of disability and of the specific needs involved by different forms of disability should be aimed at by *all* citizens, regardless of whether or not they are disabled. At the same time, the term disability should not be employed as a 'catch-all' definition. Although the disability movement has increasingly gained power and credibility as a contemporary social activity, we should be aware of differences within the movement itself: what being disabled means for individuals from diverse social and ethnic backgrounds, and with diverse sexual orientations.

The discourse of alterity manifests itself in all its complexity in the context of debates on colonialism and postcolonialism. These terms are historically associated with the politics of imperialism: a state's forceful extension of its powers through the conquest and exploitation of other territories. Since at least the Renaissance, imperialism has justified its oppressive practices by dressing them up as civilizing agents, endowed with cultural and racial superiority. The doctrine of Social Darwinism has supported this agenda by applying the idea of natural evolution to the development of human-made societies and governments. In the early part of the twentieth century, the most thorough critiques of imperialism found its roots in economic factors. In *Imperialism in the Highest Stages of Capitalism* (1915), for example, V. I. U. Lenin (1870–1924) argued that imperialism results from monopoly capitalists' determination to maximize their profits by exploiting foreign regions – using their raw materials, strengthening existing markets through the introduction of new goods made from such materials, and augmenting their investment opportunities. Although it is generally accepted that economic matters have played a key role in the development of modern imperialism, and although Lenin's theories remain influential, more recent critics have tended to focus on other, non-economic, factors, as well. Especially important are the issues of nationalism and race.

Nationalism underpins imperial and colonial domination by promoting notions of territorial and ideological supremacy. Nationalism as a discourse pivots on the notion that certain groups of people are bound together by shared racial, historical and linguistic connections. These are associated with a particular territory. The term territory does not refer merely to a geographical area but also, more importantly, to a political and cultural organization: a nation state. Such a space is both physical and conceptual, a region whose boundaries must be guarded against alien intrusions, and an ideology to be exalted and divulged.[5] The issue of race is closely linked with that of nationalism: the classification of people on the basis of racially distinctive features (most notoriously, the colour of their skin) has been instrumental to the construction of national and territorial identities. The advancement of a nation state's ideology through imperial and colonial power is virtually inseparable from issues of race, racial relations and racial prejudice. In order to assert the status of a nation as superior, something else – an Other – must first be branded as inferior. The colonizer's inflated sense of self can only be sustained in contrast with a non-self. Racial difference has been ruthlessly harnessed to the construction of social identities and related power structures: the more remote, primitive and exotic a colonized population could be made to appear, the more legitimate its exploitation and repression would seem to be. Despite decolonization, the process whereby once dependent territories have achieved the status of sovereign states, neocolonialist and neoimperialist programmes retain their hold: notably, in the more or less direct control of Third-World economies and native traditions by foreign governments.

Violence is a structural component of colonialism and racism. It operates, with various degrees of brutality, to oppress the Other. Yet, the violence perpetrated by the controlling agents is artfully

---

[5] ☞ For various definitions of space, see Part III, Chapter 3, 'Space'.

covered up, while the violent acts performed by the oppressed are publicized in full colour as terrorism, sedition and crime. Violence is an important issue in the writings of Franz Fanon (1925–61), one of the major proponents of Third-World revolution. In *Black Skin, White Masks* (1952), Fanon examines the far-reaching repercussions of racism and colonialism and advocates the necessity of extreme measures in the emancipation of black people. Freeing the oppressed from the colonizer's extensive infringement on their rights is viewed as a collective catharsis capable of renewing humanity in its entirety (Fanon 1967). In *The Wretched of the Earth* (1961), Fanon argues that the promotion of justice and, no less vitally, the psychological liberation of the oppressed requires recourse to violence (Fanon 1964). Fanon's writings do not celebrate violence for its own sake. In fact, he arrives at the conclusion that violence is an inevitable weapon through a thorough examination of colonial relations. In the structure of these relations, violence is endemic: the colonizer deploys violence against the colonized, and the colonized often deploy it against one another, driven by frustration and despair. Both forms of violence serve to perpetuate existing structures of exploitation. It is by directing violent action against the oppressor that the 'wretched of the earth' may change radically their material circumstances and, at the same time, overthrow crippling definitions of their otherness.

According to Edward Said (b. 1935), such definitions are promulgated by Orientalism: the phenomenon whereby the East has been constructed by the West since at least the Renaissance by recourse to various discourses (literature, historiography, sociology, anthropology, geography). Orientalism's objective is to validate Western values, political and economic systems and structures of domination, by positing as Other anyone and anything apparently at odds with Western institutions. The factors that make the Other especially menacing are its difference and its mysterious aura. According to Said, the strategies through which the Other is constructed are fundamentally textual, for images and stereotypes of the Orient have traditionally been emplaced through writing. Moreover, the West has often tried to make sense of an unfamiliar East by assessing it against an existing body of texts and their explanations of faraway worlds. Said underscores the textual dimension of alterity by pointing out that Orientalism's imaginary Other first comes into being 'when a human being confronts at close quarters something relatively unknown and threatening and previously distant. In such a case one has recourse not only to what in one's previous experience the novelty resembles but also to what one has read about it.' The Other is evaluated in relation to narratives because human beings tend 'to fall back on a text when the uncertainty of travel in strange parts seems to threaten one's equanimity' (Said 1988: 295). All Orientalist texts are ultimately fictional: accounts about the East, its inhabitants and its cultural traditions endeavour to present their contents as self-evident *facts* but what they invariably supply is actually a cluster of mythical presuppositions.

Although people often associate the most sinister forms of oppression with overtly physical brutality, it should not be forgotten that the Other has also been repressed through less explicit – yet no less deleterious – strategies than violence. This is confirmed by the exclusion of non-Western artists from the Canon. Until relatively recently, art history and aesthetic appreciation have been dominated by a Eurocentric outlook which has alternately excluded the Other as primitive, savage and, at best, naive, or incorporated it into Western art and its own ideological agendas. For example, so-called 'primitive' artefacts from African tribal cultures and Australian Aboriginal art have influenced significantly and often invigorated Western art by providing many Western artists with new ideas, styles and techniques, as well as with the means of challenging traditional approaches to the work of art. Limited knowledge of the cultural contexts in which 'primitive' themes and artefacts grow can result in myriad misconceptions and stereotypes. It could be argued, for instance, that an artist like Gaugin was merely romanticizing what he saw as the primitive spirit from a Western stand point. Picasso, for his part, has sometimes been accused of lacking adequate knowledge of the ethnographic connotations carried by the tribal sculptures which his works famously imitate. Nevertheless, it is undeniable that both artists have been substantially energized by their encounters with non-western cultures, and that their experience of the Other has enabled them to challenge many established conventions.

It is also worth noting that Western definitions of art have traditionally tended to group all non-Western works into one single category, despite their historical and geographical diversity, thus imposing a spuriously coherent identity upon the Other's creative achievements. This tendency can be traced back to the Renaissance, when the objects brought back to Europe by voyagers and explorers were invariably assessed against Western notions of beauty and taste, and automatically classified as strange and inexplicably different: as Other. Artefacts drawn from diverse parts of the globe were hence unified under one universal label: they were considered objects of curiosity, and indeed collected and put on display in cabinets of curiosities. The art of other cultures, in this context, could only be understood as a more or less outlandish deviation from the norms associated with European art, and it was not unusual to take the exotic character of non-Western artefacts as symptomatic of their producers' inferiority and lack of aesthetic refinement. Since the early nineteenth century, museums have further sustained the ordering and classification of non-Western artefacts according to their geographical and historical origins, and to their thematic and compositional attributes. Museological practices and methodologies have obviously changed since the institution of the early museums. However, it can hardly be denied that for a long time their primary tendency was to present non-Western cultures as alien and, concomitantly, to rely on racial and social stereotypes to make them intelligible to a Western public.

In the context of Postmodernism, globalization – and the attendant flattening of space and time – have contributed to the erosion of some traditional distinctions between Western and non-Western art forms. This could be seen as a healthy move. Yet, we should not lose sight of the fact that crucial cultural differences still obtain. Indeed, while many cultures across the planet may show symptoms of the 'postmodern condition'[6] – a concern with crisis, an emphasis on social disintegration, speculations about apocalyptic and post-apocalyptic scenarios – the ways in which the condition is experienced and articulated in art vary hugely from culture to culture due to historical, political and environmental factors. As Homi K. Bhabha points out, 'The globe is shrinking for those who own it; for the displaced or the dispossessed, the migrant or refugee, no distance is more awesome than the few feet across borders or frontiers (Bhabha 1996: 321).

[6] This concept is discussed in Part III, Chapter 2, 'The Aesthetic'.

Otherness is a basic ingredient of all social identities. According to Julia Kristeva (b. 1941), an adequate understanding of alterity must imply an understanding of the concept of 'difference' as an internal condition, rather than a matter of external attributes (such as a person's apparent gender or the colour of her/his skin). The Other is in us. When a culture, society or community marginalizes certain individuals as Other, what it attempts to exclude or repress is actually a part of itself which it finds difficult to understand, let alone accept. As psychoanalysis emphasizes,[7] an individual's identity is made precarious by the fact that disparate drives, both conscious and unconscious, are constantly competing with one another within its territory. The identity of a whole culture is comparably unstable due to ongoing tensions and conflicts within its fabric. No culture, however totalitarian its political regime may be, is ever unified. From this recognition, a troubling sense of vulnerability and impermanence ensues. In order to combat this feeling of insecurity, societies create distinctions between those parts of themselves which they cherish and wish to retain as theirs, and those which they abhor and aim at expelling. The excluded parts go to constitute the Other. We should never forget that when we discriminate against, or indeed abuse, other people, we are really rejecting facets of ourselves which we deem incompatible with our quest for plenitude and stability. We brand some people as Other, find them threatening and react to them violently because we have difficulties negotiating the stranger in us. A society's treatment of strangers mirrors the individual's attitude to his/her unconscious fears and desires. Both the stranger and the unconscious elude rational and familiar explanations. Indeed, what makes the Other disturbing is its indeterminateness: it appears not to belong to any of the categories legitimized by a culture to preserve its identity. Anxieties produced by the inability to assign a place to this ubiquitous entity escalate as we are reminded of our own strangeness to ourselves and of our own incompleteness: 'Confronting the foreigner whom I reject and with whom at the same time I identify, I lose my boundaries, I no longer have a container ... I lose my composure. I feel "lost", "indistinct", "hazy"' (Kristeva 1990: 187).

Kristeva argues that instead of trying to make sense of the

---

[7] ☞See Part II, Chapter 2, 'Subjectivity'.

Other as a menace or, at best, a nuisance to be kept at bay, we should learn to respect what we cannot know or understand. Fear of the Other far too often degenerates into blind hatred: fascism, racism, genocide, and a fetishistic attachment to national identities, languages and territories. But there is also another danger: that of incorporating and integrating others into the dominant structures of a culture, thus denying their differences and, indeed, their right to difference. Kristeva, by contrast, aims at celebrating the Other's difference, and the polyphonic character of cultures capable of respecting difference. It is by accepting the unknown in us that we are most likely to learn how to accept and value the unknown in others.

CHAPTER 6

THE GAZE

The concept of the gaze describes a form of power associated with the eye and with the sense of sight. When we gaze at somebody or something, we are not simply 'looking'. The gaze probes and masters. It penetrates and objectifies the body. A lot of the time, we simply 'see' things: we register certain sensations to do with light, colours and shapes without any ulterior motives. Sometimes we 'observe' things: we look at them carefully in order to find out about them in detail. Then there are times when we 'glance' at things: our eyes skim over them and caress their surfaces in a casual way. But when we gaze at things, our aim is to control them. This chapter explores the discourse of the gaze with reference to the role played by the sense of sight and the dynamics of looking in the genesis of social identities.

The power of the gaze owes much to the tendency in Western thought to enthrone sight as the most sophisticated of the five senses due to its supposedly closer association with the mind than with the body. Sight has conventionally been idealized on the basis of its ability to distance the act of perception from the body's materiality.[1] This notion has been refuted by critics who argue that sight itself is tactile. Walter Benjamin (1892–1940), for example, maintains that when we look at artworks and even ordinary objects, particularly those which impress us most, we become involved in a tactile exchange. We are able to communicate with these objects insofar as they push themselves forward and touch us, as it were (Benjamin 1985: 42). The Italian Futurist

---

[1] The relationship between the senses, especially sight, and the mind/body issue is addressed in detail in Part III, Chapter 1, 'The Mind'.

Filippo Marinetti (1876–1944) advocates the principle of *Tactilism* as a means of liberating the most eminently erotic features of the sensorium. He argues that all experience proceeds from the sense of touch: even 'a visual sense is born in the fingertips'. Indeed, 'sight, smell, hearing, touch, and taste are modifications of a single keen sense: touch, divided in different ways and localized in different points' (Marinetti 1972: 120).

However, it is undeniable that the power of the gaze is ancient, and this is testified by both folklore and mythology. In the domain of popular tradition, it often manifests itself as the evil eye: the power to bewitch and even kill by looking. Classical mythology abounds with references to the eye's mysterious and often fatal powers: the Gorgons' gaze is said to turn their victims into stone and their chief, Medusa, is supposed to have been destroyed by Perseus thanks to his ability to avoid her gaze and to behold her shape in a reflection. Eurydice, the wife of the legendary poet Orpheus, is the pathetic casualty of a loving gaze, her own husband's. Orpheus obtains Eurydice's release from Hades after her untimely death on the condition that he will not look at her as she follows him back to the upper world. Inadvertently turning to look at his beloved wife towards the end of their journey, Orpheus consigns her back to the underworld forever after. In biblical mythology, the power of the gaze to turn against itself is famously encapsulated by the story of Lot's wife who, looking back on the cities of Sodom and Gomorrah against God's command, is metamorphosed into a pillar of salt. In popular etiquette, the power of the gaze is implicitly acknowledged by the injunction not to stare at others. For centuries, this precept was gender-inflected, for it was the staring woman, in particular, that was considered rude and immodest. Linked to this code of conduct is the importance of vestimentary uniforms as a means of homogenizing people (in schools, armies, prisons, etc.) so that they will not attract the eye of other members of their group. At the same time, paradoxically, uniforms cause their wearers to look different to those who do not belong to their category, and thus become either the active subjects or the passive objects of the gaze depending on their position in a given power structure.

According to Michel Foucault (1926–84), the operations of power are inseparable form the dynamics of the gaze. Foucault traces a shift from pre-modern societies, where the powerful advertise their authority by putting themselves on display, and thus awing the impotent masses into submission, to modern formations, where power is relatively invisible and controls us by seeing everything whilst remaining unseen. Modern societies rely on surveillance rather than spectacle. Foucault attributes these changes to social and economic transformations triggered by the Industrial Revolution, and the elaboration of strategies geared towards the rationalization and modernization of the subject. In particular, the disintegration of the feudal/agrarian setup produces free-floating subjects, no longer anchored to traditional notions of community and identity, and gives rise to modern disciplining practices centred on a technology of the body that makes people useful and docile by subjecting them to visual control. Central to the modern setup is the structure of the *Panopticon*: an ideal prison (whose architectural principles may also be employed in the construction of schools, hospitals and barracks) where each inmate is subjected to an unrelenting gaze without being able to see his/her observer.[2] The gaze, argues Foucault, also plays a vital role in the medical field. Here, again, a shift can be noticed from pre-modern cultures, where the body is subjected to a merely external analysis of its surfaces, to modern cultures, where (especially through the refinement of the arts of autopsy and dissection) the body's inner functionings become available to the scientific gaze.

In examining the ideological deployment of visual strategies for disciplinary purposes, a distinction must be drawn between the role of the observer and the role of the spectator. Jonathan Crary highlights this distinction with reference to the etymological roots of the two terms: 'Unlike *spectare*, the Latin root for "spectator", the root for "observe" does not literally mean "to look at" … *observare* means "to conform one's action, to comply with", as in observing rules, codes, regulations, and practices. Though obviously one who sees, an observer is more importantly one who sees within a prescribed set of possibilites, one who is embedded in a system of conventions and limitations' (Crary 1990: 18). This may well be what Jacques Lacan (1901–81) has in mind when he speculates that the world of inanimate objects is not passive but

<hr />

[2] ☞ See also Part II, Chapter 1, 'Ideology' and Part II, Chapter 2, 'Subjectivity'.

actually looks back at the perceiver. What we see is always, in other words, a function of what and how we are meant to see. The inanimate world watches us to the extent that there is inevitably someone or something that expects us to see things in certain ways (Lacan 1978). As Norman Bryson puts is: 'When I look, what I see is not simply light but intelligible form .... For human beings collectively to orchestrate their visual experience together it is required that each submit his or her retinal experience to the socially agreed description(s) of an intelligible world. Vision is socialized, and visual reality can be measured and named, as hallucination, misrecognition, or "visual disturbance". Between the subject and the world is inserted the entire sum of discourses which make up visuality' (Bryson 1988: 91).

The socialization of vision has traditionally relied, at least in the west, on practices meant to unify vision. The codification of perspective[3] has played a vital role, in this respect, by positing the possibility of an abstract and objective way of seeing, centred on the totalizing gaze of one disembodied and de-eroticized Eye/I. As Martin Jay points out, the most famous strategies used to geometricalize and hence rationalize space as the emanation of a discerning eye posit that eye 'as singular, rather than the two eyes of normal binocular vision. It was considered in the manner of a lone eye looking through a peephole at the scene in front of it. Such an eye was, moreover, understood to be static, unblinking and fixated, rather than dynamic ... thus producing a visual take that was eternalized, reduced to one "point of view"' (Jay 1988: 7–8). The belief in one correct way of seeing, corresponding to one equally correct way of representing the world, is logically untenable, since the disembodied Eye/I does not actually exist. Vision, however idealized, is always attached to a contingent, rather than transcendent, being – not to mention the fact that each of a person's eyes sees differently. The camera obscura also contributed to the definition of the viewing subject between 1500 and 1700, as an apparatus supposed to guarantee objective truth. The mind is here figured as a sealed space in which images are reviewed by an inner eye. Everything is processed, known and possessed within this one self-enclosed space, independent from

[3] ☞Perspective, both as a concept and as a technique, is discussed in Part I, Chapter 4, 'Representation'.

external reality and carefully insulated from the life of the senses. Like perspectivalism, the camera obscura rests on the principles of monocularity (vision pertaining to one eye) and desensualization. These principles are supposed to aid the constitution of a rational and knowledgeable subject, and to socialize vision according to shared cultural values.

A crucial shift in the theorization of vision occurs in the early nineteenth century, as the human body acquires unprecedented centrality. The development of the discipline of physiology, in particular, encourages a recognition of the relationship between categories of knowledge and biological/anatomical structures. At the same time, the putative unity of vision is radically challenged by the discovery that the nerves related to different senses are distinct, and that the same cause generates quite different sensations from one nerve to another. The sense of sight will register electricity, for example, quite differently from the sense of touch. The subject cannot process the world in one single way (as perspectivalism and the camera obscura maintained) but must depend on multiple channels, often with unexpected and disorienting effects.

The social dimension of vision is emphasized by Jean-Paul Sartre (1905–80),[4] who asserts that an individual's gaze is inevitably caught in an intersubjective network of perception. Human identity itself, for Sartre, is a product of the gaze. This idea is conveyed through a simple, yet disturbing, parable. Sartre walks into a park and, noticing that he is alone, derives pleasure from the realization that he is wholly in control of the field of vision: he is free to gaze at and thus master his surroundings without interferences. Suddenly, as another person enters the park, the situation alters drastically. Sartre is no longer a solitary viewer but is actually forced to share the visual field with someone else. This intrusive Other shatters the illusion of mastery initially enjoyed by the solitary viewer and turns him into the spectacle of another's gaze. What the interfering stranger challenges is not only Sartre's visual mastery, however. Indeed, the unity and coherence of his whole being are called into question by the intruder's appearance on the scene: 'the intruder becomes a kind of drain which sucks in all the former plenitude, a black hole pulling the scene away from the watcher self into an engulfing void' (Bryson 1988, 89). While stressing that nobody is ever the sole master of the visual domain, Sartre simultaneously argues that we are never free to look at the world through purely subjective lenses of our own making because we have to share our vision with others. Our very sense of identity depends on the presence of another person: in begrudging the stranger's interference, Sartre is nonetheless convinced that the intruder, in gazing at us, also recognizes and hence ratifies our existence. Sartre also points out that the felt gaze – namely, the sensation of being watched – is frequently more powerful than an actual pair of eyes intent on staring at us. The most embarrassing visual experience is said to be the one in which we are caught spying through a keyhole: that is, the situation in which we are watched watching.

In recent years, the gaze has been examined in relation to the findings of Freudian and Lacanian theory. Psychoanalytically speaking, the gaze is associated with four principal concepts: scopophilia, voyeurism, fetishism and sadism. Let us look at the basic features of each. Scopophilia (from the Greek *scopein* = 'to look' + *philia* = 'love') refers to the experience of pleasure that arises from the act of looking. Voyeurism (from the French *voyeur* = 'one who sees') denotes the sense of excitement produced by viewing other bodies, preferably unclothed or engaged in sexual intercourse. While in scopophilia the object of the gaze simply elicits pleasure, in voyeurism it does so to the extent that it can be seen as a specifically sexual or erotic entity. Fetishism (from the Latin *facere* = 'to make' or *facticius* = 'artificial') describes the tendency to feel strongly (even obsessively) attracted to objects or corporeal attributes associated with a sexual partner, rather than to her/his actual body. In fetishism, the object of the gaze is an idealized token of eroticism. Commonly thought of as an exotic object, the fetish is not necessarily outlandish in either geographical or cultural terms. What makes it unusual is its uncanny identity, based on the attribution of great value to an ordinary object. Sadism (a term associated with the writings of the Marquis de Sade [1740–1814]) refers to the proclivity to derive pleasure from the observation of another person's pain, generally regardless of whether this has been inflicted by the observer her/himself or by somebody else. Here, the object of the gaze only pleases to the extent that it is subjected to cruelty and violence.

Several psychoanalytically oriented critics have examined the gaze in terms of gender relations, proceeding from the premise that its operations play a key part in the construction and perpetuation of sexual power structures. Sexuality is inextricably intertwined with power and power, in turn, is inseparable from the eye. Laura Mulvey has made a seminal contribution to contemporary debates on the discourse of the gaze in relation to psychoanalysis and sexuality through her examination of the politics of vision in mainstream Hollywood cinema (Mulvey 1989). This tradition is said to pivot on an asymmetrical distribution of power which inscribes woman as the image and man as the bearer of the look. Mulvey argues that female characters in Hollywood narrative cinema are generally controlled by the male gaze on two related levels. Firstly, the male protagonist objectifies the heroine through his gaze. Secondly, the male spectator identifies with the filmic hero and uses his own gaze to frame the heroine as a passive object. Mulvey argues that the male urge to control woman stems, in a psychoanalytical frame of reference, from the fact that her lack of a penis implies the threat of castration and is thus a source of anxiety. Men have two options available in coping with this anxiety and both rely on the objectification of woman through the gaze. Objectification can take two forms and from each a particular stereotype of femininity ensues. On the one hand, woman may be devalued, demonized as the quintessential symbol of sexual corruption. Characterized as the overpowering and vampiric beast to be repressed, the demonic woman fuels male fantasies of containment of the female body. This option is connected with sadism. On the other hand, woman may be over-valued as a fetish. This stereotype embodies the male desire to transform the female body into a desexualized icon to be placed on a pedestal and worshipped from a distance. This second option is termed fetishistic scopophilia, and its function is to keep at bay the threat posed by woman as a reminder of the possibility of castration by turning her into a passive and silent object of worship.[5]

Although the spectator's identification with the filmic hero plays an important part in the dynamics of the gaze, it should be noted that identification is inevitably based on an illusion, a misrecogni-

---

[5] The castration complex is described in Part II, Chapter 2, 'Subjectivity' in the context of a general discussion of Freudian theory.

tion.[6] As Christian Metz indicates, this misrecognition is akin to the one experienced by the Lacanian infant when it beholds its reflection in the mirror as a coherent body image and joyfully identifies with it. The identification is illusory for the infant is, at this stage, an incoherent jumble of drives, and the unified self it perceives therefore does not coincide with its authentic reality (Metz 1982). In cinema, spectators misrecognize their situation by regarding themselves as the subjects responsible for the production of the cinematic sign (*I make the film by perceiving it*), while in fact they are themselves constructed by the symbolic order of cinema both as institution and as equipment.

Pursuing a line reminiscent of Mulvey's work, Lynda Nead emphasizes the male urge to control a supposedly dangerous femininity through the power of the gaze in her study of the female nude in Western art. Kenneth Clark's seminal investigation of the nude argues that the most salient feature of this genre is its ability to convey an idealized and purified version of corporeality, and that it is in Classical art that the 'balance between an ideal scheme and functional necessities' is most satisfyingly achieved (Clark 1985: 17). The Greeks are said to have given to 'the cult of physical perfection a solemnity and a rapture which have not been experienced since' (Clark 1985: 29). Nead argues that the nude, especially in its female version, is a more complex phenomenon than Clark seems to indicate. Indeed, this genre carries crucial ideological connotations that revolve around the discourse of the gaze and, relatedly, around gender relations based on the dynamics of sight. If the nude is the supreme symbol of civilization, aesthetic excellence and accomplishment, it is also, more importantly, 'a means of containing femininity and female sexuality'. This strategy of containment is motivated by the fact that femininity and female sexuality are considered undisciplined and excessive within patriarchy, and that the female body is seen as disturbing and even obscene because of its lack of clear boundaries. Hence, the nude is introduced primarily for the purposes of 'controlling this unruly body and placing it within the securing boundaries of aesthetic discourse' (Nead 1992: 2). While the obscene body respects no boundaries and arouses tumultuous

---

[6] This concept is examined in Part II, Chapter 1, 'Ideology' in relation to Althusser and in Part II, Chapter 2, 'Subjectivity' in relation to Lacan.

passions, the nude as conceptualized by high art offers a sanitized version of feminity for consumption by a male viewer: it frames the flesh, conceals its flaws and, above all, achieves 'a kind of magical regulation of the female body' (Nead 1992: 7).

The discourse of nudity is inseparable from that of the gaze. The aestheticized nude is expected to offer a reassuring image of plenitude and balance, and to discipline potentially unruly sexual energies. The gaze of its viewer (traditionally conceived of as a male spectator) sustains the aesthetic project of containment by possessing the image and subjecting its surfaces to visual penetration. The image is desirable, ultimately, because there is no risk of it fighting back. The image's ability to convey a sense of wholeness is paramount at all times. It is for this reason, argues Nead, that the defacing of Velasquez's *The Toilet of Venus* (National Gallery, London) by the militant suffragist Mary Richardson in 1914 was construed by the media as a 'sensation murder' (Nead 1992: 38) and perceived as an assault on the whole nation's patriarchal ideals by a deviant female. The *injured* female figure is a disturbing intimation of disunity and fragmentation: a breach of the mythical seamlessness that the gaze unrelentingly seeks.

Nead also interrogates the relationship between nudity and *nakedness* and the different visual responses they elicit. In Kenneth Clark's classic account,

To be naked is to be deprived of our clothes and the word implies some of the embarrassment which most of us feel in that condition. The word nude, on the other hand, carries, in educated usage, no uncomfortable overtone. The vague image it projects into the mind is not of a huddled and defenceless body, but of a balanced, prosperous, and confident body: the body re-formed. ... In the greatest age of painting the nude inspired the greatest works.
(Clark 1985:1)

John Berger, for his part, inverts the binary opposition proposed by Clark and contends that 'To be naked is to be oneself' (Berger 1972: 54). According to Nead, both Clark's and Berger's positions are inadequate since both ultimately fail to confront the body's inevitable inscription in systems of representation and signification: the fact that the body, whether nude or naked, is never defin-

able as a purely natural entity for its significance is an effect of
cultural practices and established codes of vision. For Nead,

> The discourse on the naked and the nude, so effectively formu-
> lated by Kenneth Clark and subsequently reworked, depends
> upon the theoretical possibility, if not the actuality, of a
> physical body that is outside of representation and is then
> given representation, for better or for worse, through art; but
> even at the most basic levels the body is always produced
> through representation. Within social, cultural and psychic for-
> mations, the body is rendered dense with meaning ... . There
> can be no naked "other" to the nude, for the body is always
> already in representation.
> (Nead 1992:16)

Elizabeth Bronfen argues that an extreme example of the subjection of the female body to a powerful (male) gaze designed to keep
the fear of woman at bay is supplied by the Western idealization
of the female corpse (Bronfen 1992). As Dea Birkett points out in
her review of Bronfen's *Over Her Dead Body*, 'From the Pre-
Raphaelite Ophelia floating serenely in a pool of lilies to today's
hard-boiled crime fiction, the female corpse is a ghostly vision of
loveliness. ... Gorgeous female corpses make mortality more
bearable. It is feminine and beautiful, you can cover up the knowledge that real death is ugly. Death as someting disturbing, disrupting, can be translated into something soothing' (Birkett 1992). But
how is the female body to be rescued from this fate of visual
objectification? Some argue that it should be removed from representation altogether, for in patriarchy images of women are inevitably subjected to a repressive and sexist gaze. This suggestion is
radical but by no means progressive for it merely perpetuates a
history of exclusion. The search for alternatives goes on. Mean-
while, we must never allow ourselves to forget that the discourse
of the gaze is not merely about looking. In fact, it is primarily
about the consequences of how we use the sense of sight.

PART III

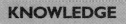

KNOWLEDGE

INTRODUCTION

Understanding, information, learning: these are some of the ideas commonly associated with the ubiquitous term knowledge. This Part offers illustrative case studies of six themes connected with the production and consumption of knowledge. Knowledge has to do with the ability to understand and absorb data, to divulge them as information, and to store them as a baggage of learning. Knowledge is based on an ongoing exchange of signals and messages. These can be grasped and processed as long as they are recognized as (at least potentially) meaningful – that is, as components of an established system of codes and conventions. Examining the issue of knowledge, therefore, requires us to explore the mechanisms through which knowledge is produced, the contexts in which it originates, the channels through which it is shared, and the value systems that legitimate it or else disqualify it.

The mind (understood both as a concrete organ, the brain, and as an abstract function, thought) is almost automatically associated by many with the production and consumption of knowledge. However, neither philosophy nor medicine nor psychoanalysis have yet ascertained the exact nature of the relationship between physiological and psychological processes. Matters are complicated further by the difficulty of establishing the role played by the senses in the acquisition of knowledge. Associated with the body and with matter, the senses have often been deemed inferior to the mind. Yet, sense experience is also supposed to provide the basis of lofty feelings and refined responses, most notably in the context of aesthetic theory.

As argued in Part I, human beings and their environments are significant only insofar as they are invested with symbolic meanings by particular cultures. Part II shows that such meanings are produced by multiple discourses that determine our social identities. Likewise, the meaning of knowledge is inseparable from the cultural circumstances in which a particular form of knowledge emerges. Scientific and technological developments, in particular, have had a momentous impact on how knowledge should be defined and interpreted – what it actually consists of, its meaning, its usefulness, and the range of its plausible applications.

Chapter 1 examines a range of approaches to 'The Mind' proposed by various disciplines to explain possible interrelations amongst the brain, consciousness, identity and structures of perception and knowledge. Chapter 2, 'The Aesthetic', focuses on forms of knowledge centred on sense experience and on variable notions of taste and value. In Chapter 3, diverse definitions of the concept of 'Space' are explored so as to show how knowledge never occurs in a vacuum but rather requires the existence of a shared context, be it 'real' or 'virtual'. Chapter 4 examines the influence of 'Time' on both individual and communal perceptions, memories and histories. Chapter 5 concentrates on 'The Machine' as a concurrently ideological and aesthetic phenomenon, assessing its impact on changing approaches to knowledge. In Chapter 6, the concept of 'The Simulacrum' is investigated to illustrate the interplay of reality and illusion in the production and dissemination of knowledge.

CHAPTER I

THE MIND

Strictly speaking, we all have a mind. However, the universality of the mind as an attribute of each and every human person – and, according to some, of each and every living creature – does not mean that there is a universally valid definition of what the mind really *is*. This is borne out by the fact that different cultures and traditions view the mind in very diverse ways. Moreover, various disciplines study and describe the mind from often radically different viewpoints: philosophy, psychology, physiology and psychiatry, for example, all have something to say about the subject but their evaluations hardly cohere into one single definition. The aim of this chapter is to delineate some of the main critical approaches to the mind. The essay gives an elementary introduction to the history and problems of the 'philosophy of mind', highlighting the interaction between various branches of philosophy (metaphysics, epistemology, moral philosophy, political philosophy) and other fields, such as psychology, cognitive science, linguistics and technology.

Although, as already mentioned, the mind is the object of study of several disciplines, many people will primarily associate its study with the discipline of psychology. Psychology focuses on the processes of thinking, perceiving and feeling. These do not only involve a dialogue between the mind and tangible people and objects but also the interaction between mental phenomena and intangible experiences that may not bear any immediate relation to the real world: fantasies, memories, desires, dreams and illusions, for example. As a result, we can never fully rationalize our mental functionings for these are inevitably affected by unconscious drives and by bodily states of which we are unaware.[1] It is often difficult to explain what and how we think, perceive and feel. More difficult still is explaining why, given that consciousness is frequently blind to the sources of our mental processes. The dilemmas faced by psychology indicate that the mind eludes totalizing definitions. This is borne out by the ambiguity of the very term from which 'psychology' derives, namely *psyche*. In Classical philosophy, this concept is varyingly described according to overarching principles of either transcendence or immanence. The first seeks to divorce the spiritual dimension from matter, whereas the second sees the spiritual as grounded in material reality. Plato, embracing the transcendental view, sees the psyche as the animating force of each living thing and as the immortal principle of life. Aristotle, opting for immanence, views it as the source of perception, movement, reproduction and self-nutrition, as well as thought. Related to the concept of the *psyche* is that of the soul, which Plato regards as the immaterial part of a human being, united only temporarily to a body, and Aristotle, conversely, sees as inseparable from the body and as an attribute not only of humans but also of plants and other animals. These two approaches point to a tendency to define the mind either in opposition or in relation to the body.

Evaluating the relationship between the body and the mind is one of philosophy's most challenging tasks. Arthur Schopenhauer (1788–1860) underscores this point by describing the mind–body problem as the *world knot*: a puzzle beyond human comprehension. Developing a trend that can be traced back to Plato, whose fundamental premise is that material forms are flawed and that truth resides in the realm of disembodied Ideas, Western thought has been consistently dominated by a dualistic mentality. This pivots on the separation of the mental from the physical. Empiricism, on the one hand, asserts that mental and physical functions are separate but that both are properties of the body. Rationalism, on the other hand, discredits the corporeal dimension by combining the idea that body and mind are separate with the postulate that the mind is superior to the body. Rationalist dualism is most famously associated with the writings of René Descartes (1596–

[1] ☞This idea is central to the development of psychoanalysis, as discussed in Part II, Chapter 2, 'Subjectivity'.

1650), who views the body as a material substance with physical properties (such as shape and size) and the mind as an immaterial substance with abstract properties (such as thinking and feeling). Authentic knowledge, argues Descartes, may only be obtained by disregarding the senses. The assertion that the mental is superior to the physical is radically debunked by the theories of Friedrich Nietzsche (1844–1900), who claims that all concepts – including abstract ideas such as thought and reason – are actually functions of biology and that knowledge, accordingly, stems from corporeal needs and priorities. Western civilization has insistently repressed the body's faculties through moral, religious and scientific laws meant to make us obedient, servile, ashamed of our deepest instincts and reluctant to express our creativity. However, Nietzsche maintains, our mental processes have no reality independently of our physical structures.[2]

Let us briefly consider some of the main approaches to the mind/body issue available today. Physical monism argues that all mental and physical phenomena depend on the laws of biology and physics. Functionalism believes that mental states should not be identified with fixed physical properties but rather studied in terms of the functions that link a physical experience with a mental state. Neutral monism contends that everything, including nature, is a mental construct. Psychophysical parallelism maintains that the mind and the body run parallel courses without affecting each other. Psychophysical interactionism, finally, states that mental and bodily events can only be explained in relation to one another.

Central to the mind–body problem is the issue of sensory perception. Indeed, it is not just the body in general but specifically the sensorium that Western thought has repeatedly marginalized. On the one hand, it can be argued that mental contents are produced through the mind's processing of the impressions it receives from the senses and that the mind would be empty and inactive if it could not rely on the senses. On the other hand, the mind appears capable of constructing images – indeed whole worlds – that do not have any obvious connection with the life of the sensorium: this militates in favour of the mind as an autonomous entity. However, it is hardly deniable that, whichever option

[2] ☞ See Part II, Chapter 2, 'Subjectivity'.

prevails, Western thought has tended to prioritize the mind over the senses on the basis that its immaterial status transcends and surpasses the physical realm to which the senses are bound. Moreover, the senses have time and again been differentiated and hierarchically organized according to their proximity to either the mind or the body.

The contention, as old as ancient Greek philosophy, that the senses are both central to human life and a fallible source of information has traditionally rendered their languages and histories ambiguous. This ambiguity has recurrently justified the subordination of the sensorium to the mind, in the belief that whilst the latter discloses ideas, the former may only disclose things. If this has generally led to the exclusion of the senses from both philosophy and the social sciences, it is also worth observing that not all five senses have been equally neglected. In fact, the sensory hierarchies fabricated by legion theoreticians throughout the history of Western thought have, by and large, tended to accord sight a privileged status. Prioritized by Plato as an index of human excellence, the sense of sight is further equated by Aristotle to the metaphysical concept of illumination. With the advent of the Enlightenment, the desensualization of knowledge promulgated by Descartes again grants sight a superior role in the sensory hierarchy: the eye celebrated by Cartesian rationalism, moreover, is a fundamentally disembodied instrument which processes images within the sealed chamber of the mind. Christianity, for its part, has conventionally associated sensory experience with the path to damnation, as succinctly typified by the eating of the forbidden fruit. In arguing that although the senses should not be regarded as ends in themselves but rather as means to a loftier end, Christian mythology has also proposed hierarchical distinctions between those senses which may be used to the glory of God, and those which are, conversely, most likely to lead to indulgence and sin. Sight and hearing belong to the former category because they are associated with God's 'Word' and its translation into flesh. Smell, taste and touch, to various degrees, epitomize the danger of sensory abuse, be it in the form of gluttony or lust.

With the growing recognition by contemporary psychologists and philosophers of the vital part played by the body in the acquisition of knowledge has come a parallel acknowledgment of the irreducible importance of the senses. This position is vividly summarized by Anthony Synnot: 'The conceptual and existential significance of the sensorium is obvious. We are social beings, and we communicate in and with and through the senses. Long before we are rational beings, humans are sensing beings. Life without the senses does not make sense' (Synnott 1993: 128). However, even critics keen on rehabilitating the life of the sensorium against a history of rampant neglect concede that such a life has been – perhaps irrevocably – depleted. Italo Calvino, for instance, observes: 'Modern man perceives certain things but fails to intercept others: olfaction is atrophied, taste is limited to a restricted range of sensations. And as far as our sight is concerned, given our habit of reading and interpreting fabricated images, it no longer has the ability to distinguish details, traces, signs, the way the tribal man no doubt was able to' (Nascimbeni 1984: 3). The erosion of the material dimension by electronic technology could be held responsible for further distancing the mind from the senses.[3]

Philosophical speculations about the mind are clearly as old as thought itself. Philosophy of mind as a discrete branch of philosophy, however, has emerged relatively recently. Early theorizing about the mind occurs within various subfields of philosophy, such as metaphysics (the study of the most fundamental features of reality), epistemology (the theory of knowledge), moral philosophy (the study of the codes and principles of moral conduct) and political philosophy (the evaluation of social organizations). Thus, for example, Plato's *Republic* integrates the study of the mind in a project concerned with the structuring of particular forms of government (political philosophy), while Aristotle often subsumes the study of the mind to the assessment of concepts of virtue and reason (moral philosophy). The philosophy of mind as a distinct area emerges in the nineteenth century and in the first half of the twentieth century.

The birth of psychology as an independent scientific discipline in the late 1800s is a seminal development in the emergence of philosophy of mind. The origins of scientific psychology are commonly associated with the founding of Wilhelm Wundt's psychological laboratory in Leipzig in 1879. An equally crucial development is

---

[3] Relevant to this idea is the discussion presented in Part III, Chapter 5, 'The Machine'.

the publication by Franz Brentano (1838-1917) of his *Psychology from an Empirical Standpoint* (1847). Central to Brentano's theories is the notion of 'intentionality' (from the Latin *intendere* = 'to aim' or 'to point towards'). According to the principle of intentionality, mental states (beliefs, desires, expectations, hopes) aim at, or point towards, an object. In thoughts such as 'I wish that goblins existed' and 'I believe that candy is sweet', 'goblins' and 'candy' are the objects of the wish or belief: they indicate what the wish or belief is about. The propositional ideas articulated by 'that goblins existed' and 'that candy is sweet' are the content of the wish or belief. Brentano argues that psychology must classify methodically all the mental states of which people are capable and the intentional objects and contents linked to those states. Intentionality, for Brentano, is the most distinctive feature of mental states: it is not possible to wish, believe, hope, etc, except by wishing, believing, hoping, etc, something.

Brentano also emphasizes that we should make a distinction between the act of thinking and the contents of thought, since they occupy different levels of reality. For example, if I think about vampires, my thinking is real (it is an act I am actually engaged in) but the content of my thought (most people would maintain) is not. Ultimately, it could be argued that the only reality we can be more or less sure of pertains to our ability to think. The reality of what we think about is always questionable. Relatedly, we are not in a position to prove why or how our minds are capable of pointing towards objects which – so common sense will have us believe – do not obtain. As psychoanalysis has shown (Freud, incidentally, attended Brentano's courses while at medical school), not all mental states are conscious. As a result, we can never be certain what the mind is intent on aiming at, or pointing towards. Beliefs, wishes, desires and countless other mental states often develop beyond the threshold of awareness.

Another important development in the early history of philosophy of mind is the publication of *Principles of Psychology* (1890) by William James (1842-1910). James proposes a scientific study of the mind based on establishing the ways in which thoughts and feelings relate to particular conditions of the brain. James identifies the mind with consciousness and introspection – the faculties whereby a person is aware of the mental states s/he is experiencing. Yet, he also stresses that it is generally difficult to single out a mental state from myriad others because consciousness is not a series of frozen frames separated by clean breaks but rather a continuous flow in which past, present and future coalesce.[4] James's description of consciousness as a flow of impressions and experiences (stream of consciousness) is embodied in the works of modernist writers such as Virginia Woolf, Henry James and James Joyce, where mental states gain significance from their association with other, often unconscious, thoughts, and rationality constantly shifts towards the penumbra of consciousness. James also differentiates the 'I', the ultimate thinker, from the 'Me'. The 'Me' encompasses the material being, with its body and physical properties; the social being, with the images of itself which the subject projects onto the world; and the spiritual being, with its intellectual faculties and achievements. The 'I' is not permanent for it continually merges with various 'Me's' and with different incarnations of itself over time. The mind, in this context, offers fertile ground for the growth of multiple personalities.

Moving on from the founders of modern psychology, the next crucial stage in the history of the philosophy of mind is represented by the theories of John Dewey (1859–1952). Dewey seeks to bridge the gap between philosophical and scientific approaches to the mind. He maintains that the dualism of mind and body, and indeed the distinction between the organism and its environment, must be rejected. The mind's operations should, accordingly, be explored in terms of philosophical issues related to ethics and politics, and to scientific issues related to biology, chemistry and physics. The mind is neither a wholly abstract concept of the kind proposed by Descartes nor an exclusively physiological bundle of reflexes and responses to its material surroundings. In fact, it is a product of ongoing processes of selection and adaptation based simultaneously on theoretical speculation and physical circumstances.

A further important contribution to the development of philosophy of mind comes with Gilbert Ryle (1900–76), whose *The Concept of Mind* (1949) argues that philosophers inspired by Cartesian Rationalism have spuriously ideated the mind as the body's spectral counterpart. He uses the phrase 'the ghost in the machine' to illustrate this position, 'the machine' signifying the

---

[4] Compare Bergson's concept of 'duration' in Part III, Chapter 4, 'Time'.

material object, the body and 'the ghost' the immaterial entity or mind that inhabits it and operates it from within. At the same time, Ryle disputes the validity of conventional distinctions between scientific laws and everyday beliefs, arguing instead that the two can be consistently related to each other, and that establishing such a relationship is essential to any study of mental processes. Ryle also disputes the assumption that individuals have a privileged and immediate access to their own mental states. Moreover, these states are said to arise not from a non-physical substance but rather from the physical organism's own inclinations. The mind as such, ultimately, is erased from Ryle's agenda. As D. W. Hamlyn observes, for Ryle 'to speak of the mind is really to speak of a set of dispositions possessed by intelligent beings' and these do not consist of 'inner processes' but of 'dispositions to beaviour' (Hamlyn 1990: 314). Although Ryle himself rejects the behaviourist label, his views sometimes echo those put forward by behaviourism in its various forms. This doctrine is characterized by the assertion that the 'behaviour of any organism, from an amoeba to a human being' should be 'described and explained in terms of the organism's *responses* to the *stimuli* presented by features of the environment' (Lyons 1970: 31; emphasis in original). J. B. Watson (1878–1958), the founder of behavioural psychology, maintains that the existence of things, including the mind, can only be postulated if they can be observed and measured.[5]

Since the second half of the twentieth century, attempts to define the mind have been problematized by the emergence of Artificial Intelligence. Amongst other issues raised by this momentous phenomenon is the question as to whether the mind itself could be conceived of as a computer. To attempt to answer this question, it is necessary to consider some of the mechanisms through which the mind tends to process data. In performing systematic acts of selection and exclusion comparable to those carried out by computers, the mind often produces not clarifying messages but rather a heightened awareness of the world's intricacy. The segmentation of any complex whole only yields further complications in each of the segments. Analysis is conventionally

---

[5] For the relationship between behaviourism and language, see Part I, Chapter 1, 'Meaning'.

expected to make life more manageable, by breaking complex situations down to their minutest components and details. The hope is that although a complex state of affairs cannot be explored, let alone understood, as a whole, it may become intelligible once its individual parts have been singled out and separated from one another. Yet, analysis may turn out to make reality only more complex and unyielding.

This is no more obviously (and frustratingly) the case than when the human mind itself is assumed as the object of analysis. In trying to make sense of the mind's complexity, one may begin by dividing it into its constituent parts, to be investigated one at a time. Alas, each part proves as complicated as the initial whole, because no single element can be properly grasped independently of its connections with countless others. One could still argue that the various pieces combine on the basis of a limited, albeit enormous, set of available rules. We may not be in a position to detail the mind down to its individual segments, but may still be able to fix the principles according to which its elements interact with one another. To back up this idea, the metaphor of the mind as a chessboard can be introduced: the billions of particles which make up the human mind could be compared to the thirty-two pieces on the chessboard, and the interactions amongst disparate mental processes to the moves available for the game of chess. Things happen only as a result of certain pieces performing certain moves, in accordance with given possibilities of combination. However, even this neat map of the human mind as a chessboard does not exhaust all the options implicit in our mental lives. No individual subject is ever going to live long enough to experience all the possible moves and plays of which the mind is potentially capable – and believing that there are rules for those moves and plays offers inadequate consolation.

The analogy between the human mind and a computer system may be more successful. Computers count on two fingers, after all, and can therefore digest complexity virtually instantly. But how well-equipped is the mind to achieve comparably astonishing results? And, conversely, to what extent are computers furnished with a temperament likely to enable them to reproduce all mental faculties? These issues are addressed explicitly in 'The Burning of the Abominable House', a short story written by Italo Calvino in response to the question, raised by IBM in 1973: could a narrative be produced by using a computer? The tale's protagonist, a computer expert, sets out to orchestrate his murder plot by trying to establish the number of alternative ways in which his computer could process and combine a given set of data: characters, their personalities and proclivities, their possible reasons for committing the crime, the weapons which could have been employed. Although technology enables the writer to work out a large number of plausible combinations and permutations of these and other related factors, it is not ultimately capable of transforming the creative process into a purely mathematical exercise. Calvino's author, in spite of himself, cannot help identifying with his four characters and imagining their faces, bodies and gestures, wondering about their hidden motives, evoking stage sets jammed with graphic images and physical detail: 'Half I'm concentrating on constructing algebraic models where factors and functions are anonymous and interchangeable, thus dismissing the faces and gestures of those four phantoms from my thoughts; and half I am identifying with the characters, evoking the scenes in a mental film packed with fades and metamorphoses' (Calvino 1996: 161).

The idea that a computer-like construct is incapable of functioning like a human mind has also been advocated by the philosopher of mind and language John Searle (b. 1932). Searle has tried to demonstrate his assumption through an experiment known as *Chinese Rooms*. Here, we have a room with two windows and an instruction manual. Pieces of paper bearing marks upon them come in through one window and, following the available instructions, we match them against other pieces of paper which we then send out through the other window. Searle argues that this is how a computer works, output consisting of a response to input guided by given rules. However, the relationship between input and output, Searle maintains, does not necessarily entail thought or understanding: the pieces of paper we receive may bear Chinese signs (a metaphor for any language we may not know) and we could still match them against others and produce output without having the faintest idea of what contents we are dealing with (Searle 1981). The idea that a computer's intelligence is not creative is corroborated by Buick and Jevtic: 'Even expert systems and software that learn from experience aren't capable of the paradigm shifts that transform data into knowledge or experience into wisdom' (Buick and Jevtic 1995: 158). Relatedly, it has been argued that mental processes cannot be treated purely as computational processes. This is because computation hinges on the handling of symbols and codes as syntactical elements devoid of semantic import,[6] while mental processes involve the tendency to relate signs to meanings through interpretation. Symbols and codes can be decoded by the mind according to their place in a structure. However, insofar as the mind encompasses not only coldly analytical powers but also desires, fantasies and fears, the quest for meaning will always exceed the demands of syntactical coherence.

The mind ultimately remains something of a mystery, not simply to the extent that we cannot fully understand its operations but also, more importantly, to the extent that we do not know what exactly we need to know in order to attain that understanding.

[6] Syntax and semantics are defined in Part I, Chapter 1, 'Meaning'.

THE AESTHETIC

This chapter examines a cross-section of definitions of the aesthetic, and of related approaches to artistic representation, ranging from Classical times to Postmodernism. Attention is drawn to the diversity of opinion surrounding the aesthetic experience and its relation to broader cultural issues. For some critics, aesthetics is wholly independent of social and moral values while for others, it is inseparable from politics and ideology. The second position has been gaining increasing credence due to the recognition that the aesthetic has often served to harness individual interests to a consensus of feeling and taste, and thus produce a sense of cohesiveness in societies that are actually riven by competitiveness and selfishness.[1]

Coined by the German philosopher Alexander Baumgarten (1714–62), the term 'aesthetic' derives from the Greek word *aesthesis* ('perception by the senses', 'feeling' or 'sensitivity'). As a distinctive subfield of philosophy, aesthetics seeks to determine how humans respond to beauty (in both art and nature) and whether the perception of beauty, or taste, is a universal or rather a subjective faculty. Aesthetics examines the processes through which objects and phenomena are experienced by the senses, and is concerned with pure feelings of pleasure or displeasure elicited by sense experience rather than with the practical functions of things or with factual information about them. Critics are still

---

[1] ☞For further detail on this topic, see the discussion of Terry Eagleton's theories on the aesthetic in Part II, Chapter 1, 'Ideology'.

divided over the issue of whether the aesthetic may be objectively defined as a category or mode of perception. This uncertainty is largely due to the fact that there is no general consensus about what beauty exactly consists of. Furthermore, it results from a fundamental inability to define the essential characteristics of a work of art and indeed to establish what distinguishes art from other cultural phenomena.

In addressing the daunting question 'what is art?', some critics have resorted to the opposition between 'high' culture and 'mass' culture, and others to the opposition between 'fiction' and 'reality'. In a traditional perspective, art would seem to belong to the camps of high culture and fiction. However, these definitions are highly subjective and still do not explain either what constitutes a work of art or what aesthetic responses the work is supposed to trigger. According to Ian Ground, what makes a text or representation artistic cannot be defined on the basis of the materials employed to produce it or even on the basis of how those materials are processed, since art tends to utilize the same raw materials as other cultural practices which are not considered artistic (Ground 1989). It could then be suggested that what ultimately distinguishes a work of art from other objects is its tendency to foreground its constructed status: it is in these terms that we may draw a distinction between a heap of bricks on a building site and Carl Andre's *Equivalent VIII*, the arrangement of bricks hosted by the Tate Gallery.

In the domain of Western philosophy, speculations about the aesthetic have been dominated by two main concepts: expression and imitation. The doctrine of expression postulates that a work of art expresses its creator's individual emotions. Lev Tolstoy (1828-1910) maintains that if these emotions are sincere, they will spread amongst the work's viewers/readers as if by infection or contagion (Tolstoy 1930). Benedetto Croce (1866-1952) and R. G. Collingwood (1889–1943) propose a more complex interpretation of the idea of art as expression, based on the belief that the artist's emotions do not produce an involuntary contagion but actually require conscious attention on the part of the perceiver. Art becomes a form of intuition (Croce 1909) or imagination (Collingwood 1938), enabling humans to grasp qualities of objects which escape ordinary perception.

Imitation is closely bound up with realism, and an evaluation of

this doctrine and practice is therefore necessary.[2] Generally under
stood as the imitation of a solid and empirically quantifiable
reality, realism has been recurringly commended as a crucial
advancement in the history of art and aesthetics. Evolution-
oriented critics, in particular, view the introduction of realistically
conceived figures in the fourth century BC, the discovery of fore-
shortening techniques and the creation of impressive *trompes-l'oeil*
as indicative of progress in comparison with the stylizing tendencies of pre-Classical art, with its predilection for rigid and non-
naturalistic forms. However, realism has not been uniformly
praised by Western philosophers. In fact, one of the first thinkers
concerned with assessing the role of art and aesthetics, Plato (c.
428–347 BC), sees imitation, or mimesis, as the measure of art's
baseness rather than its greatness. In the *Republic*, the art of
poetry and, by implication, all other representational or mimetic
arts, is condemned as a mystifying illusion and as the copy of a
copy.[3] Indeed, art is said to imitate the forms of nature and since
nature is already a second-rate copy of the Pure Forms or Ideas, it
is automatically relegated to the conditions of a shadow of a
shadow. Plato argues that art is only tolerable if it advances religious and ethical causes: 'the only poetry that should be allowed
in a state is hymns to the gods and paeans in praise of good men;
once you go beyond that and admit the sweet lyric or epic muse,
pleasure and pain become your rulers instead of law and the
rational principles commonly accepted as best' (Plato 1987: 437).
Mimesis is also associated with impersonation: the artist is said to
flee his true personality and to assume a false identity. This is a
major crime in Plato's system, for he regards the preservation of
one's true self and the perfection of one's social role as a fundamental obligation.

Aristotle (384–322 BC)[4] departs from Plato's theories by
contending that art does not imitate the particulars of nature but
actually represents general and universal characteristics. This
makes it more dependable than history itself. Aesthetic pleasure is

[2] Realism is also examined in Part I, Chapter 4, 'Representation' and in Part I,
Chapter 6, 'Textuality'. See also the discussion of 'naturalization' in Part II,
Chapter 1, 'Ideology'.
[3] See also Part I, Chapter 4, 'Representation', Part III, Chapter 1, 'The Mind'
and Part III, Chapter 6, 'The Simulacrum'.
[4] See also Part III, Chapter 1, 'The Mind'.

generated by the realistic representation of objects, so that even supposedly ugly things end up possessing beauty in virtue of their accurate depiction of reality. Aristotle, unlike Plato, also praises art's ability to evoke powerful emotions through the principle of catharsis ('purification', 'cleansing'). People's exposure to feelings and passions of a universal nature will help them come to terms with disturbing facets of human experience and achieve a deeper understanding of the world. The realistic representation of the feelings involved is of vital importance in this context.

However, realism cannot be reduced to an exclusively aesthetic or representational phenomenon. In fact, it has a material ideological dimension, and this is demonstrated not only by specific works of art but also by the circumstances of their production and consumption. Given its ability to depict objects with great precision and abundance of detail, realism has proved especially fashionable over the centuries amongst social classes eager to convey their wealth in tangible ways. This can already be observed in Classical times. For example, the copies of realistic Greek paintings found in many Roman villas are not only works of arts but also commodities made 'to be displayed in the houses and gardens of the educated' (Gombrich 1990: 120), and to communicate their owners' economic power and cultural refinement. Similarly, the development of highly sophisticated realistic techniques in the Renaissance can be related to this epoch's political climate and ideological priorities. Both the merchant princes of the Italian city states and the courts of the new nation states use art as a means of advertising their power through glamorous and spectacular displays, designed to idealize the ruler and to awe the viewer into submission. At the same time, the Renaissance witnesses the dawn of capitalism. Realistic techniques, in this context, are favoured by the rising mercantile classes for they are capable of conveying their material wealth: they depict objects as solid properties in all their richness of colour and texture and thus express a tangible sense of prosperity.

Shifting approaches to art and to the aesthetic experience are intimately connected with diverse views regarding the imagination. Indeed, the history of aesthetics could be seen as the history of changing attitudes towards this faculty. The ancient Greeks call the imagination *phantasia* (from *phos* = 'light') to suggest that mental images are not just delusions but also a form of illumination. The imagination supplies us with the initial images (*phantasms*) from which all further thought proceeds, and hence plays a vital role in the formation of knowledge. However, Western culture has often been unsympathetic to the imagination and its products and considered those 'phantasms' as the figments of an eccentric or unhealthy mind. In keeping with his theory of inspiration, Plato disparages the imagination as the attribute of a lunatic possessed by demonic powers. By highlighting art's cathartic function, Aristotle sees the imagination in more positive terms. Various Renaissance philosophers, whilst distrusting the imagination's tendency to get out of control, nonetheless concede that it has a didactic function: if properly harnessed, it can help us grasp fundamental truths. It is in order to consolidate this redeeming feature that several Renaissance poets and critics engage in the composition of apologies of the creative arts. These texts often propose that works of the imagination are useful, albeit fictitious, by defining the artist's job 'in terms of verisimilitude rather than truth or falsehood' (Cocking 1991: xii).

The late seventeenth and eighteenth centuries, moulded by the principles of the Enlightenment, generally associate the imagination with superstition, ignorance and prejudice. Keen on establishing the methods through which objective knowledge of the world may be gained, the Rationalist philosopher René Descartes (1596–1650) champions the notion that the imagination is conducive to errors of judgment.[5] The Empiricist philosopher Thomas Hobbes (1588–1679) sees the imagination as the receptacle of images left in the mind once sense impressions have been processed. What makes the imagination dangerous is its capacity to invent totally imaginary creatures and objects and to distort reality in extravagant and baffling ways. Both Rationalism and Empiricism, then, are basically suspicious of imaginative powers. It is not until the Romantic period that the imagination comes to be regarded as a positive attribute. The poet and artist William Blake (1757–1827), for example, celebrates it through the creation of alternative worlds which challenge radically the tyranny of reason and its specious ethical values. Samuel Taylor Coleridge (1772–1834) proposes a distinction between the *primary* imagination, a superior power which enables us to perceive reality as coherent by reconcil-

[5] See also Part II, Chapter 2, 'Subjectivity' and Part III, Chapter 1, 'The Mind'.

ing opposites, and the *secondary* imagination, which dissolves familiar forms to reshape the world in an idealized fashion. Fancy, by contrast, only deals with fragmentary images and hence supplies a disconnected picture of reality. The Romantic imagina-'tion is also a means of collapsing conventional boundaries. William Wordsworth (1770–1850), for instance, argues that the imagination enables us to merge with the objects we perceive by fostering a constant interaction between self and non-self. Percy Bysshe Shelley (1792–1822) maintains that love is the ultimate power through which we may identify imaginatively with others, while John Keats (1795–1821) speculates about the imaginative dissolution of individual identity through the figure of the chameleon poet, the artist able to let his personality be filled by other creatures.

Romantic approaches to the imagination and aesthetics are indebted to Kant and to German Idealism. Immanuel Kant (1724–1804) draws an important distinction between the world as we perceive it and the world of ideas.[6] The first is termed *phenomenal* (from the Greek *phenomenon* = 'appearance') because our perception of objects does not disclose a knowledge of their intrinsic essences (of things-in-themselves) but only superficial appearances. The second is termed *noumenal* (from the Greek *noumena* = 'ideas') and refers to the realm of essences. We believe in this world because reason assures us of its existence, and we are able to speculate about it because we are endowed with free will. Yet, it is ultimately beyond our grasp. The gap between the noumenal and the phenomenal is bridged by the aesthetic because in the aesthetic experience, though tied to the appearance of things, we also sense a design in them that alludes to the superior world of *noumena*. Kant argues that the aesthetic judgment is characterized by three vital attributes: it places value on the individual insofar as the perception of beauty is inevitably subjective; it is disinterested because it is not concerned with material gratification; it is universal because what pleases humans aesthetically is always related to the apprehension of a form or pattern. Kant also distinguishes between two forms of aesthetic feeling: the beautiful or the

---

[6] Immanuel Kant is also discussed in Part I, Chapter 1, 'Meaning'. The concept of 'phenomena' is further examined in Part I, Chapter 5, 'Reading' in relation to the doctrine of Phenomenology.

sublime. A beautiful object is precisely defined and its elements are harmoniously balanced. A sublime object, by contrast, is limitless and unsettles ordinary perception through either its overwhelming size or its extreme energy.

German Idealism (from the Greek *idein* = 'to see') moves beyond Kant by denying the existence of things-in-themselves and by arguing that human beings create reality by perceiving it. G.W.F. Hegel (1770–1831), in particular, maintains that the world emanates from the Spirit (human consciousness in its entirety) and that its construction follows a historical trajectory dominated by principles of evolution and progress.[7] Moreover, history is dialectical: progress takes place as a result of two conflicting ideas or phenomena (thesis and antithesis) becoming reconciled into a new synthesis. In applying the dialectical model to art and aesthetics, Hegel states that the tension between ancient Symbolic art (primitive and formless) and Classical art (formally refined yet too reliant on the physical world) is resolved in the synthesis of Romantic art, as a representation of spiritual values that transcend the senses. Ultimately, for Hegel, all forms of art and aesthetic appreciation will dissolve, superseded by philosophy as the culmination of the Spirit's evolution towards pure consciousness.

However, neither art nor aesthetics has yet come to an end. If anything, over the last hundred years at least, they have proliferated at an unprecedented rate. This is most explicitly borne out by the flourishing of avant-garde movements, with their insistent flaunting of aesthetic conventions and academic precepts. Originally a military term, referring to the foremost of an army, avant-garde was employed in nineteenth-century France to designate politically progressive groups, and thereafter to describe artists and thinkers who lead the way. Despite their ideological and stylistic differences, all avant-garde trends challenge tradition and accepted ways of seeing. Moreover, it is through their practices, to a considerable extent, that the concept of Modernism comes into being.

Modernism is a comprehensive term for an international tendency which arises in poetry, painting, architecture, music, fiction, drama and other arts in the last years of the nineteenth

---

[7] ☞Hegel's approach to history is also explored in Part II, Chapter 1, 'Ideology' and Part III, Chapter 4, 'Time'.

century and subsequently influences the character of most twentieth-century art. Of the several movements which Modernism
embraces, Symbolism, Impressionism and Decadence develop
around the turn of the twentieth century; Fauvism, Cubism, Post-
impressionism, Futurism, Constructivism, Imagism and Vorticism
in the period leading to the First World War and during the
conflict; and Expressionism, Dada and Surrealism during and
after the war. According to David Britt, Modernism's *multiplicity*
is its message' (Britt 1989: 8; emphasis in original). However, its
various movements are linked by common factors: above all, by a
more or less drastic dissociation of art and aesthetics from nineteenth-century assumptions and especially from the conventions of
realism. Disputing the notion that artistic representations may
supply a faithful reflection of reality, and indeed the idea that such
a reality is widely shared and recognized, Modernism is generally
characterized by an anti-mimetic spirit. This is combined with
technical self-awareness: the work of art does not efface the
process of its production by claiming to be a photographic representation of reality but rather foregrounds itself as an artificial
construction. Lacking faith in the notion that reliable truths may
be obtained through the empirical observation and measuring of
natural phenomena, Modernism undermines the very existence of
a static reality. Modernist artists underscore that there are other
ways of being true to life than simply providing descriptive
accounts of the world. The psychological realism cultivated by
many of these artists, for example, is a means of reaching towards
the representation of inner dimensions of experience that are very
real indeed, yet often submerged.

Not surprisingly, modernist practices were often deemed scandalous at the time of their inception. As David Britt observes: 'The
Impressionists gave great offence by showing what was perceived,
rather than what the artist knew ought to be there. Seurat and his
successors, who included the Fauves and the Futurists, used this
vital freedom to show a new kind of *perceived* image: hieratic,
dynamic, or transcendental, but always expanding the possible
versions of the world of perception. The quasi-scientific idea of a
solid world "out there" ... was something that artists were the
first to modify' (Britt 1989: 7–8; emphasis in original). Cubism
caused further shock by claiming that an object does not possess
one absolute shape, for it can be perceived and represented from

various angles and each angle will yield different forms and meanings. Cubist works aim at depicting as many of the possible shapes of an object within one image, thus alerting us to its multiplicity. It is also noteworthy that not all modernist artists perceive the modern world through the same lenses. Thus, while some are enthusiastic about technology as a celebration of human energy, others condemn it as a dehumanizing force. While some revel in the modern city as a treasurehouse of novelties, others view it as a teeming swamp filled with depravity.[8]

The modernist challenge to the realist ethos is taken a stage further by the aesthetics of Postmodernism.[9] Suspicious of totalizing versions of the world, Modernism nonetheless trusts art's ability to offer epiphanic insights into reality and the human condition. Postmodernism, by contrast, does not rely on the possibility of unearthing profound truths. Modernism endeavours to voice the ineffable, and to express those aspects of reality that are most difficult to represent, such as the continuous stream of thoughts and feelings. In this respect, it follows a well-established aesthetic tradition that invests art with the power to reveal what ordinary language is incapable of grasping. Postmodernism, for its part, seeks to highlight the unpresentable itself. According to Jean-Francois Lyotard, 'The postmodern' could indeed be defined as 'that which, in the modern, puts forward the unpresentable in presentation itself' and 'that which searches for new presentations ... in order to impart a stronger sense of the unpresentable' (Lyotard 1987: 81). The 'new presentations' of which Lyotard talks are works that do not abide by any given rules, and deny the possibility of ever arriving at final, redemptive visions of wholeness and truth. Postmodern works, though characterized by considerable variety, share certain basic features. Firstly, they tend to reject coherent patterning and allow disparate elements to crowd the textual collage in random, discontinuous and unpredictable ways. Secondly, they communicate a sense of open-endedness that negates the classic realist view of the text as a closed structure, capable of conveying notions of harmony and order. Thirdly,

---

[8] ☞ The ideological connotations of Modernism are examined in Part II, Chapter 1, 'Ideology' with reference to Marxist theory.
[9] ☞ Postmodernism is also assessed in Part II, Chapter 2, 'Subjectivity' in relation to the issue of social identity.

they subscribe to a cyclical or circular conception of time and history which implies that any image of stability is no more than an ephemeral stage in the endless process of building up and tearing down. Drawing from the contemporary world and from past traditions, from high culture and from mass culture, from disparate parts of the world regardless of national and ethnic barriers, the postmodern text comes across as eminently polyphonic: it speaks with and through many voices simutaneously. In the domain of architecture, for example, many cities have witnessed an explosion of shopping centres and malls packed with details redolent of Classical buildings (keystones, arches, friezes, columns, fountains, vaults and domes) yet made entirely of glass and metal.

Furthermore, Postmodernism stresses that meaning incessantly slides, for signs only ever lead to yet more signs. Images and stories are inevitably related to other images and stories (intertextuality) and always liable to be divorced from their original contexts, appropriated and placed in novel contexts. Not only do texts continually incorporate and modify one another: they also determine cultural existence, for all knowledge is ultimately a product of narratives. For Lyotard, this is demonstrated by the fact that even scientific knowledge – which has traditionally endeavoured to deny the value of narratives and downgraded them as ignorant and backward – can only assert itself as a reliable form of knowledge by resorting to narratives. Fredric Jameson criticizes Postmodernism in comparing the postmodern subject to a schizophrenic patient doomed to live in a perpetual present devoid of historical depth (Jameson 1991). However, Jameson also contends that narrative is an epistemological category, one of the coordinates (like space and time) within which we form a knowledge of the world. We only receive the world in the guise of stories (Jameson 1981). Thus, Jameson implicitly corroborates one of Postmodernism's principal aesthetic lessons: the idea that stories determine what we can think, and therefore know, in practically any area.

Some welcome Postmodernism as a liberating phenomenon, viewing its iconoclastic eclecticism as playful and its emphasis on multiplicity, pluri-culturalism and difference as an imaginative repudiation of traditional ideals of stability and uniformity. Others condemn Postmodernism's irreverent experiments with tradition, in the belief that they stifle authentic creativity and simply assert that everything goes, thus embodying the spirit of capitalism. Everything is put on the same level: Classical art and MTV, religion and fashion, politics and sport. No object has any inherent value of its own but only becomes valuable insofar as it can be commodified, circulated and recycled. Knowledge itself, argues Lyotard, is less and less conceivable as an end in itself. Knowledge matters insofar as its components can be packaged into bundles of data and sold. Computer technology is clearly instrumental to this mercantilization of knowledge, and, relatedly, to the pursuit of performativity. This concept is succinctly described by Madan Sarup as 'the best possible input/output equation. Scientists, technicians and instruments are bought not to find truth, but to augment power' (Sarup 1988: 124).

Whether we welcome or denounce it, it is undeniable that Post-modernism interrogates drastically many time-honoured Western myths – authority, authorship, truth – and may therefore offer us alternative ways of negotiating our place in the transitory and often disorienting scenes of contemporary culture. Indeed, it may help us adjust to the troubling recognition that the worlds we inhabit are neither safe nor clearly bounded, that we live on the threshold between past and future, and that our condition is one of permanent wandering.

CHAPTER 3

SPACE

Where are things? What is their size? How much room is there for
them and in them? These are simple questions we ask ourselves all
the time – when we are trying to find something, to gauge whether
an item of furniture or clothing will 'fit', or to ensure what a file in
our PC can accommodate. Yet, these are also questions that have
preoccupied philosophers for centuries in their explorations of the
nature of knowledge. One of the first and most influential attempts
to explain space scientifically and systematically was made by the
Greek mathematician Euclid (330?–270? BC), who is often consid-
erd the father of geometry. Euclidean space is an idealization of
perceived space. Space perception is the process whereby people
locate the positions, sizes and distances of objects. These are never
fixed but rather depend on the situation of the perceiver. For
example, the perceived size of an object depends on its proximity
to, or distance from, its observer. Euclidean geometry, by contrast,
seeks to make space (of two or three dimensions) uniform and
stable. It conceptualizes space in terms of figures endowed with
invariant properties. Euclidean space is an abstract ideal or model,
since real space is actually variable, open to interpretation, determined by how it is seen and represented.

Visual representations of space inevitably entail an element of
distortion. Indeed, 'distortion' is the technical term used to
describe the methods through which the round earth is visualized
on a flat surface through the stretching of certain areas and the
shrinking of others.[1] Cartography (the science and art of map-

---

[1] ☞The distortion of space in two-dimensional representation is also discussed in
Part I, Chapter 4, 'Representation' in relation to the law of perspective.

making) has no choice but to distort reality in visualizing it. A classic example is supplied by Ptolemy's *Geography*. The map of the world presented in this text includes Europe, northern Africa and most of Asia, as well as twenty-six maps of specific areas. Ptolemy exaggerated the land mass from Spain to China and underestimated the size of the ocean. This was probably a totally innocent mistake. Yet, its cultural repercussions were momentous – especially when one considers that it encouraged Columbus to undertake the famous voyage of 1492.

Geographical maps are never wholly neutral and objective representations of space, for they aim at rationalizing the world in systematic ways and hence fix into stable images worlds which are actually constantly changing. However, maps are often presented as accurate in order to lend a sense of permanence to our perception of space, and foster the illusion that space can be exhaustively explored and possessed. Maps do not merely describe the world: in fact, they construct it according to specific cultural requirements and this makes them important ideological tools. As Gustav Metzger observes, maps are products of particular ideological programmes. For instance:

> The 'T-in-O' maps were more statements of faith rather than a description of the world – they anchored faith. They described faith, they produced a feeling of security within the believers. The Hubble photographs support similar functions. Out there in the indescribable galaxies is a world so inhospitable to humanity that the imagination freezes. The Hubble photographs bring that immensity within our grasp, and so give a measure of comfort; ease a transition towards the new ...
> Maps and globes have always been more than merely descriptive. They are articles of faith, advancing the nation and culture producing them.
> (Metzger 1998:107)

Maps are abstract constructs based on the selection (more or less arbitrary) of specific details from a contingent geographical situation. However, as D. R. F. Taylor points out, they ask to be taken as 'holistic' representations of 'geographical reality' and hence as objective pictures of the world (Taylor 1989: 115).

Understanding the ideological significance of maps can help us grasp the objectives of geography itself as a discipline concerned with the relationship between natural and human worlds and with both natural and constructed differences between different parts of the planet. Geography was dominated for a long time by a concern with the uniqueness of particular regions, places and people. In the 1960s, several geographers shifted their attention to universal (rather than regional) laws supposedly determining the social organization of space. This shift was no doubt useful because it tried to focus on general principles rather than on localized details, and hence on the ways in which spatial organization affects human behaviour in the world at large. However, it often ignored important cultural differences to do with both the environmental and the political circumstances of particular regions. Although it may be possible to identify broad tendencies in space-related behaviour, these are bound to be played out in very different ways in disparate locations. Moreover, certain putatively 'universal' laws must be quizzed. For instance, the traditional Western distinction between public space as the sphere of action, production and political involvement, and private space as the domain of consumption and reproduction, has been radically questioned by theorists who contend that such a geographical distribution is shaped by economically inequitable and sexually divisive practices.

According to some philosophers, space is a physical reality that is not affected by the things that occupy it or by how these are perceived. This position is advocated by Isaac Newton (1642–1727), for example. Other philosophers, such as Immanuel Kant (1724–1804), argue that objects exist as products of the perceiver's imagination and that they become distinct insofar as they are seen to occupy different chunks of space. These concerns are still with us today, as evinced not only by science and philosophy but also by fictions featuring spaces with extra dimensions that defy the laws of physics. Anthropocentric and humanist philosophies tend to assume that human beings are the measure of all things and that space, relatedly, is the setting of human actions: a stage that humans can design and control. Yet, things are not quite so straightforward since both personal and communal spaces are often fluid. Their boundaries are difficult to ascertain and their material reality is called into question by the fact that much of the time we are only able to visualize space through abstract sets of data. As a result, the humanist notion of space is hard to sustain. This is testified by recent scientific developments and especially by ongoing research in the field of space psychology – namely, the branch of psychology concerned with establishing how the human brain and the organism generally adjust to their environment and to stressful or hostile circumstances. Particularly important, in this respect, is the research carried out by space psychologists concerned with how astronauts adapt to the difficulties of living in outer space. Ideologically, space travel has been a means of asserting political and economic power, national ideals and scientific expertise. It has also been a way of promoting the idea that human beings are in a position to conquer the mysterious realms stretching beyond the Earth's atmosphere. Yet, it has also been clear that tailoring humans for space is an elaborate process, sometimes resulting in tragic failures, and that astronauts, though often construed as national heroes, are inevitably bodies, vulnerable to the disorienting effects of weightlessness, space-motion sickness, hypothermia and artificial day/night cycles leading to modifications of the biological clock. Moreover, many ordinary people often find their spatial situations disorienting, alienating and even terrifying, as testified by the pervasiveness of syndromes such as claustrophobia, agoraphobia and acrophobia.

The complexity of space both as a concept and as a physical reality is testified by the fact that there is no single and universally accepted definition for this term. The multi-accentuality of space has been problematized by the increasing recognition that space is not an immaterial idea but rather the embodiment of cultural, political and psychological phenomena. Space is always, to some degree, social. Its organization and the ways in which it is experienced and conceptualized contribute vitally to the mapping of individual lives and social relations. The acknowledgment of the social dimension of space is a relatively recent occurrence. Indeed, as Henri Lefebvre remarks, 'Not so many years ago, the word "space" had a strictly geometrical meaning: the idea it evoked was simply that of an empty area. ... To speak of a "social space", therefore, would have sounded strange' (Lefebvre 1974: 1). Although the concept of *social space* is now widely adopted, there is still a tendency to think about space as something fixed and unaffected by changing social practices. According to Steve Pile, 'the concept of space which remains dominant is ultimately a mathematical one: social relations are said to be stretched out over space, but space does not stretch ... space remains a stubbornly passive backdrop' (Pile 1996: 145). This ongoing commitment to the idea of space as an immutable area can be related to the projects of traditional geography and cartography. Here, the scientific mapping of space according to stable coordinates has served to promote a broader agenda of cultural stability. Maps are laden with ideological and psychological connotations. They result from complex practices whose primary aim is to rationalize the world in systematic and reliable ways. Thus, although maps are never fully accurate – since they fix into images a shifting reality – and although they are abstract constructs that only ever grasp a contingent context, they are nonetheless passed off as objective and timeless articulations of reality.

Lefebvre has underscored the pluri-dimensionality of space by suggesting that it is important to distinguish between spatial practice (based on how the world is perceived); the representation of space (based on how the world is conceived, or thought about); and representational space (based on how the world is lived by our bodies). Lefebvre stresses that 'the lived, conceived and perceived realms should be interconnected, so that the "subject", the individual member of a given social group, may move from one to another without confusion'. However, he concedes that the three realms only 'constitute a coherent whole' in 'favourable circumstances, when a common language, a consensus and a code can be established' (Lefebvre 1974: 40). In other words, although it is tempting to ideate space as a dimension in which people may harmonize their perceptions, thoughts and bodily experiences, there is no ultimate guarantee that this will actually happen. This can be attributed to the fact that the outside world has no inherent solidity but rather comes into being as a result of a plethora of contingent impressions, mental processes and actions. These are neither organically integrated with one another nor objective. In his study of the city, D. C. D. Pocock argues that the fluidity of space is indeed related to its openness to subjective readings: 'Of the several kinds of meaning which may attach to a building or townscape – concrete, functional, emotional, symbolic – it is the symbolic interpretations, rather than intrinsic spatial attributes, which are important in city personality' (Pocock 1973: 256).

Much traditional philosophizing about space is informed by the myth of the *terra incognita*: a fantasy of discovery, ultimate knowledge and penetration, on the one hand, and a tale about mystery and otherness, on the other. The ambivalent status of this myth intimates that even in an exhaustively explored and mapped-out world, space still retains obscurities and secrets. Discovery does not yield final knowledge but rather the desire, forever renewed and forever deferred, for further knowledge. As J. K. Wright observes: 'if there is no *terra incognita* today in the absolute sense, so also no *terra* is absolutely *cognita*', since 'the unknown stimulates the imagination to conjure up mental images of what to look for within it, and the more there is found, the more the imagination suggests for further search' (Wright 1947: 4). Any *terra incognita*, therefore, is both empirical and imagined, as borne out by Huxley's intriguing metaphor:

> our mind still has its darkest Africas, its unmapped Borneos
> and Amazonian basins ... A man consists of ... an Old World
> of personal consciousness and, beyond a dividing sea, a series
> of New Worlds – the not too distant Virginias and Carolinas
> of the personal subconscious ... the Far West of the collective
> unconscious, with its flora of symbols, its tribes of aboriginal
> archetypes; and, across another, vaster ocean, at the antipodes
> of everyday consciousness, the world of Visionary Experience.
> ... Some people never consciously discover their antipodes.
> Others make an occasional landing.
> (Huxley 1977: 69–70)

Along similar lines, David Lowenthal argues that 'every image and idea about the world is compounded of personal experience, learning, imagination, and memory. The places that we live in, those we visit and travel through, the worlds we read about and see in works of art, and the realms of imagination and fantasy each contribute to our images of nature and man' (Lowenthal 1961: 260).

Space is always a matter of partial and relative geographies based on both conscious and unconscious experiences. To this extent, we should question the idea that certain ways of perceiving and representing space are more correct than others. All configurations of space are effects of subjective responses that combine elements of realism and fantastic distortions. This approach to space challenges many of the prejudices harboured by traditional geography – as voiced by Lowenthal, for example. He maintains that people's spatial abilities vary enormously and that 'the most fundamental attributes of our shared view of the world are confined ... to sane, hale, sentient adults' (Lowenthal 1961: 244). Idiots, psychotics, children and, to some extent, women, are excluded from the spatial consensus which shapes dominant conceptions of space. 'Geography', argues Steve Pile, 'has left behind its more primitive, childlike, feminized world-views' (Pile 1996: 12). These marginalized perspectives are rehabilitated by the intimation that though personal geographies are supposed to lack the objectivity of publicly shared notions of space, they nonetheless play a vital role: that of reminding us that even the most rigorously rationalized world is traversed by dreams and fantasies. Jonathan Raban emphasizes this point by positing imagined space as somewhat more substantial than scientific space: 'The city as we might imagine it, the soft city of illusion, myth, aspiration, nightmare, is as real, maybe more real, than the hard city one can locate in maps and statistics, in monographs on urban sociology and demography and architecture' (Raban 1974: 10).

Several geographers propose a distinction between the phenomenal environment (the real world) and the behavioural environment (our perception of the world according to cultural codes and conventions). The two are actually interconnected, for the world only acquires significance as long as its elements are organized into patterns. In behavioural geography, a central role is played by the notion of the *image* (a cognitive structure or visual map), as the mental factor which mediates between behaviour and environment. Behavioural geography, in endeavouring to theorize the relationship between spatial behaviour and its causes, often relies totally on the psychology of individual perception without taking into account social structures. The danger implicit in this approach is that it is oblivious to the constructedness of spatiality.

Moreover, space always contains hidden dimensions. This is demonstrated by Michel Foucault's study of heterotopias. In 'Of Other Spaces' (presented in lecture form in 1967), these are described as 'something like counter-sites, a kind of effectively enacted utopia in which the real sites, all the other real sites that can be found within the culture, are simultaneously represented, contested, and inverted'. While utopias are nowhere lands, hetero topias are real, albeit concealed, places: they are 'outside of all places, even though it may be possible to indicate their location in reality' and are capable of juxtaposing several incompatible spaces in a 'single real place' (Foucault 1986: 24). Heterotopias may be obscured from view for a variety of reasons: they may be sacred or forbidden locations, privileged sites or pockets of illegal and deviant activities. Foucault's study suggests that space is never a uniform reality. In fact, disparate realities meet and merge within its uncertain boundaries to create a hybrid and composite world.

This is typified by the contemporary city. Rationalized by elec- tronic technology as a neat computational grid, urban reality is nevertheless often messy and sprawling. The postmodern metropo- lis stands out as a mixture of sanitized virtual spaces and spaces of physical decay and anarchy: the immaterial geography of computer networks is at all times interwoven with a corporeal geography of pollution and decay. The postmodern city will be discussed further later in this chapter. Let us first consider the significance of the bodily dimension of space. One of its main implications is the mutual transformation of architectural and organic bodies. On the one hand, human beings can be conceived of as artificial structures: here humanity is architecturalized. On the other hand, it is possible to think about buildings as bodies: here architecture becomes humanized. Above all, it could be argued that cities themselves both are and have bodies. The city is born, grows, conceives, reproduces and dies; it has sex, as suggested by the idea of the city reaching a climax; it follows certain diets; it develops diseases, neuroses and disabilities, such as congestion, tumorous overgrowth, hyperactivity and the fear of alien infractions; it exhibits anabolic and catabolic processes, corresponding to its creative and destructive moments; it has both naked and clothed facets, both sealed and leaky elements, and adorns itself, either uniformly or eclectically; it contains idealized and monumental body parts to be proudly flaunted, and secret, intimate parts to be cautious or ashamed of; finally, it bears the signs of the passing of time as so many indentations, folds, lines and wrinkles in the tissue of its architectural make-up. The city's body is also gendered. Many a historical account of the birth of the urban corpus describe it as a product of the transition from the male world of hunting to the female world of sedentary life.

According to Mumford, the association of early urban existence with the female body is corroborated by the sexual symbolism of various architectural structures: 'the house and the oven, the byre and the bin, the cistern, the storage pit, the granary, ... the moat, and all inner spaces, from the atrium to the cloister' (Mumford 1991: 21). However Mumford, while granting woman a central role in the inception of city life, also emphasizes the enduring dominance of the male hunter, now metamorphosed into the mighty protector of the walled citadel. The reduction of female powers signalled by the reintroduction onto the scene of the virile, martial hero is mirrored, argues Mumford, by the demise of 'the earliest religious myths', based on dominating female figures often endowed with 'savage attributes' and the creation of myths which commend female 'tenderness, beauty, erotic delight' (Mumford 1991: 36–7).

The city is also a specifically textual body. Indeed, it is a network of narratives that we ourselves weave as we move through it. Michel de Certeau describes walking as a means of constantly remapping space by creating ever new routes through it, without recourse to rigidly compartmentalized identities, bodies, subject positions and relations of power and knowledge (Certeau 1984). *The Practice of Everyday Life* emphasizes 'the innumerable ways in which walking in the streets mobilizes other subtle, stubborn, embodied, resistant meanings. The streets become haunted by the ghosts of other stories ... . The city becomes a ghost town of memories without a language to articulate them because walking is a transient and evanescent practice. The proper spaces created for the city by the view from above – whether embodied in the visual regimes of the panoptic gaze or cartography – are interrupted' (Pile 1996: 226).[2] De Certeau's walker is not just *any* walker but, specifically, a *flâneur*, the prototype of the male voyeur, strolling aimlessly around, seeing all while retaining his anonymity. The *flâneur* is powerful and vulnerable at the same time. His uncertain condition is a corollary of his relation to the urban spectacle: the ability to hold innumerable images within his masterful field of vision is also an implicit admission that in the absence of those images, he would plausibly

[2] For details on the 'panoptic gaze', see Part II, Chapter 2, 'Subjectivity' and Part II, Chapter 6, 'The Gaze'.

evaporate. The *flaneur* incarnates the ambivalence of the develop
ing city: he is an apparently all-powerful observer, seeing everything whilst remaining virtually unseen, and a lonely and
dispossessed onlooker, excluded from any human relationship
other than casual contact with the formless crowd.[3]

The following section focuses on postmodernist approaches to
space and on their material manifestation in the contemporary
city. Mumford's study foregrounds the negative repercussions of
metropolization by emphasizing the transition from a model of
the city based on the principle of implosion, namely the mobiliza-
tion of disparate activities in the service of the human community,
to a cultural scenario dominated by rhythms of explosion: 'the city
has burst open and scattered its complex organs over the entire
landscape' (Mumford 1991: 45). *The City in History* does not fail,
however, to acknowledge the positive potentialities of explosion –
those elements of plurality and difference which are central to
postmodern versions of the deterritorialized city. Indeed,
Mumford is especially eager to stress the repressive and destructive
drives of urban formations devoted to the imperative of totalizing
unity, and is hence implicitly willing to concede emancipatory
powers to the disunified city construct. If the 'proliferation of
metropolitan tissue' (Mumford 1991: 598) is horrifying because it
denies, cancer-like, the benefits of organic growth, it is also the
case that the traditional city could often only function through
blockage and exclusion: 'in many instances the city tends to encase
the organic, many-sided life of the community in petrified and
overspecialized forms that achieve continuity at the expense of
adaptation and further growth. The very structure of the city itself
... may in the past have been in no small degree responsible for
this resistance. In the end it has made physical disintegration –
through war, fire, economic corrosion or blight – the only way of
opening the city up to the fresh demands of life' (Mumford 1991:
599).

Various critics have argued that the postmodern city problematizes conventional notions of both space and time. Postmodernism
as a broad cultural phenomenon has complicated the already intri-
cate time–space relationship by positing a diffuse geography

---

[3] For a detailed discussion of the relationship between power and the sense of
sight, see Part II, Chapter 6, 'The Gaze'.

wherein space engulfs time and motion, and by underscoring the vital part played by memory in the apprehension of space. Memory represents not so much a personal attribute or possession as the receptacle for a collective imagination in which even the most intimate thoughts are endlessly translatable into public signs. In contemporary culture, space seems to have taken over time, largely as a result of a widespread tendency to interrogate the validity of history and, particularly, its metaphysical codification on the basis of concepts of progress and rational evolution. Furthermore, the pervasiveness of electronic systems of signification and communication has fostered a progressive flattening of both spatial and temporal depth by making an astonishing amount of data simultaneously available across the immaterial realm of cyberspace.

Broadly definable as the sum total of the data produced and disseminated by electronic means, cyberspace is at once a space and not a space. It is a medium rather than a location. Besides, it is conceptual rather than geographical, for the physical situation of the people and of the technological tools that produce it is irrelevant to its operations. Cyberspace also underscores the idea that space is not a fixed backdrop against which human activities take place, since it does not pre-exist either the individuals or the moves that occupy it but is actually constructed by them. Whether or not cyberspace qualifies as a *place*, it is undeniable that its pervasiveness has questioned radically traditional conceptions of spatiality and, in the process, redefined our understanding of communities. Some believe that cyberspace compartmentalizes people by inducing them to communicate only with those who share their interests and desires. Others maintain that it offers unprecedented opportunities for global interactivity. Amongst cyberspace's detractors are critics who see the ambition to grab everything that can be known into an all-encompassing electronic matrix as reminiscent of older fantasies about the conquest of space and colonial myths of absolute control. This view is countered by those who accredit cyberspace with the ability to forge a sense of cohesiveness in societies where people feel they do not belong anywhere. The communities inaugurated by cyberspace, for these writers, are deemed capable of promoting fresh forms of learning and knowledge and means of communication unfettered by repressive divisions based on race, gender, age and status.

Whichever way we look at it, digital technology has inevitably eroded the assumption that space coincides with a given reality. The experiences it affords are of the order of the virtual, the simulated and the hyperreal.[4] However, it would be preposterous to argue that the reality of space has been called into question exclusively by postmodernism and cyberculture, since there is plenty of evidence for the tendency in Western culture to capitalize on imaginary spaces: the Nation, Mother Earth, the Empire and the Heavenly City, for example.

Postmodern architecture makes spatial boundaries unstable. This is epitomized by the idea of the balcony space: a space which turns the inside into the outside and the outside into the inside. The balcony problematizes the commonplace link between building and dwelling, for it is structurally connected with a building, yet it is hardly conceptualizable as a dwelling place. At best, it operates as a medium for interaction between the private and public spheres; it does not foster, clearly, the cult of space as protected habitation. Perversely, perhaps, the balcony simultaneously supports and shakes the pillars of domesticity.

Celeste Olalquiaga provides one of the most exhaustive accounts of the postmodern megalopolitan body which, whilst acknowledging its threatening connotations, simultaneously highlights its knack for provoking radical and potentially healthy redefinitions of time and memory, place and space: 'The ability of cultural imagery to adapt itself to new requirements and desires can no longer be mourned as a loss of cultural specificity in the name of exhausted notions of personal or collective identities. Instead, it must be welcomed as a sign of opening to and enjoyment of all traditional culture worked so hard at leaving out' (Olalquiaga 1992: 55). Olalquiaga also stresses the need to conceive of identity not as a demarcated territory but rather as a fragmentary map. The unfamiliar, the foreign and the alien are not exterior to the self, the city and the body: if there indeed is anything other in and to human subjectivity, that is our foreignness to and alienation from *ourselves*. This can be read as an invitation to take up multiple subject positions and resist stifling categorizations. *Megalopolis* incarnates postmodernism's ambivalences, ambiguities and inconsistencies, its dismissal of hierarchies, neglect of boundaries

[4] ☞See Part III, Chapter 6, 'The Simulacrum'.

and eclectic and irreverent juxtaposition of disparate motifs. Olalquiaga associates the postmodern city with images of displacement
and boundlessness. The rise of the postmodern expanse is indisso-
ciable from the 'transformation of time into space, emptiness into
saturation, body into electronics, and absence into presence' (Olalquiaga 1992: xx). The association of the city with a scenario of
waste and abjection, moreover, is a reminder that death 'is lived as
a permanently present condition' (Olalquiaga 1992: 69).

The concept of space has been made especially hard to define by
momentous developments in modern physics. Whilst in Newton's
system an event's situation in space is supposed to be independent
from its duration in time, the theories of Albert Einstein (1879–
1955) have demonstrated that there is no absolute way of separating and measuring the space and time of an event because these
change according to the motions of the event's observers. Thus, if
space is a fluid category due to the diversity of its social, psychological and scientific connotations, it is made all the more fluid by its
inseparability from the axis of time.[5] More recently, the inseparability of space and time has been emphasized by studies of the
contemporary urban environment as a site of cultural and
economic conflict. Mike Davis's *City of Quartz*, in particular,
concentrates on the city of Los Angeles as a fragmentary and
contradictory location. Los Angeles is not one city, argues Davis,
but rather a galaxy of competing city states beset by 'social
anxiety', racial violence, economic disparity, environmental
'malice' and ever-increasing 'social polarization' (Davis 1992: 6 7).
This galaxy plays the 'double role of utopia *and* dystopia for
advanced capitalism' (Davis 1992: 18): it is concurrrently an
economically and racially invigorating city of '*sunshine*' (Davis
1992: 27) and an apocalyptic, '*noir*' setting – as famously presented
by Ridley Scott's *Blade Runner* (Davis 1992: 21; emphasis in
original). Paradoxically, the city's 'dystopianization' serves to
increase its appeal and to turn it into the kind of space that
'American intellectuals love to hate' (Davis 1992: 21). Simultaneously, as the book's subtitle (*Excavating the Future in Los
Angeles*) suggests, space is inextricable from time. Just as space is
discontinuous, so is time. There is no linear progression from the
past through the present to the future. Indeed, the future is

[5] The space-time issue is discussed in detail in Part III, Chapter 4, 'Time'.

already buried in the past, in the history, mythography and
economy of the city. 'The best place to view Los Angeles of the
next millennium', Davis maintains, 'is from the ruins of its alternative future' (Davis 1992: 3). In the historical and mythological
debris of postmodern spaces such as Los Angeles, disparate
temporal dimensions continually interact in much the same way as
data do in a digital hypertext.

CHAPTER 4

TIME

This chapter supplies a selection of interpretations of the concept of time by focusing on three central issues: the ways in which our grasp of time influences our perception of the world; the relationship between time and space; the relationship between time and history.

Philosophical assessments of time fall into two main categories: the static view and the dynamic view. The first can be traced back to Parmenides and Zeno, who argue that temporal change is an illusion. Parmenides (c. 480 BC) arrives at this conclusion as a result of his speculations about the foundations of knowledge. His reasoning, incidentally, anticipates the theories of René Descartes (1596–1650).[1] Starting from the premise that thinking happens, and that its objects must exist, Parmenides argues that any philosophical position is bound to be incoherent if it refers to non-existent entities. He then defines the attributes of what truly exists: wholeness, consistency and a capacity to remain unchanged. Real objects do not come into being and then cease to exist. In fact, they always obtain, steadily and immutably. Zeno of Elea (c. 470 BC) likewise states that temporal change is impossible. He uses various parables to demonstrate this point. All are based on the idea that time and space are interconnected and that since both are endlessly divisible, no apparent progress through time and space can actually lead to a goal or produce change. In the imaginary anecdote known as the 'race-course', it is argued that a runner may never reach his destination for he cannot run the full length of the course without first running half of it, or half of it

---

[1] ☞ See Part II, Chapter 2, 'Subjectivity'.

before running a quarter of it, and so on. The divisibility of space is interminable and time, as a result, comes to something of a standstill. In the story of 'Achilles and the tortoise', Zeno maintains that if a slow runner (such as the tortoise) is given a start by a fast runner (such as Achilles), the fast runner will never catch up: he will have to cross an interminable sequence of portions of time and space, like the runner in the previous illustration. The flight of an arrow, relatedly, cannot be regarded as a temporal occurrence for the arrow's movement across a stretch of space can be broken up into an infinite number of successive moments.

The dynamic approach to time goes back to the theories of Heraclitus of Ephesus (c. 500 BC) who maintains that life is a process of constant becoming. Everything flows: we cannot step into the same river twice for we cannot be touched twice by the same waters. This fluid conception of time is paralleled by a relativistic attitude to life in general: the waters that nourish fish will very possibly kill a human being; a sloping road runs uphill and downhill seamlessly and simultaneously.[2] According to Heraclitus, reality is continually modified by the passing of time, because new elements are added to it from one moment to the next.

Scientists divide time into periods of equal length: this is normally referred to as 'clock-time'. However, various theorists and philosophers have argued that this abstract version of time does not reflect the way in which we actually experience its passing. Henri Bergson (1859–1941) is an especially influential figure in this debate. Central to Bergson's philosophy are the concepts of duration and *élan vital*. Bergson uses the term duration to describe time as it is actually experienced: that is to say, not moment by moment but as a continuous flow in which past, present and future are not truly distinguishable. Scientists generally regard time as a homogeneous medium in which all instants have the same value and magnitude. Bergson, conversely, posits duration as an ever-changing and heterogeneous phenomenon that cannot be cut up into instants. In treating time as homogeneous and divisible, science equates time to space. Bergson rejects this spatialization of time, 'in favour of the continuous flow of time as it appears to consciousness' (Hamlyn 1990: 287).

---

[2] Compare this idea with Wittgenstein's theories, as discussed in Part I, Chapter 1, 'Meaning'.

Spatialized time does not allow for real development. Time as flow or duration, by contrast, is based on principles of constant change (the occurrences that form it are unrepeatable) and creativity. As John Mullarkey points out, for Bergson 'time must be creative: if it isn't inventive, it isn't time at all. In real time each new moment is qualitatively different from the last' (Mullarkey 1999: 9). Bergson's views bear affinities to William James's notion of the stream of consciousness. For James (1842–1910), consciousness is ever-changing and continuous – that is, it cannot be chopped up into discrete pieces.[3]

Bergson also maintains that consciousness tends towards the future as a result of a vital spirit (*élan vital*). Thus, development over time cannot be reduced – as argued by Darwinism – to the evolution of a species on the basis of the survival of the fittest. A species does not survive and evolve merely as a result of mechanisms of competition and selection centred on its genetic characteristics. The Bergsonian life force is not only a physical attribute but also a mental/spiritual one. Perception is, to a large extent, a function of bodily needs and automatic responses to physical stimuli. Yet, it is also a function of consciousness: specifically, of our capacity to project mental images onto the objects we perceive. In *Creative Evolution*, originally published in 1907, Bergson suggests that not only individuals but the universe as a whole should be viewed in developmental terms. Just as any one moment in the flow of consciousness is unrepeatable, so is any one moment in cosmic history. Each moment consists of a total history which no other moment can share in exactly the same way (Bergson 1998).

In considering the distinction between time as a scientific construct and time as it is actually lived, it is also worth noting that many scientific approaches to time often seem hardly relevant to the temporal experiences of non-professionals. Their postulates appear esoteric, remote or, at best, only graspable by huge leaps of the imagination. For example: what is a lay person supposed to make of the idea that 15,000 million years ago the cosmic egg blew up? Or of tachyons, namely particles deemed faster than light? Or of naked singularities – occurrences of matter so tightly compressed that they lack a horizon and clear location in time?

[3] ☞ James's theories are discussed in Part III, Chapter 1, 'The Mind'.

Western culture is strictly structured in relation to time. The routines and schedules which dominate both family life and professional life (by and large) require us to make constant reference to clocks. Psychologically, the dividing of time into regular units can be seen as a way of keeping at bay the knowledge of death: it is almost as if, by chopping up the line that inevitably leads to death, the end could be postponed. Yet, humans also long for continuity and often regard its breach as an assault on their psychological and physical coherence. This is why time-gap experiences are so unsettling. When we find ourselves somewhere and have no conscious recollection of how we have got there, of how time has passed or of what we have been doing since we last looked at the clock, we experience the uncanny feeling that we are just waking up although, of course, we have been awake all the time. Time gaps produce mysterious blanks in our awareness of the passing of time. The phenomenon of time error should also be considered as a factor capable of unsettling our hold over temporality. This phenomenon refers to the tendency to register the second of two sensory stimuli of equal intensity occurring in quick succession as greater than the first, due to its greater impact on short-term memory. Neither stimulus – be it visual, auditory, olfactory, gustatory or tactual – is actually stronger than the other. It is its position in time that lends it magnitude. Both time gaps and errors show that time rules us in unexpected ways. Any effort on our part to measure it and compartmentalize it is unlikely to supply us with any means of ultimate control.

Furthermore, even the finite interval of time in which the mind is supposed to be conscious of what is happening 'now' is only a specious present, a shadowy frontier between the remembered past and the anticipated future. Several philosophers and scientists claim that this interval is real and has a temporal duration of its own, and this is proved by our ability to perceive continuous movement. However, most of us – in the day to day course of events – would find it extremely arduous to pinpoint and quantify the 'now' as separate from the past that underlies it and the future towards which it tends. Indeed, various critics have stressed that the idea of an absolute 'now' should be relinquished. In this context, any perception of the distinction between past and future experiences is deemed wholly subjective, for occurrences considered past in one frame of reference are considered future in another. Related to this issue is the work of the idealist philosopher John McTaggart Ellis (1866–1925), who contends that the present is not a dimension that moves, along a sequence of occurrences, from the past to the future. In fact, the phenomenon of temporal unfolding – argues McTaggart – is based on future events becoming present and then receding into the past. Hence all events could be regarded simultaneously as past, present and future (Broad 1933).

Since the beginning of the twentieth century, reality has undergone momentous reassessments. These are largely connected with important redefinitions of the relationship between temporality and spatiality. Albert Einstein's theory of relativity is plausibly the one revolutionary idea of which even those least versed in matters of physics, cosmology and astronomy will have heard. In demonstrating the underlying connections amongst the most fundamental natural phenomena – namely, light, time and space – in what is commonly termed a Unified Field Theory, Einstein concurrently undermined Newtonian physics[4] by showing that all motion is relative, and Euclidean geometry by showing that space is neither flat nor distinguishable from time, for we actually inhabit a curved space–time continuum. The Special (or Restricted) Theory of Relativity of 1905 found its primary realm of applicability in the field of microscopic physics and demonstrated that there is no absolute frame of reference in the universe. In fact, there are many frames of reference, whose motions are relative to one another. The place and time of an event depend on how they are perceived by varyingly moving observers, and are not separable but actually constitute a four-dimensional continuum. The General Theory of Relativity of 1916 is mainly applicable to cosmology and astrophysics and it is here that the notions that space–time is curved and that the curvature is produced by matter acquire special prominence. In this context, Einstein's objective was to establish the most basic field equations which would enable scientists to calculate the space–time curvature on the basis of a particular distribution of matter.

This project spawned a long series of experiments, such as the ones seeking to establish curvature degrees in relation to the deflection of starlight by the Sun. This is not the place to enter

---

[4] ☛See Part III, Chapter 3, 'Space'.

into the details of such experiments and their findings. It is worth stressing, however, that relativity theory has had a profound impact on contemporary notions of reality – amongst not only scientists but also creative writers and artists – and particularly in the domain of cosmology. Relativity theory lies behind the Big Bang theory, whereby the universe is supposed to be expanding from an originally condensed state – a theory which has been gaining increasing support against the Steady State theory which maintains the idea of continuous matter-creation throughout the cosmos. Last but not least, general relativity somewhat prophesied one of the most intriguing astral phenomena – black holes: 'These theorized objects', Clifford M. Will explains, 'are celestial bodies with so strong a gravitational field that no particles or radiation can escape from them, not even light – hence the name. Black holes most likely would be produced by the implosions of extremely massive stars, and they could continue to grow as other material entered their field of attraction. Some scientists have speculated that supermassive black holes may exist at the centres of some clusters of stars and of some galaxies, including our own' (Will 1995: 6).

Scientific theories characterized by a move away from Newtonian physics, then, interrogate the separation between the physical and the non-physical at the same time as they challenge linear notions of time and space. According to Victor Seidler, one reading of this state of affairs points to the plausibility of a drastic rethinking of 'the relation between a "superior" Western science' and putatively ' "backward" ' traditions of a mystical character, for in refiguring reality in both its temporal and spatial dimensions, post-Newtonian physics posits 'a different vision of progress' (Seidler 1998: 25). Progress is no longer conceivable as the linear, forward march of enlightened reason. Both time and space, in fact, acquire circular and cyclical connotations reminiscent of Eastern philosophical and mythological systems. Moreover, in redefining the relationship between time and space, relativity theory has inaugurated new forms of scientific inquiry. The most prominent ones show that the concept of time is inextricably intertwined with the concepts of energy and matter. Time is inseparable from the particles that register its passing. Those particles, in turn, can only be properly analysed by registering their changes over time.

Some of the most crucial consequences of relativity theory are noticeable in its association with quantum mechanics. Quantum theory has been developing since 1900, following Max Planck's assertion that light is emitted from its sources in *quanta*, that is, discrete amounts. Einstein corroborated this idea through his work in the field of photoelectricity. Planck and Einstein showed that light is capable of behaving as both waves and particles, which suggests that even those aspects of so-called reality which we are most likely to take for granted (like light) have no one definitive identity for they may be concurrently thought of as energy and as matter. Planck and Einstein's speculations on light paved the way for subsequent developments in the field of quantum mechanics. This branch of modern physics emerged in the 1920s through the work of scientists such as Born, Dirac, Heisenberg, Jordan and Schrodinger. Heisenberg, in particular, postulated that the position of a particle cannot be accurately measured, and that its momentum is uncertain and always likely to exceed the Planck's constant which binds matter to wave properties, for matter is actually absorbed, diffracted and thus modified by waves (light, sound). According to classical physics, the state of a system is determined by a fixed number of variables, such as its position in space and time. Quantum mechanics challenges this determinism by introducing elements of instability – such as the Uncertainty Principle formulated in 1927 – whereby the position and momentum of a particle are only approximately and contingently measurable. Determinism is superseded by probability; a system may only be described by stating the probability of certain events or effects taking place. As Gerald Feinberg points out, 'for systems described by quantum mechanics, even one as simple as an atom with a single electron, precise prediction of future behaviour is usually impossible. Instead, only predictions of the probability of various behaviours can be made' (Feinberg 1995: 1).

A major scientific development consists of Grand Unification, or Grand Unified Theories (GUTs). This is the study of elementary particles (i.e. the smallest constituents of matter) which seeks to demonstrate that new interactions may be discovered among the fundamental forces of nature. Grand Unification argues that there are processes in which the value attached to elementary particles is not stable, and in which even particles once thought of as immune to decay (such as protons) actually deteriorate over a protracted period of time. The boundaries between hitherto discrete natural forces are breached, as are the dividing lines between notions of life and death, immortality and corruption, continuity and mutation.

That time and space are inseparable is further indicated by the fact that increasingly accurate mechanisms for measuring time have developed in relation to changing perceptions of space. Time-measuring devices were already available in the ancient civilizations of China, Egypt, Greece and Rome (to cite but a few) but the question of accuracy only became crucial with the development of travel across large areas for commercial and colonial purposes. As long as journeys took a considerably long time, it was common to assume that days and nights occurred at the same time everywhere in the world. However, with the increasing speed of travel – especially maritime – it became clear that this was not the case and that since the longitudinal location of a ship had to be worked out by time, the precision of its clocks was of paramount importance. In 1714, Britain was so keen on securing the effectiveness of its fleet's operations as to offer a £20,000 prize to anyone able to provide an accurate clock. In 1761, John Harrison produced the first small-scale timepiece correct to half a minute per year. A momentous event in the history of time was the Curie brothers' discovery, in 1880, that crystals vibrate when electricity is applied to them and that they discharge electricity when they are hit. This marked the beginning of quartz crystal technology. As a novel way of measuring time, this technology was first employed in 1929. The ability to count electronically the vibrations of a quartz crystal has created the possibility of highly precise clocks.

That mapping out time is a difficult task is testified not only by individual perceptions and scientific developments. In fact, it is made starkly evident by the attempts made by whole cultures to record their vicissitudes through the discipline of history. There have been intimations for centuries that historiography does not represent facts neutrally and objectively. Recently, this idea has gained considerable momentum as a result of postmodern approaches to history and time, and particularly of their emphasis on the inevitably distorted and distorting character of all texts. The principles of uncertainty, relativism and probability under-scored in the scientific domain find a parallel in contemporary speculations about history. Western thought has traditionally promoted the idea of history as a linear chronology of facts, connected by a more or less obvious chain of causes and effects. Some philosophers have developed the linear conception of history by arguing that events do not unfold along a simple line that may or may not lead us in a particular direction but rather along an evolutionary trajectory. The line of history, in this perspective, traces a history of progress. This view was championed by G.W.F. Hegel (1770–1831), who saw history as the march of the Spirit towards higher and higher ends.[5]

Traditional approaches to history as a practice devoted to supplying detailed documentation about the past have endeavoured to formalize time by dividing it into periods (e.g. ancient civilizations, the Middle Ages, modernity) and into genres (such as political history, art history, the history of ideas). This mapping of time on the basis of neat categories underpins the discipline of historiography: this can be defined both as writing about history and as the history of historical writing. Since the second half of the twentieth century, historiography has been the object of increasingly lively debates, primarily as a result of an awareness, on the part of historians, that descriptions of past events are unlikely to be totally objective and uncontaminated by personal values and opinions. Historicism is an important concept, in this respect, for the contrasting definitions to which it lends itself highlight the ambiguous relationship between history and time. On the one hand, historicism stresses that each epoch should be evaluated in terms of its own values and beliefs, without any reference to the historian's own age and its principles. This position was prevalent in the late nineteenth century, especially in Germany. On the other hand, historicism denotes a belief in the existence of general laws governing historical development and a conviction that this development is deeply influenced by the growth, dissemination and acquisition of knowledge.

Postmodernism has questioned drastically both linear and evolutionary approaches to history by arguing that there is no incontrovertible evidence of either progress or of the gradual revelation of reason advocated by Hegel. Furthermore, Postmodern-

---

[5] ☞ Hegel's theory of history is discussed in Part II, Chapter 1, 'Ideology' and in Part II, Chapter 2, 'Subjectivity'.

iom aaleo: what do we really know about the past? Linda Hutcheon usefully unpacks this question in *The Politics of Postmodernism*: 'How can the present know the past it tells? We constantly narrate the past, but what are the conditions of the knowledge implied by that totalizing act of narration? Must a historical account acknowledge where it does not know for sure or is it allowed to guess? Do we know the past only through the present? Or is it a matter of only being able to understand the present through the past?' (Hutcheon 1989: 72). Some critics claim that this radical questioning of the nature of history and of historical knowledge has engendered a deep sense of insecurity about the human condition. Some go even further and view the postmodern approach to time as a nihilistic repudiation of the existence of any meaning whatsoever. However, there are also critics that welcome the postmodern position as something of a lesson in survival. By presenting the passing of time as a discontinuous and random phenomenon, in particular, that position may help us face and adjust to often unfavourable circumstances rather than allow us to indulge in idealized notions of history as a logical sequence of causes and effects. Hayden White, for example, contends that Postmodernism encourages a 'willingness to confront heroically the dynamic and disruptive forces in contemporary life. The historian serves no-one well by constructing a specious continuity between the present world and that which preceded it' (White 1978: 25). Jean Baudrillard, for his part, rejects the idea of history as an evolutionary process guided by reason and logic by emphasizing instead its interminability and repetitiveness: 'things will continue to unfold slowly, tediously, recurrently, in the hysteresis of everything which, like nails and hair, continues to grow after death' (Baudrillard 1994a: 116). Incidentally, 'hysteresis' (from the Greek word translatable as 'coming late') is the temporal phenomenon consisting of 'the lag of an effect behind its cause' (*Fontana Dictionary of Modern Thought*).

Following theoretical developments in the fields of Structuralism and Poststructuralism,[6] many contemporary historians maintain that human beings can only grasp concepts and events when these are encoded, namely articulated in textual form. This position

---

[6] ☞See Part I, Chapter 1, 'Meaning' and Part I, Chapter 2, 'The Sign'.

echoes Derrida's postulate that there is nothing outside the text.[7] This is not to deny that historical events have actually occurred. Postmodernism's aim, in fact, is to emphasize that so-called facts only exist as constructed and, relatedly, to expose the textual status of all knowledge of the past.

[7] ☞This idea is examined in Part I, Chapter 3, 'Rhetoric'.

CHAPTER 5

THE MACHINE

'Human technology', argues Douglas Rushkoff, 'should be considered no less natural than animal technology. ... A web makes it a lot easier for a spider to catch a fly, and a computer makes it easier for me to submit this column' (Rushkoff 1997: 15). In other words, technology should not be regarded as a malevolent power keen on robbing humans of their skills and creativity, or indeed capable of autonomous creativity. As Benjamin Woolley observes: 'to ascribe the computer as a medium with powers to "discover" the imaginary realm would be as absurd as ascribing the typewriter with the power to discover the world of literature' (Woolley 1993: 249). These positions are in many ways convincing. However, they are not universally embraced. J. G. Ballard, for example, suggests that we are no more in control of machines than machines are in control of us. This is borne out by his definition of the 'typewriter' in his 'Project for a Glossary of the Twentieth Century': 'it types *us*, encoding its own linear bias across the free space of the imagination' (Ballard 1992: 269; emphasis in original). Philip K. Dick problematizes further the relationship between humans and machines by proposing that: 'we humans ... are perhaps the true machines' and that it is somewhat preposterous to draw distinctions between the natural and the artificial, for: 'everything is not alive or half-alive or dead, but rather *lived through*' (Dick 1978: 219; emphasis in original). Humans operate like machines much of the time and machines, in turn, acquire an element of life through their communion with people.

The ambivalent messages embodied by the positions presented above are not just contemporary. The machine has been regarded with mixed feelings of confidence and anxiety from its earliest manifestations. This is because machines are not merely tools designed to help people carry out practical tasks. They are actually creatures endowed with ideological and psychological connotations of considerable complexity. People's ambivalent attitudes to the mechanical can be traced back to the Renaissance. One of the most ground-breaking inventions associated with this period is printing, introduced by Johan Gutenberg into Europe in 1450. Gutenberg's machine was based on the movable type (already used in Korea in 1409), a printing block for each page of a book produced by assembling individual reversed letters. The Bible was the first text reproduced by such means. Gutenberg's was a truly revolutionary achievement, which ushered in the mass reproduction of texts, the birth of the publishing industry and of modern libraries, and opportunities for the growth of education. While many showered praise upon Gutenberg's invention, as many damned it as a diabolical contraption. These conflicting views about the printing press should be assessed in relation to the context in which it was created. Although the Renaissance is often depicted as an era of energetic optimism, committed to putting the imprint of Western 'Man' around the world as a commanding presence, things are not quite so simple. This same era also witnessed the erosion of many traditional values and beliefs: a major part was played by the realization that the earth was neither flat nor the centre of the universe. By transferring the centre of the universe to the Sun, the Polish astronomer Nicolaus Copernicus (1473–1543) not only revolutionized cosmology but also intimated that anthropocentrism (the idea that 'Man' is the centre of the universe) was hard to sustain. Like the Gutenberg Revolution, the Copernican Revolution was by no means universally welcome. To cite but one famous case, Galileo was accused of blasphemy and persecuted by the Church as a result of providing scientific evidence for the gross inaccuracy of the older system.

The Renaissance was a time of doubt and uncertainty no less than it was the cradle of modernity and progress. On the one hand, the rapid flourishing of ideas and of media for their dissemination was conducive to an enthusiastic approach to both experience and knowledge. On the other hand, a drastic remapping of the world – stemming not only from scientific and technological developments but also from colonial expansion and economic change – generated considerable anxiety about people's place in society and in the cosmos at large. Old notions of stability (where human nature was deemed unchanging) gave way to the conviction that humans are prone to err – i.e. to wander and to blunder. The Renaissance experience shows that attitudes to the machine are implicated in broad cultural processes which involve a tension between tradition and change, the desire to protect the one or advance the other and, above all, the need to negotiate with both.

Ambivalent responses to the machine and to the scientific developments that underpin it continue manifesting themselves well beyond the Gutenberg and Copernican Revolutions. Thus, for example, the seventeenth-century philosopher Descartes (1596–1650) considered the machine inferior to the human mind, yet favoured as a travelling companion a female automaton named Francine. This may seem ironical – if not downright comical – when we consider that Descartes is commonly seen as the champion of modern Rationalism. However, his logic was based on the premise that science, mathematics and mechanical laws could be applied to the physical world but could not restrain the mind, which Descartes saw as superior to the body and to anything material.[1]

With the advent of industrial technology in the late eighteenth and nineteenth centuries, people's attitudes to machines became more ambiguous still. Machines could be regarded as monstrous constructs, capable of depriving humans of their usefulness and rights to creative labour. Yet, they also promised fresh opportunities for the expansion of scientific skills and imaginative powers. Thus, whilst the Luddites aimed at destroying machines, ancestors of the modern computer were being designed, notably by Charles Babbage. This point will be returned to after a brief examination of the momentous changes brought about by the Industrial Revolution. Hostile feelings towards machines were mainly caused by appalling living conditions resulting from the transition from an economy of agriculture and domestic handicrafts to the factory system. In Britain, these developments occurred in the closing decades of the eighteenth century, both the scale and the tempo of change increasing rapidly from the 1890s onwards. One of the most impressive technological innovations was James Watt's steam engine, an ear-shattering monstrosity whose spectacle would

---

[1] For further information on this topic, see Part III, Chapter 1, 'The Mind'.

easily inspire awe or even terror and make it an ominous symbol of the modern age. (One such machine operated the Albion Flour Mills in Southwark and was well-known to the poet William Blake and his contemporaries.)

The deterioration of the working people's lifestyles and standards of living, moreover, was accompanied by the ungenerous doctrines of utilitarianism and individual self-interest. Providing the philosophical justification for the manufacturers' unimpeded pursuit of profit, these doctrines would do nothing to ameliorate the labourers' dismal conditions. Ruthless measures were also proposed to control the growth of the population and the apportioning of wages. Malthus's 'Essay on the Principle of Population' (1798), for example, argued that, insofar as populations grow by geometric progression and food supplies only by arithmetical progression, the best way of curbing demographic expansion was to ensure that the working classes have fewer children. David Ricardo adopted this idea to advocate the institution of a fixed wages fund, meant to guarantee that an increase in the population, and hence in the number of people eligible for work and a salary, would result in the reduction of individual wages. Given that these ideas were inspired by the advent of industrialization, it is easy to see why the machine should be viewed by many as inimical to human welfare, let alone happiness. To many, the machine symbolized for a long time submission to an exploitative regime. While the labourers, wrenched from the land, were expected to work long hours for scanty rewards in execrable safety and sanitation conditions, the affluent had access to disposable income. This signalled the dawn of consumerism and of the modern concept of fashion.

The nineteenth century also witnessed the flourishing of forms of popular culture in which tradition and innovation, superstition and science were interwoven. Interestingly, the fairgrounds, circuses, museums and magic-lantern shows of the time evinced a fascination with the unusual, the weird and the monstrous. The new territories disclosed by a rapidly changing economy were not unproblematically approached with enthusiasm. They also elicited anxieties about their latent unnaturalness. These feelings are famously epitomized by Mary Shelley's *Frankenstein* (1818), where the 'creature' symbolizes (amongst other things) everything that humanity could deem most menacing about technology. The construction of an artificial being with the aid of technology, though inspired by benevolent intentions, may unleash extreme violence, revulsion and terror.

One of the most radical assaults on the culture of the machine was enacted by the Luddites, so named after their legendary leader Ned Ludd. These were mainly textile workers in the districts of Nottinghamshire, Yorkshire, Lancashire and Cheshire who, in the years 1811 to 1816, embarked upon the destruction of machines which they held responsible for their unemployment and poverty. As already mentioned, attitudes to the machine were ambiguous from the start. Thus, whilst some welcomed them as the means of achieving unprecedented wealth, others feared them as potentially demonic forces or committed themselves to their annihilation.

At the same time, scientific research was not merely sustaining the development of the factory system but also exploring avenues which would eventually lead from industrial technology to digital technology. The French philosopher and mathematician Blaise Pascal had already created a calculating machine in the seventeenth century. This was a system based on cogged wheels and ratchets – initially designed to help his tax-collecting father! It is with the name of Charles Babbage (1801–71), however, that the mechanical forerunners of the modern computer tend to be associated. Babbage was inspired by the work of the textile manufacturer Joseph Marie Jacquard who, in 1804, came up with the first programme based on punched cards. In the Jacquard loom, threads are raised and lowered as the shuttle passes through them according to a series of cards with holes punched into them. Keen on developing this model, Babbage focused on the possibility of producing complex interactions among the cards that could simulate human memory. He explored ways of grouping cards according to certain rules so as to ensure that a card or set of cards could be used repeatedly to solve a particular problem. Babbage's inventions, neither of them developed to his full satisfaction, were the Difference Engine and the Analytical Engine. The first could only perform the most basic operation, addition, while the second was intended to handle all operations by systematically grasping the laws of their functioning. This idea was only put to use in the 1940s with the advent of cybernetics. The starting point of modern artificial intelligence is often associated with the Turing Machine, designed by the mathematician Alan Mathison

Turing (1912–54). This consisted of a long tape of squares, some with numbers on them and others blank. It could read one square at a time and move the tape backwards and forwards to read other squares.

As the culture of the machine moved into the twentieth century, strengthened by discoveries and inventions such as electricity, the telegraph, the Morse code, the telephone and photography, reflections about the gains and losses induced by technology proliferated. Late nineteenth-century and early twentieth-century aesthetic movements go on displaying ambiguous responses to industrialization. The Arts and Crafts Movement, whilst not despising the machine wholeheartedly, sought to ensure that human labour be freed from the drudgery of factory production. William Morris (1834–96), one of the Movement's founders, opposed production for a mass market. Later artists and designers inspired by the Movement, however, thought that industrial technology had its own benefits. Modern industry was seen as a means of manufacturing economically a wide range of objects without having to sacrifice creativity and beauty. Especially influential was the Bauhaus School, founded in Weimar in 1919 by the architect Walter Gropius. Its aesthetic principles required artefacts to be both simple and stylish, practical yet elegant. Bauhaus designers believed that the mechanical age could help them achieve this aim. They designed objects suitable for industrial manufacture and utilized materials made available by new technologies, such as plastic and chrome. The Bauhaus's main intention was to marry mechanical production to principles of design.

Certain strands of Modernism cultivated a machine aesthetic based on the desire to make artefacts look like machines and mechanically produced. Technology was supposed to sustain an aesthetic based on notions of simplicity, clarity, integrity and both formal and functional economy. Some of the most enthusiastic responses to the machine surrounded the technologies of photography and cinema. What aroused special interest was the possibility that these technologies would make visible various aspects of life normally unavailable to the naked eye. Etienne-Jules Marey, for instance, carried out a series of photographic experiments in the 1870s which consisted of decomposing movement into its tiniest elements through the camera, and thus capturing a world which the eye alone could never perceive. Walter Benjamin, for his part, believed that cinema was capable of revealing hidden facets of reality – e.g. by expanding space through the technique of the close-up, by extending movement through that of slow motion, and by disclosing unexpected attributes of objects through enlargement.

However, the benefits and promises heralded by new technologies are invariably attended by as many anxieties and fears. The machine is, above all, a machinery of ambiguities. A good example of the sense of apprehension evoked by technology is supplied by Sigmund Freud: 'If there had been no railway to conquer distance, my child would never had left his native town and I should need no telephone to hear his voice; if travelling across the ocean by ship had not been introduced, my friend would not have embarked on his sea-voyage and I should not need a cable to relieve my anxiety about him' (Gunning 1991: 185). (The railway, incidentally, is the icon of modern technology around which some of the most potent myths have accrued – as a symbolic conquest of space and time, on the one hand, and as a terrifying cause of lethal accidents, on the other. Interestingly, traumatic neurosis was first diagnosed in the treatment of victims of train disasters.)

The idolatry of the machine also led some modernist and *avant-garde* movements to speculate about the ideal of a man-machine. Especially vociferous, in this area, were the Futurists. Filippo Marinetti, for example, proposed an eminently masculine machine-body based on principles of force, order, discipline and precision. An alternative approach to the relationship between the body and the machine was offered in the 1920s by the costume designer Oskar Schlemmer. He argued that humans must live in harmony with machines, yet remember that the body is a superior and immutable essence. Schlemmer was interested in the idea of the body as a machine but at the same time keen on ideating the body as an eternal structure based on geometric shapes: the head, the neck, the rib cage, the belly, arms, legs and joints could be abstractly conceived of as circles, squares, spheres, cylinders, etc.

As we move into the later part of the twentieth century, we find that the idea of the body-as-machine no longer inspires idealistic visions of the kind entertained by many modernists. In the writings of Michel Foucault, for example, the machine-body is presented as the effect of disciplining strategies meant to maximize the organism's usefulness, exploit its energies and make it pliant and docile. The control of the individual body (anatomo-politics) is then extended into the regimentation of whole populations as functional machines (bio-politics).[2]

Just as machines are alternately open to both idealization and demonization, so are the bodies associated with them. Whichever way we look at it, it is undeniable that technology has had a profound impact on how people perceive themselves and others as both minds and bodies. According to Benjamin, this has a lot to do with technology's ability to shape the ways in which people receive and process information. The information technologies of newspapers and magazines already required readers to develop interpretive skills that would enable them to filter and link disparate narratives and sets of data. Electronic technology has obviously complicated this process. It exposes us to vast arrays of data through multimedia channels, and much as we can rely on computers to sort out the relevant bits of information for us, we also need to develop the ability to know (more or less) what we are looking for, without becoming blind to unforeseen ramifications. The effects of post-industrial technologies on people's grasp of information were closely examined by Marshall McLuhan in the 1960s. He argued that 'as electrically contracted, the globe is no more than a village'. The contraction of information impacts directly on our bodies and on our perceptions of space and time: 'After 3,000 years of explosion ... the western world is imploding. During the mechanical ages we had extended our bodies in space. Today, after more than a century of electric technology, we have extended our central nervous system itself in a global embrace, abolishing both space and time as far as our planet is concerned' (McLuhan 1964: 5). What sorts of communities and messages are produced by today's electronic villages?

Welcome by some as a Brave New World, the universe opened up by computers is regarded suspiciously by those who equate it to the annihilation of traditional notions of identity, community and space. There are also those who stress the dangers of digital technology on the basis of its confusion of the real and the virtual.[3] The Gulf War is often cited as a case in point. In that

---

[2] ☞Foucault's theories are examined in detail in Part II, Chapter 2, 'Subjectivity'.
[3] ☞Related issues are addressed in Part III, Chapter 6, 'The Simulacrum'.

conflict, some pilots are reported to have made fatal mistakes as a result of misreading the digital signals meant to differentiate friends and enemies. It has also been shown that virtual interactions – though not based on face-to-face encounters – are often talked about in very physical terms. Thus, exchanges taking place in a multi-user domain (MUD) that are deemed intrusive or aggressive are referred to as 'MUD-rape'. This suggests that the apparently abstract world created by computers is not so abstract after all. Simulations may have very concrete effects indeed.

The scenario generated by computer technology is commonly tagged cyberculture. This term alludes to an environment saturated by electronic technology in which the futuristic fantasies and nightmares of classic SF (science fiction) are experienced in the here-and-now, and in which reality is not so much a tangible world as a product of computer-simulated virtual images. Its bedrock is Information Technology (IT): the media and processes through which information about people and machines can be produced, stored and transmitted by them. IT has to do with the development of systems capable of classifying and handling such data, and with their political, commercial and educational applications.

The scientific underpinning of cyberculture is the discipline of cybernetics. This word, introduced by the mathematician Norbert Wiener in 1948, derives from the Greek *kubernetes*, which means 'steersman'. Wiener's best-known text, *Cybernetics, or Control and Communication in the Animal and the Machine*, argues that control and communication should be based on steersmanship, not on dictatorship. Both organisms and machines are viewed as self-regulating systems based on control and communication. In the electronic era, in particular, the organism can be thought of as a network capable of absorbing and processing data. At the same time, the machine simulates the organism. The model on which it is designed is provided by the sensory and nervous apparatuses. The technological construct based on an understanding of the structural similarities between organisms and machines is termed cybernetic organism. This phrase suggests a more promising interpenetration of the human and the mechanical than the term 'robot'. This derives from the Czech word *robota*, used by Karel Capek in 1920 to signify 'forced labour'.

The phrase 'cybernetic organism' is also, of course, at the root of the idea of the cyborg – a figure that encapsulates many contemporary anxieties about the merging of the natural and the artificial and about the uncertainty of the dividing-line separating the human from the non-human. As a fusion of organic and mechanical elements, the cyborg features in many areas of our lives. Cyborg technologies have military and astronautical origins: in the early 1960s, their objective was to modify physical functions so as to make the human body capable of surviving in alien environments. Cyborg technologies have also been used in the medical domain through the development of prosthetics. Most of us are familiar with cyborgs as fictional figures popularized by cinema. These figures are not wholly imaginary for they embody conflicting cultural ideals. Tough and hypermasculine, the cyborg is sealed and unpolluted: it offers the ideal of a bounded body that does not eat, drink, cry, sweat, urinate, defecate, menstruate, ejaculate. Yet, the cyborg is also a hybrid, impure and often fluid compound that dramatizes contemporary fears about the collapse and violation of boundaries.

The best-known fictional interpretation of cyberculture to date is cyberpunk, the genre associated with the writings of William Gibson, Bruce Sterling, Pat Cadigan and Kathy Acker (amongst many others). The 'cyber' element indicates that this brand of SF uses computer technology – rather than spaceships and robots – as its main point of reference. The 'punk' element hints at a defiant attitude based in urban street culture. Cyberpunk's characters are people on the fringe of society, outsiders, rebels and psychopaths, struggling for survival on a junk-infested planet. Reality and identity are unstable and often reduced to commodities doomed to a fate of planned and rapid obsolescence. Cyberpunk is one of the most recent chapters in a long history recording ambivalent attitudes to technology. Cyberpunk writers often highlight technology's ability to enhance people's access to knowledge by electronic means and to strengthen their bodies in various ways. Biotechnology, for example, plays an important part in restructuring bodies, in endowing them with protective and aggressive mechanisms and even in enabling survival against all odds. At the same time, technology is portrayed as hostile – or simply indifferent – to human welfare. It is presented as capable of manipulating the most intimate mental and physical processes and of harnessing them to sinister plans that ultimately only benefit the megarich and megacorrupt.

Human beings will feasibly go on exhibiting ambivalent feelings towards technology as long as they regard machines as alien and yet tend to identify with them. People often bond with machines by associating them with the human organism in the form of metaphors. This applies to both industrial and electronic cultures. Several expressions used to describe human situations strike their roots in the world of the machine: 'to have a nervous breakdown', 'to reprogramme oneself', 'to get one's wires crossed', for example. At the same time, machines are often construed as bodies and invested with sexual attributes. The machines of the early Industrial Age have been associated with virility due to their boisterous energy. Digital technology is more ambiguous: the computer's amazing power links it to stereotypical notions of masculinity, whilst its unobtrusiveness links it to stereotypical notions of femininity. Computers are ideated as people on various levels: they have memories, suffer from viruses; break down (crash), and get married (when interconnected within a network). Concurrently, the most intimate human experiences are becoming increasingly entangled with electronic technology, as evinced – most notably – by the growing popularity of virtual sex.

CHAPTER 6

THE SIMULACRUM

The simulacrum has been a prominent concept in both the theory and the practice of the visual arts since at least Plato (fifth century BC). In the course of the twentieth century, the simulacrum gained fresh resonance as a result of technological and economic developments. These problematized the already complex relationship between reality and its simulations firstly through the flourishing of mechanical reproduction and subsequently through the electronic production of virtual worlds.

In order to grasp the idea of the simulacrum, it is first of all necessary to examine some of the major positions on the relationship between the real and the copy articulated by Western philosophy. In Plato's system, the copy is regarded as inferior to the Idea or Form that lies behind it. According to the Greek philosopher, the natural world we inhabit and experience daily as mortal creatures is itself a second-rate copy of the transcendental realm of Pure Forms. These are abstract concepts that exist independently of any of their material manifestations. The idea of 'dogness', for example, transcends the hundreds of thousands of physical dogs to be found in nature. While the individual animals are, like all living entities, subject to death and decay, the idea of 'dogness' is supposed to be immortal and eternal. The realm of Ideas, argues Plato, is the only authentic and enduring reality. Its material embodiments are merely flimsy simulacra of its undying principles. Artistic representations of the natural world, such as poems and paintings, are even further removed from reality than nature is: representations of nature are third-rate copies, the copy of a copy. It is on this basis that Plato bans artists (poets, painters) from his ideal Republic – a world ruled by philosophers committed to the pursuit of reason and truth, and hence to the dismantling of illusory simulacra.

Although Plato has influenced many subsequent developments in Western philosophy (particularly the branch of philosophy termed 'metaphysics'), more recent trends in critical and cultural theory have indicated that copies and simulacra are not unproblematically inferior to the reality which they are supposed to simulate or imitate. Furthermore, it is spurious to generalize about the relationship between reality and its representation – as though the world could only be represented in one way. The French philosopher Gilles Deleuze, for instance, has argued that the world is represented and replicated in a variety of ways. For him, it is preposterous to assume that there is only one, universally valid way of understanding the relationship between the real and its representations. Most importantly, Deleuze stresses that a distinction should be made between the copy and the simulacrum. He maintains that although the copy has traditionally been viewed as second rate, it has nonetheless been held in some esteem because of its close association with a worthy original, and thus deemed capable of offering insights into the values contained by the original. The simulacrum, by contrast, does not refer to a superior reality. In fact, it has its own reality and flaunts the authority of any original that may have inspired its construction. 'The simulacrum', Deleuze maintains, 'is not a degraded copy. It harbours a positive power which denies *the original and the copy, the model and the reproduction.* At least two divergent series are internalized in the simulacrum – neither can be assigned as the original, neither as the copy ... . There is no longer any privileged point of view except that of the object common to all points of view. There is no possible hierarchy, no second, no third. ... The same and the similar no longer have an essence except as *simulated*, that is as expressing the functioning of the simulacrum' (Deleuze 1990: 262; emphasis in original).

As a means of illustrating the difference proposed by Deleuze, a simple example may be used. A mail-order catalogue offers a range of goods inspired by the work of the painter Gustav Klimt. Some of the products are obviously 'copies': mass-produced images of his most famous paintings that can be instantly recognized as specific works created by the famous artist. These objects have a direct connection with their originals and remain utterly faithful to such originals' composition. Other products are more like 'simulacra': velvet slippers, silk ties and kimonos, and coat cardigans whose designs are based on Klimt's palette and whose patterns hark back to the artist's work but do not evince the kind of respect for the original associated with straightforward copies. These simulacra have no natural link with a pre-existing reality. They are realities in their own right and suggest that no original holds ultimate authority. The preceding example has deliberately been drawn from the sphere of mass consumption to indicate that contemporary attitudes to copies and simulacra are largely an offshoot of the forces that have moulded consumer culture.

Walter Benjamin was one of the first and most influential voices in the debate about the effects of mechanical reproduction.[1] In his famous essay 'The Work of Art in the Age of Mechanical Reproduction', Benjamin asserts that mechanically reproduced copies, such as photographs of artworks, challenge the original's uniqueness, or 'aura' (Benjamin 1969: 221). As a result, the original acquires novel meanings: its images become accessible by a wide range of people who are not necessarily experts or practitioners in the world of art. The connotations of such images, moreover, vary according to their contexts. The museum industry has increasingly benefited from this idea. It is common to see the same work of art reproduced in a variety of forms and contexts, often for advertising purposes. Thus, the products on sale in connection with an exhibition or art event tend more and more to include not only catalogues and postcards, but also stationery, garments, soft furnishings, jewellery, toys and crockery (to mention but a few examples) inspired by the works of art on display.

While the more conservative sections of the public regard the commercialization of art as distasteful evidence for a rampant consumerism, and as disrespectful of the artists' achievements, others view the displacement of the original from its privileged position as a welcome challenge to stifling traditions. However, it has also been pointed out that disseminating famous works into a plurality of contexts is not necessarily a democratic move. John Berger, for instance, maintains that although the significance of the original is dislocated by mechanical reproduction and by its translation into a plethora of commodities, its special value may

---

[1] ☞Benjamin's writings are also discussed in Part III, Chapter 5, 'The Machine'.

be simultaneously reinforced. The original may come to be perceived as the unique model behind its various copies, inspire a sense of awe and thus become the object of a 'bogus religiosity' (Berger 1972: 23). This is confirmed, according to Berger, by the devotion with which many people approach so-called masterpieces. Going to a museum to see a famous painting, for example, becomes something of a pilgrimage. In this case, the original's authority turns out to be magnified, rather than diminished, by its mass diffusion through copies and simulacra. Indeed, it is its very popularity – paradoxically – that strengthens the notion of its uniqueness and its status as an unattainable object of desire.

Simulacra and copies, therefore, serve a twofold purpose: they challenge tradition and concomitantly perpetuate traditional values. These paradoxes and ambiguities are consistently highlighted by Benjamin. He argues that 'technical reproduction can put the copy of the original into situations which would be out of reach for the original itself', that it endangers 'the authority of the object', and that 'it substitutes a plurality of copies for a unique existence' (Benjamin 1969: 220–1). Benjamin also states that 'the work of art reproduced becomes the work of art designed for reproducibility' (Benjamin 1969: 224). This suggests that the concept of the original, ultimately, only makes sense in relation to the possibility of its reproduction. This idea has been developed by Jacques Derrida: his writings deconstruct the binary opposition between the original and the copy that conventionally accords superiority to the original. Derrida shows that the word 'original' has a meaning only insofar as we can expect the original to become a non-original, namely a simulation.[2]

While foregrounding the emancipatory potential of technical reproduction, Benjamin also stresses its oppressive and repressive effects or applications. He emphasizes the revolutionary powers of reproductive technologies as an assault on cultural elitism and even a means of revealing concealed aspects of the world. However, he shows that technology can be appropriated by fascist and capitalist dispensations in order to consolidate totalitarian structures of power. Reproduction is capable of empowering despotic regimes. This is most patently borne out by political propaganda: photographic and filmic records of rallies, parades,

[2] Derrida's theories are examined in detail in Part I, Chapter 3, 'Rhetoric'.

sports tournaments, warfare, state weddings and funerals which supply spectacular displays of regimented masses. Furthermore, popular images divulged by means of mechanical reproduction are often both revolutionary and liable to be distorted by the dominant ideology. Benjamin cites the figure of Mickey Mouse as a case in point. The early Mickey-Mouse movies are revolutionary to the extent that they open up an alternative world based on the collapse of conventional boundaries. Nature and technology, organic and mechanical bodies, the animate and the inanimate, animals and people constantly merge in those films. More recently, the revolutionary opportunities held by the crossing of the nature/technology divide have been emphasized by Donna Haraway in her study of cyborgs (Haraway 1991). Yet, Benjamin also highlights the ambivalence of popular figures such as Mickey Mouse: Disney's creation was, after all, used as a mascot on German fighter planes in the Second World War. This suggests that fictional characters popularized through mechanical reproduction are never wholly fictional. In fact, they voice deep-seated cultural concerns and aspirations.

The pervasive cultural role played by simulacra in contemporary culture is thrown into relief by the writings of Jean Baudrillard, who argues that in postmodern societies simulacra do not imitate a preexisting reality but actually replace reality: 'It is no longer a question of imitation, nor even of parody. It is rather a question of substituting signs of the real for the real itself ... Illusion is no longer possible because the real is no longer possible' (Baudrillard 1994b: 19). Signs do not bear any resemblance or correspondence to the real world but rather produce their own hyperreality: an order of representation based on illusion whose power increases in direct proportion to its ability to make us forget that it is indeed illusory. 'The collapse of reality into hyperrealism', Baudrillard argues, 'entails a minute duplication of the real, preferably on the basis of another reproductive medium – advertising, photography, etc. From medium to medium the real is volatilized'. In this perspective, conventional distinctions between reality and illusion become hard to sustain: 'The unreal is no longer that of dream or of fantasy ... . The very definition of the real becomes: that of which it is possible to give an equivalent reproduction. ... It is reality itself today that is hyperrealist ... . We live everywhere already in an "aesthetic" hallucination of reality ... . "It's a circus", "It's theatre", "It's a movie", old adages .... These sayings are now obsolete' (Baudrillard 1983: 141–8).

Simulacra and simulations underpin the social system, its economic structures and its ideologies – in other words, power. Power perpetuates itself by unremittingly selling us fantasies and denying that they are fantasies. Power claims to be real and to offer people the naked truth. Moreover, it sustains this myth by blaming overtly fictional worlds (such as those of sport and entertainment) for ensnaring people into fantastic and mystifying situations. In this way, power effaces its own illusory character and uses certain aspects of culture as scapegoats. This idea is neatly summed up by the statement: 'Power is only too happy to make football bear a diabolical responsibility for stupefying the masses' (quoted on the Baudrillard *Philosophy Football* T-shirt, 1996).

Let us look more closely at the role played by the simulacrum as the underpinning of postmodern culture. Three main factors must be taken into consideration: (1) the type of society in which the simulacrum thrives; (2) the order of representation produced by the simulacrum; (3) the nature of the illusions and delusions carried by the simulacrum. According to Baudrillard, the basis of the social order is not production – as Marxism believed[3] – but consumption. We inhabit what Guy Debord has tagged the 'society of the spectacle' (Debord 1983): a world in which relationships amongst people are constantly mediated by images to be unrelentingly consumed, then discarded, then recycled, then consumed again – ad infinitum. As cultural subjects, we are controlled by being incorporated into an ongoing spectacle of consumption. Conventional assumptions about an object's function or relation to a specific place have become obsolete. That is to say, objects are no longer defined by the contexts in which they appear or by the practical purposes that they may serve. All objects are caught in a network of signs which endlessly circulate and become virtually interchangeable. Consider, as a simple example, the commodities that surround us at all times. Their meanings have little to do with their contexts and functions. The same kind of mobile phone, for instance, may be used by a businessperson as s/he speeds down a motorway to sort out a transac-

[3] ☞Marxist theories are examined in Part II, Chapter 1, 'Ideology'.

tion and by a shopper in a general store fancying a chat with a friend while deciding what to purchase. In both cases, the object's meaning has to do with its ability to confer upon its user a sense of control over her or his circumstances. Such a meaning is neither defined by a specific context nor related to a specific function. In the process, users and consumers are constructed on the basis of the contingent meanings accrued by the goods with which they associate themselves. Consumption, argues Baudrillard, manipulates objects so that they become signs, and so that signs define certain categories of people.

In this system, there are no genuine needs. The only enduring drive is the desire for consumption, for the incessant acquisition of objects that promise but never actually yield a sense of fulfilment. (An extreme instance of this drive is shown by the collector: somebody who accumulates objects out of a passion not so much for possession itself as for the attainment of a sense of personal completion.) However, the objects we relentlessly consume are presented to us (more often than not) as means of satisfying so-called natural needs. Baudrillard maintains that the idea of natural needs is actually a cultural myth promoted by capitalism. Commodities are incapable of satisfying needs because they are not so much objects as signs. In other words, although commodities appear to be concrete (as material entities), it is not from their materiality that they derive meaning but rather from their symbolic status as images. The identity of a particular object is not established by its physical properties (e.g. the materials from which it is made, its shape, colour, texture, practical utility) but by what it signifies.[4] An astounding variety of goods may serve to signify the same concepts – status, wealth, sex appeal, etc. – and this suggests that the goods themselves are somewhat interchangeable. Indeed, it is probably preposterous to talk of the identity of objects, for everything is inevitably captured into the same levelling circuit of consumption. What gets exchanged when commodities are bought and sold is not tangible stuff but rather signs, symbols and images. Any number of objects may, at any one time, be used to convey the values favoured by this or that ideology or power structure. Whatever the objects and whatever the values at

---

[4] The symbolic value of signs is discussed in detail in Part I, Chapter 2, 'The Sign' and in Part I, Chapter 4, 'Representation'.

stake, the only thing that truly matters is that the process of sign exchange must go on.

This is secured by fashion trends that incessantly recycle and reinscribe certain forms, styles and ideas, whilst displaying them under the banner of novelty. The fashion cycle is the principal code through which the culture of consumption operates. The realization that what we produce and consume consists of abstract signs rather than concrete objects has profound repercussions on our grasp of reality. Indeed, though signs are supposed to reflect reality, they actually exclude it. That is to say, signs marginalize the physical attributes of objects by according priority to their symbolic connotations. Thus, the symbolic significance of an item of clothing or furniture, a car, pet, PC or toy, for example, takes over their reality and translates it into abstract ideas. Moreover, in a culture predicated upon relentless consumption, everything is saturated with information. Many critics have described Postmodernism as a cultural phenomenon based on the rejection of meaning: a world of surfaces in which nothing is more important than anything else and everything, as a result, is bound to become equally meaningless. Baudrillard contradicts this approach by arguing that postmodern culture does not hinge on the denial of meaning but is, in fact, too full of meanings. Commodities of all sorts are invested with a surplus or excess of meaning. This produces a deep sense of disorientation (what Baudrillard sometimes refers to as 'ecstasy') and the feeling that objects are always surpassing their intended functions and aims ('hypertelia'). This is also a culture of extremes, in which practically everything is exaggerated, accelerated and distorted. The real is magnified into the hyperreal – the more real than real – and truth is displaced by simulation – the more true than true. It is in this scenario that the order of the simulacrum thrives.

Baudrillard outlines three orders of representation. The first, dominant from the Renaissance to the Industrial Revolution, is based on the idea that copies and simulations are false images that do not mirror reality but actually mask or pervert it. The second, spanning the early industrial period to the nineteenth century, introduces the notion that what signs and images mask is not reality but its absence. In the culture of mass production and reproduction, signs do not refer to reality but only to other signs. The third order is the one in which we currently live. Here, as already mentioned, signs bear no relation or resemblance to reality whatsoever: they are pure simulacra designed to sustain the order of hyperreality. Simulacra are used by the dominant powers to foster many illusions and delusions. Above all, power endeavours to consolidate itself by setting up an apparently inviolable boundary between fiction and reality. It defines certain portions of the world as fictional so as to have us believe that the rest of the world is real – when, in fact, the world in its entirety is steeped in imaginary fabrications.

The following is one of Baudrillard's best known examples. Disneyland, the critic points out, is presented as a fictional alternative to the real world to efface the fact that the culture of consumption as a whole is a kind of theme-park. A fantasy world like Disneyland is a simulacrum to the extent that it capitalizes on images that produce their own realities. Yet, Western culture in all its manifestations – including apparently serious activities, projects and pursuits – depends on simulacra no less than the famous theme-park does. Disneyland is there to avert our attention from the fact that all consumer societies are Disneylands of sorts. (Prisons, likewise, exist so as to prevent us from realizing that the world as a whole is somewhat carceral.)

Ultimately, the main function performed by the simulacrum is to challenge traditional hierarchies. It is no longer possible to conceive of the real as more fundamental and more solid than its reproductions, representations and simulations. All images, as a result, are brought to the same level. Whether we welcome or fear the culture of the simulacrum, it is practically impossible not to acknowledge its pervasiveness. For one thing, technological developments increasingly indicate that much of our daily existence is inevitably woven around computer-simulated images, virtual experiences and forms of interaction that tend to displace the reality of face-to-face contact. Computer technologies have generated forms of simulation that question radically conventional notions of origin and originality, and make the artificial, the synthetic and the fake indistinguishable from the real. Indeed, the simulated sometimes appears more vivid and authentic than reality itself. Yet, this should not be taken as a gloomy denial of the existence of reality. In fact, the erosion of traditional barriers separating the real from its simulations may contribute beneficially to our understanding and knowledge of our cultural circum-

stances. In particular, it can help us recognize that if it is the case
that the world now feels less real than it ever did before, it is also
the case that there has never been a totally certain notion of
reality.

It is vital to remember that at no point in the history of ideas
has there been an incontrovertibly reliable and universally convincing definition of the real. Plato's theories on the relationship
between reality and illusion and on that between the original and
the copy may at first suggest that he knew (or thought he knew)
the essence of reality, and took it upon himself to convince others
of the validity of his knowledge. Yet, had reality been as pure and
immutable a set of concepts as Plato claims, and had he known
this as a fact, there would not have been any need to safeguard it
from the threat of mystifying simulacra. The ways in which Plato
endeavours to present the realm of Ideas as the only authentic
reality and to insulate it from the world of illusion are reminiscent
of the colonial strategies used by states, empires and corporations
to proclaim their inviolability and superiority over the objects of
their domination. The world of the simulacrum, like the world of
the colonized, is the mysterious Other, the inexplicable non-self,
which must be kept at bay if the ruling self is to remain dominant.
In both cases, the urge to define a territory as immortal stems
from the awareness, however submerged, that anything can die,
more or less finally or abruptly. There would be no need to celebrate a philosophical doctrine or geographical region as inviolable
if anxieties about its vulnerability were not lurking in the background.[5]

At the same time, it could be argued that even theories which,
like Baudrillard's, have announced the dissolution of the real have
not necessarily gone all the way. There is a chance that future
simulation techniques will modify our understanding of reality
well beyond the point envisaged in Baudrillard's writings. Baudrillard's simulacra, much as they may come across as hallucinations
now, might seem to have the solidity of marble monuments a few
decades hence. Technological developments have increasingly
dissociated reality from traditional notions of solidity and
certainty and will no doubt go on doing so. Some find this state of
affairs lamentable, others find it daunting, others still find it

[5] For further discussion of these issues, see Part II, Chapter 5, 'The Other'.

exciting. In any case, it is undeniable that those developments are capable of opening up alternative approaches to the real and, concomitantly, of redefining our roles as both consumers and producers.

REFERENCES

Abrams, M. H. (1953), *The Mirror and the Lamp*, Oxford: Oxford University Press.

Adler, K. and M. Pointon (eds.) (1993), *The Body Imaged: The Human Form and Visual Culture Since the Renaissance*, Cambridge: Cambridge University Press.

Adorno, T. (1977), *Aesthetics and Politics*, London: New Left Books.

—— (1984), *Aesthetic Theory*, London: Routledge.

Adorno, T. and M. Horkheimer (1986), *Dialectic of Enlightenment*, trans. J. Cumming, London: Verso.

Althusser, L. (1972), 'Ideology and Ideological State Apparatuses', in *Lenin and Philosophy and Other Essays*, London: New Left Books.

Austin, J. L. (1962), *How To Do Things With Words*, Oxford: Oxford University Press.

Ballard, J. G. (1992), 'Project for a Glossary of the Twentieth Century', in J. Crary and S. Kwinter (eds.), *Incorporations*, New York: Zone.

Barthes, R. (1967a), *Writing Degree Zero*, trans. A. Lavers and C. Smith, London: Cape.

—— (1967b), *Elements of Semiology*, trans. A. Lavers and C. Smith, London: Cape.

—— (1972a), *Mythologies*, trans. A. Lavers, London: Cape.

—— (1972b), *Critical Essays*, trans. R. Howard, Evanston, IL.: Northwestern University Press.

—— (1975), *S/Z*, trans. R. Miller, London: Cape.

—— (1977), 'The death of the author', in *Image, Music, Text*, trans. S. Heath, Glasgow: Fontana.

—— (1990a), *The Pleasure of the Text*, trans. R. Miller, Oxford: Blackwell.

—— (1990b), *A Lover's Discourse*, trans. R. Howard, London: Penguin.

—— (1990c), *The Fashion System*, trans. M. Ward and R. Howard, Berkeley, CA: University of California Press.

Barton, L. (1996), 'Sociology and disability: some emerging issues', in L.

Barton (ed.), *Disability and Society: Emerging Issues and Insights*, New York: Longman.

Baudrillard, J. (1983), *Simulations*, trans. N. Dufresne, New York: Semiotext(e).

—— (1994a), *The Illusion of the End*, trans. C. Turner, Cambridge: Polity Press.

—— (1994b), 'The Precession of Simulacra', in *Simulacra and Simulations*, trans. S. Faria Glaser, Ann Arbor, MI: University of Michigan Press.

Beauvoir, S. de (1953), *The Second Sex*, Harmondsworth: Penguin.

Belsey, C. and J. Moore (eds.) (1997), *The Feminist Reader*, London: Macmillan.

Benjamin, W. (1969), 'The work of art in the age of mechanical reproduction', in *Illuminations*, trans. H. Zohn, New York: Schocken.

—— (1985), 'Moscow Diary', trans. R. Sieburth, *October* 35.

Berger, J. (1972), *Ways of Seeing*, London and Harmondsworth: BBC and Penguin.

Bergson, H. (1998), *Creative Evolution*, trans. A. Mitchell, New York: Dover.

Bhabha, H. K. (1996), 'Postmodernism/Postcolonialism', in R. S. Nelson and R. Shiff (eds.), *Critical Terms for Art History*, Chicago, IL and London: Chicago University Press.

Birkett, D. (1992), Review of *Over Her Dead Body*, *The Guardian*, 1 October.

Bordo, S. (1990), 'Reading the slender body', in M. Jacobus, E. Fox Keller and S. Shuttleworth (eds.), *Body/Politics*, London: Routledge.

Borges, J. L. (1970), *Labyrinths*, trans. J. E. Irby, Harmondsworth: Penguin.

Bostock, P. (1999), *The Cricket*, London: Minerva Press.

Boyer, C. (1996), *CyberCities*, New York: Princeton Architectural Press.

Bristow, J. and A. R. Wilson (eds.) (1993), *Activating Theory: Lesbian, Gay, Bisexual Politics*, London: Lawrence & Wishart.

Britt, D. (ed.) (1989), *Modern Art*, London: Thames & Hudson.

Broad, C. D. (1933), *An Examination of McTaggart's Philosophy*, Cambridge: Cambridge University Press.

Bronfen, E. (1992), *Over Her Dead Body*, Manchester: Manchester University Press.

Bryson, N. (1983), *Vision and Painting: The Logic of the Gaze*, London: Macmillan.

—— (1988), 'The gaze in the expanded field', in H. Foster (ed.), *Vision and Visuality*, Seattle, WA: Bay Press.

Buick, J. and Z. Jevtic (1995), *Cyberspace for Beginners*, Cambridge: Icon.

Butler, J. (1993), *Bodies that Matter: On the Discursive Limits of Sex*, London and New York: Routledge.

Calvino, I. (1987), *The Literature Machine*, trans. P. Creagh, London: Secker & Warburg.

—— (1993), *If on a Winter's Night a Traveller*, trans. W. Weaver, London: Everyman's Library.

—— (1996), 'The Burning of the Abominable House', *Numbers in the Dark*, trans. T. Parks, London: Vintage.

Carter, A. (1979), *The Sadeian Woman*, London: Virago.

Certeau, M. de (1984), *The Practice of Everyday Life*, trans. S. Rendall, Berkeley, CA and London: University of California Press.

Chomsky, N. (1957), *Syntactic Structures*, The Hague: Mouton.

—— (1965), *Aspects of the Theory of Syntax*, Cambridge, MA: MIT Press.

Clark, K. (1985), *The Nude*, London: Penguin.

Cocking, J. M. (1991), *Imagination*, London: Routledge.

Collingwood, R. G. (1938), *The Principles of Art*, Oxford: Clarendon Press.

Crary, J. (1990), *Techniques of the Observer*, Cambridge, MA: MIT Press.

Croce, B. (1909), *Aesthetics as Science of Expression*, trans. D. Ainslie, London: Methuen.

Cubitt, S. (1998), *Digital Aesthetics*, London: Sage.

Davis, M. (1992), *City of Quartz: Excavating the Future in Los Angeles*, London: Vintage.

Debord, G. (1983), *Society of the Spectacle*, Detroit, MI: Black & Red.

Deleuze, G. (1990), 'Plato and the Simulacrum', in C. V. Boundas (ed.), *The Logic of Sense*, New York: Columbia University Press.

Deleuze, G. and F. Guattari (1988), *A Thousand Plateaus: Capitalism and Schizophrenia*, trans. B. Massumi, London: Athlone.

De Man, P. (1979), *Allegories of Reading*, New Haven, CT and London: Yale University Press.

—— (1988), 'The resistance to theory', in D. Lodge (ed.), *Modern Criticism and Theory*, London: Longman.

—— (1990), 'Roland Barthes and the Limits of Structuralism', *Yale French Studies*, 77: 177–90.

Derrida, J. (1976), *Of Grammatology*, trans. G. C. Spivak, Baltimore, MD: Johns Hopkins University Press.

—— (1978), *Writing and Difference*, trans. A. Bass, London: Routledge & Kegan Paul.

—— (1981), *Positions*, trans. A. Bass, London: Athlone.

Dick, P. K. (1978), 'Man, android and machine', in P. Nicholls (ed.), *Explorations of the Marvellous*, Glasgow: Fontana/Collins.

Dworkin, A. (1981), *Pornography*, London: Women's Press.

Eagleton, T. (1990), *The Ideology of the Aesthetic*, Oxford: Blackwell.

Easthope, A. (1983), *Poetry as Discourse*, London: Methuen.

REFERENCES

Eco, U. (1979), *The Role of the Reader*, Bloomington, IN: Indiana University Press.

Ewing, W. A. (1994), *The Body: Photoworks of the Human Form*, London: Thames & Hudson.

Fanon, F. (1964), *The Wretched of the Earth*, New York: Grove.

—— (1967), *Black Skin, White Masks*, New York: Grove.

Feinberg, G. (1995), 'Quantum Mechanics', *The 1995 Grolier Multimedia Encyclopaedia*, Grolier Electronic Publishing.

Fish, S. (1980), *Is There a Text in This Class?*, Cambridge, MA: Harvard University Press.

Foucault, M. (1973a), *The Order of Things: An Archaeology of the Human Sciences*, New York: Vintage/Random House.

—— (1973b), *Madness and Civilization*, trans. R. Howard, New York: Vintage/Random House.

—— (1979), *Discipline and Punish: The Birth of the Prison*, trans. A. Sheridan, New York: Vintage/Random House.

—— (1986), 'Of Other Spaces', *Diacritics* 16.1, Spring: 22–7.

—— (1988), 'What is an Author?', trans. J. V. Harari, in D. Lodge (ed.), *Modern Criticism and Theory: A Reader*, London: Longman.

—— (1990), *The History of Sexuality*, vol. I, London: Penguin.

Friedan, B. (1963), *The Feminine Mystique*, New York: Dell.

Genette, G. (1988), 'Structuralism and Literary Criticism', in D. Lodge (ed.), *Modern Criticism and Theory: A Reader*, London: Longman.

Gombrich, E. H. (1990), *Art and Illusion*, Oxford: Phaidon.

Gramsci, A. (1971), *Selections from the Prison Notebooks*, trans. Q. Hoare and G. Nowell Smith, London: Lawrence & Wishart.

Greer, G. (1970), *The Female Eunuch*, London: MacGibbon & Kee.

—— (1999), *The Whole Woman*, London and New York: Doubleday.

Ground, I. (1989), *Art or Bunk?*, Bristol: Bristol Classical Press.

Gunning, T. (1991), 'Heard over the phone', *Screen* 32.3, Summer.

Hamlyn, D. W. (1990), *The Penguin History of Western Philosophy*, London: Penguin.

Haraway, D. (1991), *Simians, Cyborgs and Women: The Reinvention of Nature*, London and New York: Routledge.

Hawkes, T. (1977), *Structuralism and Semiotics*, London: Methuen.

Helman, C. (1992), *The Body of Frankenstein's Monster: Essays in Myth and Medicine*, New York and London: W. W. Norton Company.

Hutcheon, L. (1989), *The Politics of Postmodernism*, London: Routledge.

Huxley, A. (1977), *Heaven and Hell*, London: Grafton.

Iser, W. (1988), 'The reading process: a phenomenological approach', in D. Lodge (ed.), *Modern Criticism and Theory*, London: Longman.

Jakobson, R. (1960), 'Closing statement: linguistics and poetics', in T. A. Sebeok (ed.), *Style in Language*, Cambridge, MA: MIT Press.

Jakobson, R. and M. Halle (1956), *Fundamentals of Language*, The Hague: Mouton.

Jameson, F. (1981), *Narrative as a Socially Symbolic Act*, London: Methuen.

—— (1991), *Postmodernism, or the Cultural Logic of Late Capitalism*, London and New York: Verso.

Jay, M. (1988), 'Scopic regimes of modernity', in H. Foster (ed.), *Vision and Visuality*, Seattle, WA: Bay Press.

Kierkegaard, S. (1974), *Fear and Trembling* and *The Sickness Unto Death*, trans. W. Lowrie, Princeton, NJ: Princeton University Press.

Kojeve, A. (1969), *Introduction to the Reading of Hegel: Lectures on the Phenomenology of Spirit*, New York: Basic Books.

Kristeva, J. (1974), *Séméiotiké: Recherches pour une semanalyseis*, Paris: Seuil.

—— (1982), *Powers of Horror: An Essay on Abjection*, trans. L. Roudiez, New York: Columbia University Press.

—— (1984), *Revolution in Poetic Language*, trans. M. Waller, New York: Columbia University Press.

—— (1987), *Tales of Love*, trans. L. Roudiez, New York: Columbia University Press.

—— (1989), *Black Sun: Depression and Melancholia*, trans. L. Roudiez, New York: Columbia University Press.

—— (1990), *Strangers to Ourselves*, trans. L. Roudiez, New York: Columbia University Press.

—— (1992), *The Samurai*, trans. B. Bray, New York: Columbia University Press.

—— (1996), 'The ethics and practice of love', in R. M. Guberman (ed.), *Julia Kristeva: Interviews*, New York: Columbia University Press.

Kroker, A. and D. Cook (1988), *The Postmodern Scene*, London: Macmillan.

Lacan, J. (1970), 'Of structure as an inmixing of otherness prerequisite to any subject whatsoever', in R. Macksey and E. Donato (eds.), *The Structuralist Controversy*, Baltimore, MD: Johns Hopkins University Press.

—— (1977), *Ecrits: A Selection*, trans. A. Sheridan, London: Tavistock.

—— (1978), *The Four Fundamental Concepts of Psychoanalysis*, trans. A. Sheridan, London and New York: W. W. Norton.

Lakoff, G. (1987), *Women, Fire, and Dangerous Things*, Chicago, IL: University of Chicago Press.

Laqueur, T. (1992), *Making Sex: Body and Gender from the Greeks to Freud*, Cambridge, MA: Harvard University Press.

Lefebvre, H. (1974), *The Production of Space*, Oxford: Blackwell.

Lowenthal, D. (1961), 'Geography, experience and imagination', *Annals of the Association of American Geographers* 51.

REFERENCES

Lukacs, G. (1972), 'The Ideology of Modernism', in D. Lodge (ed.), *Twentieth-Century Literary Criticism*, London: Longman.

Lyons, J. (1970), *Chomsky*, London: Fontana/Collins.

Lyotard, J.-F. (1987), *The Postmodern Condition: a Report on Knowledge*, trans. G. Bennington and B. Massumi, Manchester: Manchester University Press.

Macherey, P. (1977), 'Problems of Reflection', in *Literature, Society and the Sociology of Literature*, Colchester: University of Essex Press.

Manguel, A. (1997), *A History of Reading*, London: Flamingo.

Marinetti, F. (1972), *Let's Murder the Moonshine: Selected Writings*, Los Angeles, CA: Sun and Moon Classics.

Marx, K. (1973), *Grundrisse*, Harmondsworth: Penguin.

—— (1975), *Early Writings*, Harmondsworth: Penguin.

Marx, K. and F. Engels (1974), *The German Ideology*, London: Lawrence & Wishart.

McIntosh, M. (1993), 'Queer theory and the war of the sexes', in J. Bristow and A. Wilson (eds.), *Activating Theory: Lesbian, Gay and Bisexual Politics*, London: Lawrence & Wishart.

McLuhan, M. (1964), *Understanding Media: the Extensions of Man*, London: Routledge.

Mennell, S. (1991), 'On the civilizing of appetite', in M. Featherstone, M. Hepworth and B. Turner (eds.), *The Body: Social Process and Cultural Theory*, London: Sage.

Merleau-Ponty, M. (1962), *Phenomenology of Perception*, trans. C. Smith, London: Routledge & Kegan Paul.

Metz, C. (1982), *The Imaginary Signifier: Psychoanalysis and the Cinema*, trans. C. Britton *et al.*, Bloomington, IN: Indiana University Press.

Metzger, G. (1998), 'The artist in the eye of the storm', in J. Wood (ed.), *The Virtual Embodied: Presence/Practice/Technology*, London and New York: Routledge.

Millett, K. (1977), *Sexual Politics*, London: Virago.

Mullarkey, J. (1999), *Bergson and Philosophy*, Edinburgh: Edinburgh University Press.

Mulvey, L. (1989), *Visual and Other Pleasures*, London: Macmillan.

Mumford, L. (1991), *The City in History*, Harmondsworth: Penguin (originally published 1961).

Nascimbeni, G. (1984), 'Colloquio con lo scrittore in occasione dell'uscita di *Cosmicomiche vecchie e nuove*', *Corriere della Sera*, 5 December.

Nead, L. (1992), *The Female Nude: Art, Obscenity and Sexuality*, London and New York: Routledge.

Nietzsche, F. (1967), *The Will to Power*, trans. W. Kaufmann, New York: Random House.

REFERENCES

Olalquiaga, C. (1992), *Megalopolis*, Minneapolis, MN: University of Minnesota Press.

Pile, S. (1996), *The Body and the City*, London and New York: Routledge.

Plato (1987), *The Republic*, Harmondsworth: Penguin.

Pocock, D. C. D. (1973), 'Environmental perception: process and product', *Tijdschrift voor Economische en Sociale Geografie* 63: 251–7.

Poole, R. (1990), 'Embodiment', in A. Bullock and O. Stallybrass (eds.), *The Fontana Dictionary of Modern Thought*, London: Fontana.

Potterton, H. (1977), *The National Gallery, London*, London: Thames & Hudson.

Raban, J. (1974), *Soft City*, London: Hamish Hamilton.

Raphael, M. (1980), *Proudhon, Marx, Picasso: Three Studies in the Sociology of Art*, London: Lawrence & Wishart.

Rorty, R. (1989), *Contingency, Irony and Solidarity*, Cambridge: Cambridge University Press.

Rushkoff, D. (1997), 'Organic engines', *The Guardian*, 26 June.

Said, E. (1988), 'Crisis (in orientalism)', in D. Lodge (ed.), *Modern Criticism and Theory*, London: Longman.

Santayana, G. (1940), *Realms of Being*, vol. II, New York: Columbia University Press.

Sartre, J.-P. (1956), *Being and Nothingness*, trans. H. E. Barnes, New York: Philosophical Library.

Sarup, M. (1988), *An Introductory Guide to Post-structuralism and Postmodernism*, Hemel Hempstead: Harvester Wheatsheaf.

Schilder, P. (1935), *The Image and Appearance of the Body*, New York: Dover.

Schopenhauer, A. (1969), *The World as Will and Representation*, trans. F. J. Payne, New York: Dover.

Searle, J. (1981), 'Minds, brains and programs', in J. Haugeland (ed.), *Mind Design*, Cambridge, MA: MIT Press.

Seidler, V. (1998), 'Embodied knowledge and virtual space', in J. Wood (ed.), *The Virtual Embodied*, London and New York: Routledge.

Shklovsky, V. (1988), 'Art as Technique', in D. Lodge (ed.), *Modern Criticism and Theory: a Reader*, London: Longman.

Smyth, C. (1992), *Lesbians Talk Queer Notions*, London: Scarlet Press.

Synnott, A. (1993), *The Body Social*, London and New York: Routledge.

Taylor, D. R. F. (1989), 'Postmodernism, deconstruction and cartography', *Cartographica* 26: 3–4.

Tolstoy, L. (1930), *What is Art?*, Oxford: Oxford University Press.

Varela, F. J. (1992), 'The Reenchantment of the concrete', *Zone* 6.

Warren, K. (ed.) (1997), *Ecofeminism: Women, Culture, Nature*, Bloomington, IN and Indianapolis, IN: Indiana University Press.

Waugh, P. (1992), 'Stalemates?', in B. Regan (ed.), *The Politics of Pleasure*, Buckingham and Philadelphia, PA: Open University Press.

White, H. (1978), 'The burden of history', *Tropics of Discourse*, Baltimore, MD and London: Johns Hopkins University Press.

Will, C. M. (1995), 'Relativity', *The 1995 Grolier Multimedia Encyclopaedia*, Grolier Electronic Publishing.

Williams, R. (1977), *Marxism and Literature*, Oxford: Oxford University Press.

Wimsatt, W. K. and M. C. Beardsley (1972), 'The Intentional Fallacy' and 'The Affective Fallacy', in D.Lodge (ed.), *Twentieth-Century Literary Criticism: a Reader*, London: Longman.

Wittgenstein, L. (1973), *Philosophical Investigations*, trans. G. E. M. Anscombe, Oxford: Blackwell.

—— (1975), *Tractatus Logico-Philosophicus*, trans. D. F. Pears and B. F. McGuinness, London: Routledge.

Wollstonecraft, M. (1986), *A Vindication of the Rights of Woman*, Harmondsworth: Penguin.

Woolfe, K. (1998), 'It's not what you wear: fashioning a queer identity', in D. Atkins (ed.), *Looking Queer: Body Image and Identity in Lesbian, Bisexual, Gay and Transgender Communities*, New York and London: Harrington Park Press.

Woolley, B. (1993), *Virtual Worlds*, London: Penguin.

Wright, J. K. (1947), 'Terrae Incognitae: the place of the imagination in geography', *Annals of the Association of American Geographers* 37.

FURTHER READING

PART I: LANGUAGE AND INTERPRETATION

I: Meaning

General introductory texts
Green, K. and G. Le Bihan (1996), *Critical Theory and Practice: a Source-book*, London and New York: Routledge.
Hacker, P. M. S. (1997), *Wittgenstein*, London: Phoenix.
Hawkes, T. (1977), *Structuralism and Semiotics*, London: Methuen.
Lycan, W. G. (2000), *Philosophy of Language*, London and New York: Routledge.
Lyons, J. (1970), *Chomsky*, London: Fontana/Collins.
McGinn, M. (1997), *Routledge Philosophy Guidebook to Wittgenstein and the Philosophical Investigations*, London: Routledge.
Maher, J. and J. Groves (1999), *Introducing Chomsky*, Cambridge: Icon.
Polanyi, M. and H. Proch (1977), *Meaning*, Chicago, IL and London: University of Chicago Press.

Philosophy of language
Bartley, III, W. W. (1974), *Wittgenstein*, London: Quartet.
Deleuze, G. and F. Guattari (1994), *What Is Philosophy?*, London and New York: Verso.
Devitt, M. and K. Sterelny (1999), *Language and Reality*, Oxford: Blackwell.
Fann, K. T. (1969), *Wittgenstein's Conception of Philosophy*, Berkeley, CA: University of California Press.
Fogelin, R. J. (1995), *Wittgenstein*, London: Routledge.
Sluga, H. and D. G. Stern (eds.) (1996), *The Cambridge Companion to Wittgenstein*, Cambridge: Cambridge University Press.

Thihor, A. (1987), *Words in Reflection*, Chicago, IL and London: Chicago University Press.
Warnock, G.J. (1991), *J. L. Austin*, London: Routledge.

Linguistics
Benveniste, E. (1971), *Problems in General Linguistics*, Miami, FL: University of Miami Press.
Bloomfield, L. (1935), *Language*, London: Allen & Unwin.
Chomsky, N. (1997), *Barriers*, Cambridge, MA: MIT Press.
Fowler, R. (1977), *Linguistics and the Novel*, London: Methuen.
Halliday, M. A. K. (1973), *Explorations in the Functions of Language*, London: Edward Arnold.
—— (1978), *Language as Social Semiotic: the Social Interpretation of Language and Meaning*, London: Edward Arnold.
Minnis, N. (ed.) (1973), *Linguistics at Large*, London: Paladin.
Sapir, E. (1921), *Language*, New York: Harcourt Brace.
Saussure, F. de (1974), *Course in General Linguistics*, trans. W. Baskin, London: Fontana.
Whorf, B. L. (1956), *Language, Thought and Reality*, Cambridge, MA: MIT Press.

2: The Sign

General introductory texts
Barry, P. (1999), *Beginning Theory*, Manchester: Manchester University Press.
Belsey, C. (1980), *Critical Practice*, London: Methuen.
Cobley, P. and L. Jansz (1999), *Introducing Semiotics*, Cambridge: Icon.
Hawkes, T. (1977), *Structuralism and Semiotics*, London: Methuen.
Hodge, R. and G. Kress (1988), *Social Semiotics*, Cambridge: Polity Press.
Kress, G. and T. van Leeuwen (1990), *Reading Images*, Deakin University Press.
Sarup, M. (1988), *An Introductory Guide to Post-structuralism and Post-modernism*, London: Harvester Wheatsheaf.

Studies of major theorists
Bradford, R. (1994), *Roman Jakobson: Life, Language, Art*, London and New York: Routledge.
Brunning, J. and P. Forster (eds.) (1997), *The Rule of Reason: the Philosophy of C. S. Peirce*, Toronto: University of Toronto Press.
Culler, J. (1976), *Saussure*, London: Fontana.
Leach, E. (1970), *Levi-Strauss*, London: Fontana.
Norris, C. (1987), *Derrida*, London: Fontana.

The Sign from Saussure to Poststructuralism
Bennett, T. (1979), *Formalism and Marxism*, London: Methuen.
Erlich, V. (1955), *Russian Formalism: History, Doctrine*, The Hague: Mouton.
Jameson, F. (1972), *The Prison-House of Language*, Princeton, NJ: Princeton University Press.
Leitch, V. (1983), *Deconstructive Criticism*, London: Hutchinson.
Lodge, D. (1977), *The Modes of Modern Writing: Metaphor, Metonymy and the Typology of Modern Literature*, London: Edward Arnold.
Lodge, D. (1981), *Working With Structuralism*, London: Routledge & Kegan Paul.
Powel, T. (1992), *The Feud of Language: A History of Structuralist Thought*, Oxford: Blackwell.
Scholes, R. (1974), *Structuralism in Literature*, New Haven, CT and London: Yale University Press.
Silverman, K. (1983), *The Subject of Semiotics*, Oxford: Oxford University Press.
Sturrock, J. (1980), *Structuralism and Since*, Oxford: Oxford University Press.

3: Rhetoric

General introductory texts
Collins, J. and B. Mayblin (2000), *Introducing Derrida*, Cambridge: Icon.
Culler, J. (1987), *Derrida*, London: Fontana.
Easthope, A. (1980), *Poetry as Discourse*, London: Methuen.
Hobson, M. (1998), *Jacques Derrida: Opening Lines*, London and New York: Routledge.
Johnson, C. (1997), *Derrida*, London: Phoenix.
Norris, C. (1982), *Deconstruction: Theory and Practice*, London: Methuen.
Wolfreys, J. (1988), *Deconstruction - Derrida*, London: Macmillan.

Approaches to rhetoric and deconstruction
Bakhtin, M (1986), *Speech Genres and Other Late Essays*, Austin, TX: University of Texas Press.
Beardsworth, R. (1996), *Derrida and the Political*, London and New York: Routledge.
Berman, A. (1988), *From the New Criticism to Deconstruction*, Chicago, IL: University of Illinois Press.
Butler, J. (1997), *Excitable Speech: a Politics of the Performative*, London and New York: Routledge.
Critchley, S. (1992), *The Ethics of Deconstruction*, Oxford: Blackwell.

De Man, P. (1983), *Blindness and Insight*, London: Methuen.
Derrida, J. (1976), *Of Grammatology*, trans. G. C. Spivak, Baltimore,
MD: Johns Hopkins University Press.
Empson, W. (1930), *Seven Types of Ambiguity*, London: Chatto &
Windus.
Norris, C. (2000), *Deconstruction and the 'Unfinished Project of Moder-
nity'*, London: Athlone.
Searle, J. (1969), *Speech Acts*, Cambridge: Cambridge University Press.
Tsohatzidis, S. L. (1994), *Foundations of Speech Act Theory: Philosophical
and Linguistic Perspectives*, London: Routledge.
Ulmer, G. L. (1992), *Applied Grammatology*, Baltimore, MD and London:
Johns Hopkins University Press.

4: Representation

General introductory texts

Barnard, M. (1998), *Art, Design and Visual Culture: an Introduction*,
London: Macmillan.
Berger, J. (1972), *Ways of Seeing*, London: Penguin.
Brookeman, C. (ed.) (1996), *Art and Society*, Todmorden, Lancs.: Altair
Publishing.
Lacey, N. (1998), *Image and Representation*, London: Macmillan.
Nelson, R. S. and R. Shiff (eds.) (1996), *Critical Terms for Art History*,
Chicago, IL and London: Chicago University Press.
Thomas, J. (ed.) (2000), *Reading Images*, London: Macmillan.

Representation and perception

Cummins, R. (1989), *Meaning and Mental Representation*, Cambridge,
MA: MIT Press.
Foster, H. (ed.) (1988), *Vision and Visuality*, Dia Art Foundation, Discus-
sions in Contemporary Culture, no. 2, Seattle: Bay Press.
Gombrich, E. H. (1977), *Art and Illusion: a Study in the Psychology of
Pictorial Representation*, Oxford: Phaidon.
—— (1982), *The Image and the Eye: Further Studies in the Psychology of
Pictorial Representation*, Oxford: Phaidon.
Goodman, N. (1976), *Languages of Art*, Indianapolis, IN: Indiana
University Press.
Grace, H. (ed.) (1996), *Aesthesia and the Economy of the Senses*, Sydney:
Faculty of Visual and Performing Arts, Nepean, University of Western
Sydney.
Hubert, D. (1994), *The Origin of Perspective*, Cambridge, MA: MIT Press.

Representation, politics and ideology

Barthes, R. (1977), 'The Rhetoric of the Image', in *Image, Music, Text*, trans. S. Heath, New York: Hill & Wang.

Berger, P. L. and T. Luckmann (1979), *The Social Construction of Reality: a Treatise in the Sociology of Knowledge*, Harmondsworth: Penguin.

Mitchell, W. J. T. (1986), *Iconology: Image, Text, Ideology*, Chicago, IL: Chicago University Press.

Pollock, G. (1988), *Vision and Difference*, London: Routledge.

Regan, S. (ed.) (1992), *The Politics of Pleasure*, Buckingham and Philadelphia, PA: Open University Press.

5: Reading

General introductory texts

Alsop, D. (1999), *The Practice of Reading*, London: Macmillan.

Holub, R. C. (1984), *Reception Theory: a Critical Introduction*, London: Methuen.

Freund, E. (1987), *The Return of the Reader: Reader-Response Criticism*, London: Methuen.

Suleiman, S. (ed.) (1980), *The Reader in the Text*, Princeton, NJ: Princeton University Press.

Tompkins, J. P. (ed.) (1980), *Reader-Response Criticism*, Baltimore, MD: Johns Hopkins University Press.

Representative voices

Eco, U. (1983), *Reflections on 'The Name of the Rose'*, trans. W. Weaver, London: Picador.

Harari, J. V. (ed.) (1980), *Textual Strategies*, London: Methuen.

Iser, W. (1974), *The Implied Reader*, Baltimore, MD: Johns Hopkins University Press.

—— (1979), *The Act of Reading*, Baltimore, MD: Johns Hopkins University Press.

Richards, I. A. (1924), *Principles of Literary Criticism*, London: Routledge & Kegan Paul.

Interpretation, phenomenology and existentialism

Golomb, J. (1995), *In Search of Authenticity: Existentialism from Kierkegaard to Camus*, London and New York: Routledge.

Hammond, J. and R. Keat (1991), *Understanding Phenomenology*, Oxford: Blackwell.

Inwood, M. (1993), *Heidegger*, Oxford: Oxford University Press.

Kearney, R. and M. Rainwater (eds.) (1996), *The Continental Philosophy Reader*, London and New York: Routledge.

Macann, C. (1993), *Four Phenomenological Thinkers*, London and New York: Routledge.

Petitot, J., F. J. Varela, B. Pachoud and J.-M. Roy (1999), *Naturalizing Phenomenology: Issues in Contemporary Phenomenology and Cognitive Science*, Stanford, CA: Stanford University Press.

Sartre, J.-P. (1948), *Existentialism and Humanism*, London: Methuen.

Weber, S. (1987), *Institution and Interpretation*, Minneapolis, MN: University of Minnesota Press.

6: Textuality

General introductory texts
Culler, J. (1983), *Barthes*, London: Fontana.

Febvre, L. and H.-J.Martin (1984), *The Coming of the Book*, trans. D. Gerald, London and New York: Verso.

Hopkins, C. (2000), *Thinking About Texts*, London: Macmillan.

Thody, P. and A. Course (1999), *Introducing Barthes*, Cambridge: Icon.

Approaches to the text
Brink, A. (1998), *The Novel: Language and Narrative from Cervantes to Clavino*, London: Macmillan.

Chatman, S. (ed.) (1971), *Literary Style*, Oxford and London: Oxford University Press.

De Man, P. (1979), *Allegories of Reading*, New Haven, CT and London: Yale University Press.

Harari, J. V. (ed.) (1980), *Textual Strategies*, London: Methuen.

Kristeva, J. (1980), *Desire in Language: A Semiotic Approach to Literature and Art*, trans. T. Gora, A. Jardine and L. Roudiez, New York: Columbia University Press.

Macksey, R. and E. Donato (eds.) (1970), *The Structuralist Controversy*, Baltimore, MD: Johns Hopkins University Press.

Melville, S. and B. Readings (1995), *Vision and Textuality*, London: Macmillan.

Relevant works on Barthes and Kristeva
Fletcher, J. and Benjamin, A. (eds.), (1990), *Abjection, Melancholia and Love*, London: Routledge.

Lavers, A. (1982), *Roland Barthes, Structuralism and After*, London: Methuen.

Lechte, J. (1990), *Julia Kristeva*, London: Routledge.

Oliver, K. (ed.), (1993), *Ethics, Politics and Difference in Julia Kristeva's Writing*, London: Routledge.
Reineke, M. J. (1997), *Sacrificed Lives: Kristeva on Women and Violence*, Bloomington, IN: Indiana University Press.
Sturrock, J. (1974), 'Roland Barthes – a profile', *The New Review* 1,2:13–21, May.
Thody, P. (1977), *Roland Barthes, a Conservative Estimate*, London: Macmillan.

PART II: SOCIAL IDENTITIES

I: Ideology

General introductory texts

Bottomore, T. (ed.) (1988), *Interpretations of Marx*, London: Routledge.
Eagleton, T. (1991), *Ideology*, London and New York: Verso.
—— (1997), *Marx*, London: Phoenix.
Elster, J. (1985), *Making Sense of Marx*, Cambridge: Cambridge University Press.
Wolff, J. (1982), *The Social Production of Art*, London: Macmillan.

Ideology and Marxist theory

Althusser, L. (1969), *For Marx*, Harmondsworth: Penguin.
Bennett, T. (1979), *Formalism and Marxism*, London: Routledge.
Cohen, G. A. (1978), *Karl Marx's Theory of History – a Defence*, Princeton, NJ: Princeton University Press.
Eagleton, T. (1976), *Marxism and Literary Criticism*, London: Methuen.
Eagleton, T. and D. Milne (eds.) (1985), *Marxist Literary Theory*, London: Routledge.
Jameson, F. (1971), *Marxism and Form*, Princeton, NJ: Princeton University Press.
—— (1996), *Late Marxism: Adorno, or, The Persistence of the Dialectic*, London and New York: Verso.
Jay, M. (1984), *Marxism and Totality*, Berkeley, CA: University of California Press.
Kolakowsky, L. (1978), *Main Currents of Marxism*, Oxford: Clarendon Press.
Lunn, E. (1982), *Marxism and Modernism*, Berkeley, CA: University of California Press.

Ideology and cultural theory

Arato, A. and E. Gebhardt (eds.) (1978), *The Frankfurt School*, London: Urizen.

Althusser, L. (1984), *Essays on Ideology*, London: New Left Books
Benjamin, W. (1973), *Illuminations*, trans. H. Zohn, London: Fontana.
Lovell, T. (1987), *Consuming Fiction*, London and New York: Verso.
Macherey, P. (1978), *A Theory of Literary Production*, London: Routledge.
Zizek, S. (1989), *The Sublime Object of Ideology*, London and New York: Verso.
—— (1994), *Mapping Ideology*, London and New York: Verso.

2: Subjectivity

General introductory texts

Belsey, C. (1980), *Critical Practice*, London: Methuen.
Benvenuto, B. and R. Kennedy (1986), *The Works of Jacques Lacan*, London: Free Association Books.
Deleueze, G. (1988), *Foucault*, London: Athlone.
Hayman, R. (1997), *Nietzsche*, London: Phoenix.
Hill, P. (1997), *Lacan For Beginners*, London: Writers and Readers.
Sarup, M. (1988), *An Introductory Guide to Post-Structuralism and Postmodernism*, Hemel Hempstead: Harvester Wheatsheaf.
Tanner, M. (1998), *Schopenhauer*, London: Phoenix.
Weedon, C. (1987), *Feminist Practice and Poststructuralist Theory*, Oxford: Blackwell.

Philosophical perspectives

Gardiner, P. (1988), *Kierkegaard*, Oxford: Oxford University Press.
Magee, B. (1997), *The Philosophy of Schopenhauer*, Oxford: Clarendon Press.
Magnus, B. (1996), *The Cambridge Companion to Nietzsche*, Cambridge: Cambridge University Press.
Oliver, K. (1998), *Subjectivity Without Subjects*, Oxford: Rowman & Littlefield Publishers.
Scruton, R., P. Singer, C. Janaway and M. Tanner (1997), *German Philosophers: Kant, Hegel, Schopenhauer, Nietzsche*, Oxford: Oxford University Press.
Solomon, R. C. (1988), *Continental Philosophy After 1750: The Rise and Fall of the Self*, Oxford: Oxford University Press.

Relevant works on Foucault and Lacan

Felman, S. (1987), *Jacques Lacan and the Adventure of Insight*, Cambridge, MA: Harvard University Press.
Lemaire, A. (1986), *Jacques Lacan*, trans. D. Macey, London: Routledge & Kegan Paul.

Merquior, J. G. (1987), *Foucault*, Berkeley, CA: University of California Press.

Mitchell, J. and J. Rose (eds.) (1982), *Feminine Sexuality: Jacques Lacan and the Ecole Freudienne*, London: Macmillan.

Poster, M. (1984), *Foucault, Marxism and History*, Cambridge: Polity Press.

Smart, B. (1985), *Michel Foucault*, New York: Tavistock Publications.

Smith, J. H. and W. Kerrigan (1983), *Interpreting Lacan*, New Haven, CA and London: Yale University Press.

Visker, R. (1995), *Michel Foucault: Genealogy as Critique*, London and New York: Verso.

3: The Body

General introductory texts

Atkinson, T. (2000), *The Body*, London: Macmillan.

Cavallaro, D. (1999), *The Body for Beginners*, London: Writers and Readers.

Feher, M., R. Nadaff and N. Tazi (eds.) (1989), *Fragments for a History of the Human Body, Part One*, New York: Zone.

Synnott, A. (1993), *The Body Social*, London and New York: Routledge.

Welton, D. (1998), *Body and Flesh: a Philosophical Reader*, Oxford: Blackwell.

The body, philosophy and cultural theory

Barkan, L. (1975), *Nature's Work of Art: the Human Body as Image of the World*, New Haven, CA and London: Yale University Press.

Barker, F. (1995), *The Tremulous Private Body*, Ann Arbor, MI: University of Michigan Press.

Crary, J. and S. Kwinter (eds.) (1992), *Incorporations*, New York: Zone.

Danto, A. C. (1999), *The Body/Body Problem*, Berkeley, CA: University of California Press.

Halberstam, J. and I. Livingston (eds.) (1995), *Posthuman Bodies*, Bloomington, IN: Indiana University Press.

Kuriyama, S. (1999), *The Expressiveness of the Body*, New York: Zone Books.

McWorther, L. (1999), *Bodies and Pleasures: Foucault and the Politics of Sexual Normalization*, Bloomington, IN and Indianapolis, IN: Indiana University Press.

Prosser MacDonald, D. (1995), *Transgressive Corporeality*, New York: State University of New York Press.

Sargissen, L. (2000), *Utopian Bodies and the Politics of Transgression*, London and New York: Routledge.

Scarry, E. (1985), *The Body in Pain*, New York: Oxford University Press.

The body, representation and fashion

Breward, C. (1995), *The Culture of Fashion*, Manchester: Manchester University Press.

Davis, F. (1994), *Fashion, Culture and Identity*, Chicago, IL: University of Chicago Press.

Dijkstra, B. (1986), *Idols of Perversity*, New York and Oxford: Oxford University Press.

Elkins, J. (1999), *Pictures of the Body: Pain and Metamorphosis*, Stanford, CA: Stanford University Press.

Gill, M. (1989), *Image of the Body*, London: The Bodley Head.

Hollander, A. (1978), *Seeing through Clothes*, New York: Viking Penguin.

Lucie-Smith, E. (1991), *Sexuality in Western Art*, London: Thames & Hudson.

Scholz, S. (2000), *Body Narratives*, London: Macmillan.

4: Gender and Sexuality

General introductory texts

Bristow, J. (1997), *Sexuality*, London and New York: Routledge.

Evans, J. (1995), *Feminist Theory Today: an Introduction to Second-Wave Feminism*, London: Sage Publications.

Medhurst, A. and S. Munt (eds.) (1997), *Lesbian and Gay Studies: A Critical Introduction*, London and Washington, DC: Cassell.

Nicholson, L. (ed.) (1997), *The Second Wave: a Reader in Feminist Theory*, London and New York: Routledge.

Feminist theories

Assiter, A. (1989), *Pornography, Feminism and the Individual*, London: Pluto Press.

Eisenstein, H. and A. Jardine (eds.) (1990), *The Future of Difference*, New Brunswick, NJ and London: Rutgers University Press.

Fricker, M. and J. Hornsby (eds.) (2000), *The Cambridge Companion to Feminism in Philosophy*, Cambridge: Cambridge University Press.

Gunew, S. & A. Yeatman (eds.) (1993), *Feminism and the Politics of Difference*, London: Allen & Unwin.

Kemp, S. and J. Squires (eds.) (1997), *Feminisms*, Oxford and New York: Oxford University Press.

MacKinnon, C. (1988), *Surviving Sexual Violence*, Cambridge: Polity Press.

Marks, E. and I. de Courtivron (eds.) (1980), *New French Feminisms*, Brighton: Harvester.

Moi, T. (1985), *Sexual/Textual Politics*, London and New York: Methuen.

Weedon, C. (1987), *Feminist Practice and Poststructuralist Theory*, Oxford: Blackwell.

Gender, sexuality and social identity

Allen, J. (ed.) (1990), *Lesbian Philosophies and Cultures*, Albany, NY: State University of New York Press.

Butler, J. (1990), *Gender Trouble*, London and New York: Routledge.

De Lauretis, T. (1994), *The Practice of Love: Lesbian Sexuality and Perverse Desire*, Bloomington, IN: Indiana University Press.

Mort, F. (1996), *Cultures of Consumption: Masculinities and Social Space in Late Twentieth-Century Britain*, London and New York: Routledge.

Plummer, K. (ed.) (1992), *Modern Homosexualities*, London and New York: Routledge.

Sedgwick, Eve Kosofsky (1993), *Between Men: English Literature and Male Homosocial Desire*, New York: Columbia University Press.

Smart, C. (1995), *Law, Crime and Sexuality*, London: Sage Publications.

Tiefer, L. (1995), *Sex is not a Natural Act and other Essays*, New York: Westview Press.

Weeks, J. (1985), *Sexuality and its Discontents: Meanings, Myths and Modern Sexualities*, London and New York: Routledge.

Gender, sexuality and race

Collins, P. (1990), *Black Feminist Thought*, London and New York: Routledge.

McClintock, A. (1995), *Imperial Leather: Race, Gender and Sexuality in the Colonial Context*, New York: Routledge.

Young, L. (1996), *Fear of the Dark: Race, Gender and Sexuality in the Cinema*, New York: Routledge.

5: The Other

General introductory texts

Ashcroft, B. (1995), *The Post-Colonial Studies Reader*, London and New York: Routledge.

Chambers, I. and L. Curti (1996), *The Post-Colonial Question*, London and New York: Routledge.

Moore-Gilbert, B., G. Stanton and W. Maley (eds.) (1997), *Postcolonial Criticism*, London: Longman.

Wyrick, D. (1998), *Fanon For Beginners*, London: Writers and Readers.

Young, R. J. C. (1999), *Postcolonialism: an Historical Introduction*, London and New York: Routledge.

Postcolonial criticism and theory

Balibar, E. and I. Wallerstein (1991), *Race, Nation, Class - Ambiguous Identities*, London and New York: Verso.

Bhabha, H. K. (1990), *Nation and Narration*, London: Routledge.

Boehmer, E. (1995), *Colonial and Postcolonial Literature: Migrant Metaphors*, Oxford: Oxford University Press.

Brantlinger, P. (1988), *Rule of Darkness: British Literature and Imperialism*, Ithaca, NY: Cornell University Press.

Giddings, R. (ed.) (1991), *Literature and Imperialism*, London: Macmillan.

Lazarus, N. (1999), *Nationalism and Cultural Practice in the Postcolonial World*, Cambridge: Cambridge Uiversity Press.

Lingis, A. (1994), *Foreign Bodies*, London and New York: Routledge.

Moore-Gilbert, B. (1997), *Postcolonial Theory: Contexts, Practices, Politics*, London: Verso.

Quayson, A. (1999), *Postcolonialism: Theory, Practice, or Process*, Oxford: Blackwell.

Said, E. (1993), *Culture and Imperialism*, London: Chatto & Windus.

Wodak, R., R. de Cillia, M. Reisigl and K. Liebhart (1999), *The Discursive Construction of Identity*, trans. A. Hirsch and R. Mitten, Edinburgh: Edinburgh University Press.

Colonialism, postcolonialism and gender studies

Mohanti, C. T., A. Russo and L. Torres (eds.) (1991), *Third World Women and the Politics of Feminism*, Bloomington, IN: Indiana University Press.

Morrison, T. (1992), *Playing in the Dark*, Cambridge, MA: Harvard University Press.

Parker, A., M. Russo, D. Sommer and P. Yaeger (eds.) (1992), *Nationalism and Sexualities*, London and New York: Routledge.

Sharpe, J. (1993), *Allegories of Empire: The Figure of Woman in the Colonial Text*, Minneapolis, MN and London: University of Minnesota Press.

Alterity and disability

Albrecht, G. L. (1976), *The Sociology of Physical Disability and Rehabilitation*, Pittsburgh, PA: University of Pittsburgh Press.

Mitchell, D. T. and S. L. Snyder (eds.) (1997), *The Body and Physical Difference: Discourses of Disability*, Ann Arbor, MI: Michigan University Press.

Oliver, M. (1990), *The Politics of Disablement*, London; Macmillan.

6: The Gaze

General introductory texts
Betterton, R. (ed.) (1987), *Looking On: Images of Femininity in the Visual Arts and Media*, London and New York: Pandora.
Jay, M. and T. Brennan (eds.) (1995), *Vision in Context*, London and New York: Routledge.
Melville, S. and B. Readings (1995), *Vision and Textuality*, London: Macmillan.

Seeing and society
Bryson, N. (1983), *Vision and Painting*, New Haven, CT: Yale University Press.
Debord, G. (1977), *Society of the Spectacle*, Detroit, MI: Black and Red.
Levin, D. M. (ed.) (1993), *Modernity and the Hegemony of Vision*, Berkeley, CA: University of California Press.
Miles, M. R. (1985), *Image as Insight: Visual Understanding in Western Christianity and Secular Culture*, Boston, MA: Beacon Press.
Rorty, R. (1979), *Philosophy and the Mirror of Nature*, Princeton, NJ: Princeton University Press.

The gaze and gender
Gamman, L. and M. Marshment (eds.) (1988), *The Female Gaze: Women as Viewers of Popular Culture*, London: The Women's Press.
Parker, R. and G. Pollock (eds.) (1987), *Framing Feminism: Art and the Women's Movement 1970-1985*, London and New York: Pandora.
Pollock, G. (1988), *Vision and Difference: Femininity, Feminism and the Histories of Art*, London: Routledge.
Rose, J. (1986), *Sexuality in the Field of Vision*, London: Verso.

The eye and art
Derrida, J. (1976), *The Truth in Painting*, trans. G. Bennington and I. McLeod, Chicago, IL and London: Chicago University Press.
Jacobs, M. (1979), *Nude Painting*, Oxford: Phaidon.
Lucie-Smith, E. (1981), *The Body: Images of the Nude*, London: Thames & Hudson.
Pointon, M. (1990), *Naked Authority: the Body in Western Painting 1930-1908*, Cambridge: Cambridge University Press.

PART III: KNOWLEDGE

I: The Mind

General introductory texts
Gellatly, A. and O. Zarate (1999), *Introducing Mind and Brain*, Cambridge: Icon.
Gregory, R. L. (ed.) (1998), *The Oxford Companion to the Mind*, Oxford: Oxford University Press.
Guttenplan, S. (ed.) (1996), *A Companion to the Philosophy of Mind*, Oxford: Blackwell.
Heil, J. (1998), *Philosophy of Mind: a Contemporary Introduction*, London and New York: Routledge.
Nicholson, L. (1999), *The Play of Reason*, Ithaca, NY: Cornell University Press.

Philosophy of mind and psychology
Block, N. (ed.) (1980, 1981), *Readings in Philosophy of Psychology*, vols. I and II, Cambridge, MA: MIT Press.
Churchland, P. (1988), *Matter and Consciousness*, Cambridge, MA: MIT Press.
Damasio, A. R. (1994), *Descartes' Error: Emotion, Reason and the Human Brain*, New York: Avon Books.
Dennett, D. C. and R. Hofstadter (1982), *The Mind's I*, Harmondsworth: Penguin.
Flanagan, O. (1991), *The Science of the Mind*, Cambridge, MA: MIT Press.
Fodor, J. (1981), *Representations: Philosophical Essays on the Foundations of Cognitive Science*, Cambridge, MA: MIT Press.
Honderich, T. (1988), *Mind and Brain*, Oxford: Oxford University Press.
Searle, J. (1984), *Minds, Brains and Science*, Cambridge, MA: MIT Press.
Smith, P. and O. R. Jones (1986), *The Philosophy of Mind*, Cambridge; Cambridge University Press.
Steuerman, E. (2000), *The Bounds of Reason*, London and New York: Routledge.

Mind and body
Corbin, A. (1986), *The Foul and the Fragrant*, London: Picador.
Crabbe, M. J. C. (1999), *From Soul to Self*, London and New York: Routledge.
Featherstone, M., M. Hepworth and B.Turner (eds.) (1991), *The Body: Social Process and Cutural Theory*, London: Sage.

Merleau-Ponty, M. (1962), *Phenomenology of Perception*, trans. C. Smith, London: Routledge & Kegan Paul.

Rosenthal, D. (ed.) (1987), *Materialism and the Mind-Body Problem*, Indianapolis, IN: Indiana University Press.

2: The Aesthetic

General introductory texts

Beardsley, M. (1966), *Aesthetics from Classical Greece to the Present*, London: Macmillan.

Cooper, D. (ed.) (1992), *The Blackwell Companion to Aesthetics*, Oxford: Blackwell.

Shepherd, A. (1987), *Aesthetics*, Oxford: Oxford University Press.

Townsend, D. (1997), *An Introduction to Aesthetics*, Oxford: Blackwell.

Studies on aesthetics

Abrams, M. H. (1958), *The Mirror and the Lamp*, Oxford: Oxford University Press.

Auerbach, E. (1953), *Mimesis: the Representation of Reality in Western Literature*, Princeton, NJ: Princeton University Press.

Eagleton, T. (1990), *The Ideology of the Aesthetic*, Oxford: Blackwell.

Foster, H. (ed.) (1988), *Vision and Visuality*, Seattle, WA: Bay Press.

Grace, H. (ed.) (1996), *Aesthesia and the Economy of the Senses*, Sydney: Faculty of Visual and Performing Arts, Nepean, University of Western Sydney.

Hegel, G. W. F. (1993), *Introductory Lectures on Aesthetics*, trans. B. Bosanquet, London: Penguin.

Regan, S. (ed.) (1992), *The Politics of Pleasure*, Buckingham: Open University Press.

Summers, D. (1987), *The Judgment of Sense: Naturalism and the Rise of Aesthetics*, Cambridge: Cambridge University Press.

Wolff, J. (1993), *The Social Production of Art*, London: Macmillan.

Art studies

Butler, A. (1996), *The Art Book*, Oxford: Phaidon.

Harrison, C. (ed.) (1992), *Art in Theory*, Oxford: Blackwell.

Nelson, R. S. and R. Shiff (eds.) (1996), *Critical Terms for Art History*, Chicago, IL and London: Chicago University Press.

O'Toole, M. (1994), *The Language of Art*, London: Leicester University Press.

Pointon, M. (1993), *History of Art: A Student's Handbook*, London: Routledge.

3: Space

General introductory texts
Kasinitz, P. (1995), *Metropolis*, London: Macmillan.
Legates, R. T. and F. Stout (eds.) (1996), *The City Reader*, London and New York: Routledge.
Miles, M. (ed.) (2000), *City Cultures Reader*, London and New York: Routledge.

Approaches to geography and cartography
Crang, M. (1998), *Cultural Geography*, London and New York: Routledge.
Dicken, P. (1999), *Global Shift*, London: Sage.
Gold, J. (1980), *An Introduction to Behavioural Geography*, Oxford: Oxford University Press.
Gregory, D. (1994), *Geographical Imaginations*, Oxford: Blackwell.
Haraway, D. (1997), *Modest_Witness @ Second_Millennium*, London and New York: Routledge.
Jarvis, B. (1998), *Postmodern Cartographies*, London: Pluto.
Peet, R. (1998), *Modern Geographical Thought*, Oxford: Blackwell.
Shurmer-Smith, P. and K. Hannam (1994), *Worlds of Desire, Realms of Power*, London: Edward Arnold.
Wood, D. (1992), *The Power of Maps*, Guilford: Guilford Press.

The city
Calvino, I. (1974), *Invisible Cities*, trans. William Weaver, San Diego, CA, New York and London: Harcourt Brace & Company.
Grange, G. (1999), *The City*, Albany, NY: State University of New York Press.
Jacobs, J. (1993), *The Death and Life of Great American Cities*, London: Vintage.
Massey, D. B. (ed.) (2000), *City Worlds*, London and New York: Routledge.
Watson, S. and K. Gibson (eds.) (1995), *Postmodern Cities and Spaces*, Oxford: Blackwell.

4: Time

General introductory texts
Greene, B. (2000), *The Elegant Universe*, London: Vintage.
Hawkins, S. (1988), *A Brief History of Time*, New York: Bantam Books.
Lippincott, K. (1999), *The Story of Time*, London: Merrell Holberton.

McEvoy, J. P. and O. Zarate (1999), *Introducing Quantum Theory*, Cambridge: Icon.
Pickover, C. A. (1998), *Time: a Traveller's Guide*, Oxford; Oxford University Press.
Richards, E. G. (1998), *Mapping Time*, Oxford: Oxford University Press.
Spencer, L. and A. Krauze (1999), *Introducing Hegel*, Cambridge: Icon.
Wells, N. M. (1999), *Time: an Exploration of Our Discovery and Experience of Time*, Glasgow: HarperCollins.
Waugh, A. (1999), *Time*, London: Headline.
Withrow, G. J. (1989), *Time in History*, Oxford: Oxford University Press.

Time and philosophy
Deleuze, G. (1997), *Bergsonism*, trans. H. Tomlinson and B. Habberjam, New York: Zone Books.
Grosz, E. (ed.) (1999), *Becomings - Explorations in Time, Memory and Futures*, Ithaca, NY: Cornell University Press.
Heidegger, M. (1962), *Being and Time*, trans. J. Macquarrie and E. Robinson, Oxford: Blackwell.
Horwich, P. (1987), *Asymmetries in Time*, Cambridge, MA: MIT Press.
Lucas, J. R. (1989), *The Future*, Oxford: Oxford University Press.
Poidevin, R. le and M. MacBeath (eds.) (1993), *The Philosophy of Time*, Oxford: Oxford University Press.

Time and science
Albert, D. Z. (1992), *Quantum Mechanics and Experience*, Cambridge, MA: MIT Press.
Geroch, R. (1978), *General Relativity from A to B*, Chicago, IL: Chicago University Press.
Hawkins, S. and R. Penrose (1996), *The Nature of Space and Time*, Princeton, NJ: Princeton University Press.
Lucas, J. R. and P. E. Hodgson (1990), *Spacetime and Electromagnetism*, Oxford: Oxford University Press.
Pais, A. (1982), *'Subtle is the Lord ...': the Science and Life of Albert Einstein*, Oxford: Oxford University Press.
Rees, M. J. (1997), *Before the Beginning*, Reading, MA: Addison-Wesley.
Thorne, K. (1994), *Black Holes and Time Warps*, New York: Norton.

Approaches to history and historiography
Attridge, D., G. Bennington and R. Young (eds.) (1987), *Post-Structuralism and the Question of History*, Cambridge: Cambridge University Press.
Breisach, E. (1983), *Historiography: Ancient, Medieval and Modern*, Chicago, IL: Chicago University Press.

Koselleck, R. (1985), *Futures Past*, Cambridge: Cambridge University Press

Lovejoy, A. O. (1948), *Essays in the History of Ideas*, Blatimore, MD: Johns Hopkins University Press.

Popper, K. (1957), *The Poverty of Historicism*, London: Methuen.

Spargo, T. (2000), *Reading the Past*, London: Macmillan.

5: The Machine

General introductory texts

Andermatt Conley, V. (ed.) (1993), *Rethinking Technologies*, Minneapolis, MN: University of Minnesota Press.

Brook, J. and I. A. Boal (eds.) (1995), *Resisting the Virtual Life: the Culture and Politics of Information*, San Francisco, CA: City Lights.

Hodges, A. (1997), *Turing*, London: Phoenix.

Naughton, J. (1999), *A Brief History of the Future: the Origins of the Internet*, London: Weidenfeld & Nicolson.

Rawlins, G. J. E. (1998), *Slaves of the Machine*, London and Cambridge, MA: MIT Press.

Wicks, K. (1999), *Key Moments in Science and Technology*, London: Hamlyn.

The machine and modernity

Benjamin, W. (1969), *Illuminations*, trans. H. Zohn, New York: Schocken.

—— (1978), *Reflections*, trans. E. Jephcott, New York: Schocken.

Boyer, C. (1996), *CyberCities*, New York: Princeton Architectural Press.

Lucic, K. (1991), *Charles Sheeler and the Cult of the Machine*, Cambridge, MA: Harvard University Press.

The machine and the body

Balsamo, A. (1997), *Technologies of the Gendered Body*, London and Durham, NC: Duke University Press.

Jacobus, M., E. Fox Keller and S. Shuttleworth (eds.) (1990), *Body/Politics: Women and the Discourse of Science*, London and New York: Routledge.

Springer, C. (1996), *Electronic Eros*, Austin, TX: Texas University Press.

Computers and cyberculture

Featherstone, M. and R. Burrows (eds.) (1995), *Cyberspace/Cyberbodies/Cyberpunk: Cultures of Technological Embodiment*, London: Sage.

Heim, M. (1993), *The Metaphysics of Virtual Reality*, Oxford: Oxford University Press.

Holmes, D. (ed.) (1997), *Virtual Politics: Identity and Community in Cyberspace*, London: Sage.

Jones, S. G. (ed.) (1995), *Cybersociety: Computer-Mediated Information and Community*, London: Sage.

Morrison, P. and E. Morrison (eds.) (1961), *Charles Babbage and his Calculating Engines*, New York: Dover.

6: The Simulacrum

General introductory texts

Butler, R. (1999), *Jean Baudrillard*, London: Sage.

Camille, M. (1996), 'Simulacrum', in R. S. Nelson and R. Shiff (eds.), *Critical Terms for Art History*, Chicago, IL and London: University of Chicago Press.

Caygill, H., A. Coles and A. Klimowski (1998), *Benjamin For Beginners*, Cambridge: Icon.

Gombrich, E. H. (1969), *Art and Illusion: a Study in the Psychology of Pictorial Representation*, Princeton, NJ: Princeton University Press.

Horrocks, C. and Z. Jevtic (1999), *Introducing Baudrillard*, Cambridge: Icon.

The simulacrum and philosophy

Deleuze, G. (1988), 'The Visible and the Articulable', in *Foucault*, Minneapolis, MN: University of Minnesota Press.

—— (1994), *Difference and Repetition*, trans. P. Patton, London: Athlone.

Deleuze, G. and F. Guattari (1994), *What Is Philosophy?*, New York: Columbia University Press.

Foucault, M. (1982), *This Is Not a Pipe*, trans. J. Harkness, Berkeley, CA: University of California Press.

Rosen, S. (1983), *Plato's Sophist: the Drama of Original and Image*, New Haven, CT: Yale University Press.

Hyperreality and postmodern culture

Baudrillard, J. (1981), *For a Critique of the Political Economy of the Sign*, trans. C. Levin, St Louis, MS: Telos Press.

Durham, S. (1998), *Phantom Communities: the Simulacrum and the Limits of Postmodernism*, Stanford, CA: Stanford University Press.

Jameson, F. (1991), *Postmodernism, or the Cultural Logic of Late Capitalism*, Ithaca, NY: Cornell University Press.

Lyotard, J.-F. (1984), *The Postmodern Condition: A Report on Knowledge*, trans. G. Bennington and B. Massumi, Manchester: Manchester University Press.

Wallis, B. (ed.) (1984), *Art after Modernism: Essays on Rethinking Representation*, New York: New Museum of Contemporary Art.

QUESTIONS?

The following questions are indicators of possible lines of discussion.

PART I: LANGUAGE AND INTERPRETATION

I: Meaning

i.   What is a word?
ii. How is language used in the construction of reality?
iii. How does the behaviourist approach contribute to the debate on meaning?

2: The Sign

i.   How do signs relate to meanings?
ii. In what ways has structuralist linguistics modified traditional approaches to language?
iii. How do sign systems contribute to the shaping of cultures and societies?

3: Rhetoric

i.   Examine the proposition that 'all language is rhetorical'.
ii. What does deconstruction attempt to deconstruct and why?
iii. In what ways can speech be considered a form of action?

4: Representation

i.   What are the aims and objectives of realism?

ii.   Discuss the idea that 'everything is a representation'.
iii. How do different representational techniques impact on meaning?

5: Reading

i.   Examine the relationship between the act of reading and perception.
ii. 'The text's producer is its reader.' Discuss.
iii. Working on a text of your choice, suggest two alternative and opposed meanings.

6: Textuality

i.   In what ways has the concept of text been extended by contemporary theories?
ii. 'The text is a body; the body is a text.' Discuss.
iii. To what extent is the analysis of the self related to the analysis of the text?

PART II: SOCIAL IDENTITIES

1: Ideology

i.   Examine the proposition that 'an ideology is a way of seeing the world'.
ii. How do ideologies affect the production of texts?
iii. 'Ideology constructs meanings for its subjects.' Discuss.

2: Subjectivity

i.   What is the relationship between the self and the subject?
ii. How have recent theories redefined the relationship between the subject and power?
iii. 'Subjectivity is constructed by language.' Discuss.

3: The Body

i.   How has the body been redefined by scientific developments?
ii. Examine the relationship between the body and language.
iii. How many kinds of body are there?

4: Gender and Sexuality

i. 'Gender and sexuality are culturally determined.' Discuss.
ii. How has feminist theory redefined traditional conceptions of gender and sexuality?
iii. Examine the idea that 'there are many genders and many sexualities'.

5: The Other

i. How do cultures construct various forms of otherness?
ii. Examine the links between otherness and colonialism/postcolonialism.
iii. Where is the Other?

6: The Gaze

i. What is the relationship between power and the eye?
ii. Why has Western culture traditionally prioritized sight over the other senses?
iii. Examine the connection between the gaze and gender politics.

PART III: KNOWLEDGE

I: The Mind

i. 'The mind is a universal attribute of humanity.' Discuss.
ii. What is the relationship between the mind and the senses?
iii. Where is the Mind?

2: The Aesthetic

i. What is the aesthetic?
ii. To what extent are aesthetic values shaped by ideology?
iii. Examine the relationship between modernist and postmodernist aesthetics.

3: Space

i. That is the function of maps?

ii.   Examine various interpretations of the city as a physical place and as a concept.

iii.   'Space is inseparable from time.' Discuss.

4: Time

i.   To what extent is time related to the idea of change?

ii.   How do the measuring of time and the perception of time differ?

iii.   How is time recorded by the discipline of historiography?

5: The Machine

i.   'Knowledge produces machines; machines produce knowledge.' Discuss.

ii.   What is the relationship between machines and bodies?

iii.   Why do machines traditionally elicit ambivalent responses?

6: The Simulacrum

i.   'Simulations of reality are taking over reality.' Discuss.

ii.   What is the relationship between an original and a copy?

iii.   How has electronic culture affected the notion of reality?

INDEX